CRAFTSMAN
DO-IT-YOURSELF
MONEY-SAVING PROJECT PLANNER

A NORTH COAST PRODUCTION
Published by North Coast Productions,
650 Mount Curve Blvd., St. Paul, MN 55116

Gene Schnaser, Editor and Publisher
Jeanne Fredensborg, Managing Editor
Bill Rose, Production Manager

Original illustrations by Brian Jensen
Cover and section photos by Marvin Windows
& Doors; photo inset, Sears, Roebuck & Co.

The editors of this book are dedicated to presenting information and ideas needed to plan and execute do-it-yourself activities successfully. If you have comments or suggestions, please address your correspondence to the address above. Also use the address above for inquiries relating to special editions of this book.

Note To The Reader: The information, plans, and instructions in this book have come from a variety of sources. Every effort has been made to ensure the accuracy of data presented. However, due to differing conditions, tools, and individual skills, the publisher and the staff cannot assume responsibility for any injuries suffered, damages, or losses incurred during or as a result of following this information. Before beginning any project, it is important to consider personal safety above all else. Review the plans and procedures carefully and, if any doubts or questions remain concerning your personal safety, working procedures, or use of materials, consult local experts or authorities. Also always read and observe all of the safety precautions provided by any tool, equipment, or materials manufacturer, and always follow all accepted safety procedures.

A very special thanks to the many people, companies, and organizations who assisted the staff, either directly or indirectly, in making this book a reality. For contributing their time and talents to this book: Jim Fassel and Jim Klepac of Jim Fassel Advertising; Ann Woolman of Sears, Roebuck & Co.; Mike Mangan of MKM Communications; Pamela Allsebrook of the California Redwood Association; Jim Plucker and Peggy Arnson of Marvin Windows & Doors; Rob Guzikowski of Simpson Strong-Tie Co.; John Post and Kathy Molloy of Precision Marketing Associates; Merle Henkenius of Henkenius Free-Lance; John Shaughnessy, Rich Sharp, and Joe Deckenbach of Mona, Meyer, McGrath & Gavin; Kathy Ziprik of Georgia-Pacific Corporation; Gary Green, Donna Green, and Warren Weber of Performax Products; Paige Perdue of WD40 Company; Ronald Barlow of Windmill Publishing; Mary Spencer of Little Giant Pump Co.; Holly Walters and Linda Beheler of Thompson & Formby; Lauren Holzman of Phillips-Ramsey; Richard Wright of Village West Publishing; Virginia Crum of Lilypons Water Gardens; Jenny Leavens of Deckmaster; George Washington of Flood Co.; Ron Nystrom of Supreme Decking; Don Struckel of The Beckwood Company; Keith Hobbs of Loeffler, Ketchum, Mountjoy; Michael Isser of Isser & Associates. For their valuable editorial assistance: Robert Tupper, Hugh Foster, Mark Egge, Robert Scharff, Johnny Blackwell, Don Johnson, and David Chapeau. For their advice and consul: Jim Barrett, Ron A. Bruzek, Mark Newhall, Don Rodi, Marlyn Rodi, Dwight Paulson, Barbara Bowen, and Connie Schrader. For their help in getting this book to the reader: Mary Fitzgerald, Judy Holby, Sue Levitt, and Graham Benson. For feature-by-feature credits and association and company addresses, see page 192.

CONTENTS

DO-IT-YOURSELF
PROJECTS

THE DO-IT-YOURSELF INDEX

As you plan out the deck project you hope to start soon, head to the store to pick up some plumbing parts, or pile a load of lumber into your pickup, you are probably unaware of the vast boundaries of what is referred to as "do-it-yourself" and "home improvement." Be assured that as a do-it-yourselfer you have plenty of company, and that home building, maintenance, and repair activities are supported by a massive industry with roots worldwide. Here is a collection of facts, gleaned from several sources, to help you picture some of the dimensions:

Percent of male DIYers between 35 and 44 who do projects to save money: **50%**

Dollars spent on home improvement products in the U.S. during 1994: **$125 billion**

Dollars expected to be spent on home improvement products in 1998: **$157 billion**

Number of Americans who watch Bob Vila's *Home Again* show every week: **3.4 million**

Estimated number of decks being built onto homes every year in the U.S.: **3 million**

Value of processed lumber possible to get from a 15′-dia. redwood tree: **$150,000**

Ranking of interior painting among all do-it-yourself projects: **#1**

Number of Americans who currently belong to the Sears Craftsman Club: **7 million**

Number of Americans who join the Sears Craftsman Club each month: **50,000**

Average number of electrical appliances used in the average American home in 1940: **30**

Average number of electrical appliances used in the average American home today: **80**

Total projected value of lumber products expected to be sold in 1996: **$17.9 billion**

Estimated value of all power tools sold in the U.S. in 1991: **$2.6 billion**

Percent increase in the cost of the average U.S. home since 1977: **100%**

Average cost to replace a U.S. home, not counting garage or basement, per sq. ft.: **$53**

Ratio of Craftsman full-size tablesaws sold compared to all other brands: **6:10**

Ratio of Craftsman full-size radial-arm saws sold compared to all other brands: **7:10**

Dollars paid by State Farm for damages caused by frozen pipes in 1993: **$212 million**

Feet of 2x6s ripped by Craftsman Contractor Series tablesaw in four test days: **40,000**

Amount of money spent by homeowners on an average remodeling project: **$4,000**

Total number of homes which existed in the United States in 1994: **110 million**

Percent of all American homes which were built before the year 1980: **70%**

Number copies sold of Patrick Spielman's original *Router Handbook*: **1 million**

Percent of all woodworking that is using saws for straight cuts: **80%**

Percent of all woodworking that is using saws for curved cuts: **10%**

Percent of all woodworking that is drilling, turning, shaping, and sanding: **10%**

Total number of all Sears Craftsman hand tools ever sold: **1 billion**

Average cost to replace a log home today, per sq. ft.: **$58**

Average cost to replace a masonry-earth shelter home today, per sq. ft.: **$69**

Miles covered if all Craftsman screwdrivers sold were laid end-to-end: **68,000**

Height most often recommended for workbenches built for average Americans: **34″**

Percent of American homes that had two and a half baths in 1978: **25%**

Percent of American homes that had two and a half baths in 1993: **48%**

Number of Craftsman hand tools currently marketed by Sears, Roebuck & Co.: **1,600**

Percent landfill waste consisting of lawn refuse during the 1980 growing season: **50%**

Value of a set of Craftsman collector cards originally sold for $1 in 1992: **$75**

Percent increase in the cost of lumber between the years 1991 and 1994: **100%**

Percent of homes in this country that had two-car garages in 1978: **52%**

Percent of homes in this country with two-car garages in 1993: **77%**

Percent of hardware retailers who say batteries are their top selling impulse item: **55%**

Average cost of a major kitchen remodeling project in 1994: **$20,078**

Percent of kitchen remodeling costs a homeowner is likely to recoup: **101%**

Current number of Sears Craftsman sockets being sold every year: **150 million**

Number of gallons water used by the average American every day: **80**

Percent water used by average American which is consumed by water closets: **33%**

Average cost of a bathroom addition project during 1994: **$11,441**

Percent of bathroom addition costs a homeowner is likely to recoup: **93%**

Number of items in the 1994 Craftsman Power & Hand Tools Catalog: **3,200**

Total trees required to equal all unprotected deck and fence wood in U.S.: **25 million**

Percent of U.S. homeowners who waterproofed their decks in 1992: **47%**

Percent of U.S. homeowners who waterproofed their wood fences in 1992: **27%**

Average cost of adding a master bedroom suite during 1994: **$19,210**

Percent of master bedroom addition costs a homeowner is likely to recoup: **93%**

Percent of all paint sold which is made by the top three manufacturers: **70%**

Percent of shop owners in the U.S. with a shop in the basement: **30%**

Percent of shop owners in the U.S. with a shop in the garage: **45%**

Percent of shop owners in the U.S. with a shop in a separate building: **25%**

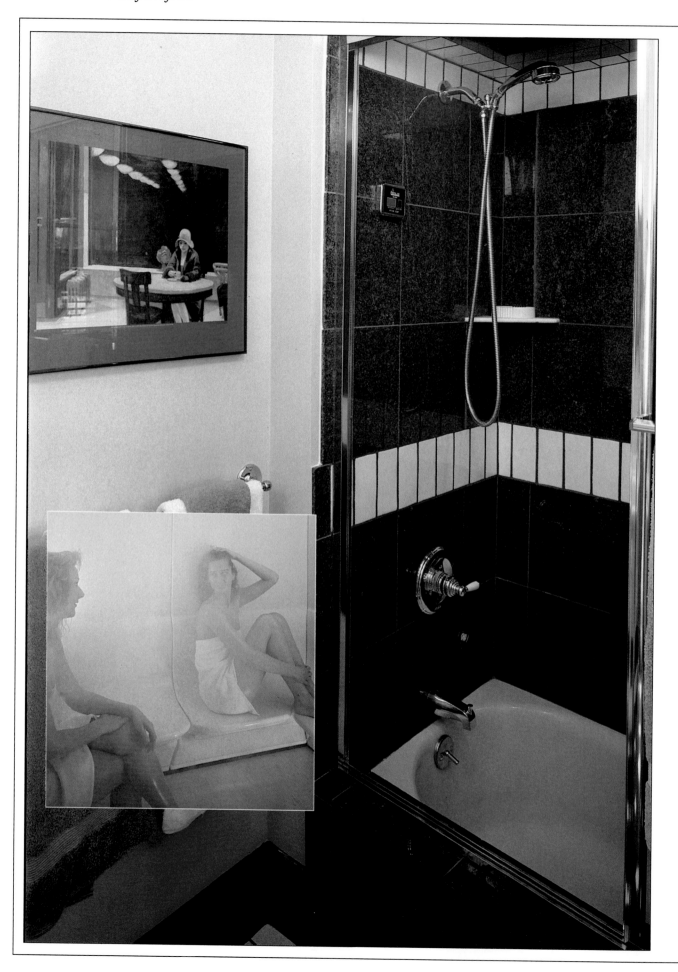

ULTIMATE SHOWER

*How To Transform A Time-Worn
Bathroom Into A Luxury Steam Spa*

Picture yourself coming home from a hard day at work and jumping into a shower that has all the attributes of a steam room at the most posh country club.

Imagine the deep-warming, therapeutic effect of being surrounded by relaxing warm clouds of steam lightly scented with the aroma of sandalwood. A quick cool-down leaves you perfectly refreshed after the day's hectic pace, and with a new sense of well-being.

Any tub or shower space can become a luxurious steam bath with simple remodeling and without using additional floor space. It's possible, even on a tight budget, to convert your bath into a private health spa.

Companies such as Finnleo make it possible by combining state-of-the-art steam generators that feed steam quietly and continuously into prefabricated acrylic/ABS modules. The models have pre-molded seating and come complete with roof, walls, corner joints, safety vapor-proof glass doors, generator, controls and all installation materials.

A steambath can be created in a custom installation, photo left, or by using prebuilt modular units of acrylic.

As these photos from U.S. Gypsum Company (USG) show, using such pre-engineered kits is especially attractive when faced with deciding how to update a tired, cramped bathroom. And the work involved

Kit components let you turn a bath into a country club spa. Steam showers are best fitted with vapor-proof doors inside a metal frame.

had no more headaches than those of a traditional remodeling.

REMODELING DECISIONS

The homeowners were on a tight budget, yet they had three major objectives: to update the bathroom's look; to maximize the room's usable space; and to squeeze as much luxury as possible into the limited space. The answer: an updated bath suite with steam shower, set off with the opulence of mahogany granite.

While the bathroom was functional, it was not an attractive room. A faux marble basin was supported by a makeshift vanity-cum-kitchen cabinet, and a large radiator dominated the small room. The floor was covered with drab vinyl. And a molded plastic shower and tub unit were ordinary, didn't hold heat, and gave the room a low-budget aura.

There were many structural considerations as well. To gain more space and open up the room, the homeowners decided the radiator had to go. Since the house had steam heat, they needed to get creative, yet be careful not to send the budget skyward.

In addition, to accommodate a steam shower, the shower area would have to be moisture-resistant. But the two-piece construction of the old shower unit risked the possibility that moisture could seep through to the bare studs behind. Continued moisture infiltration could eventually cause serious structural damage to the house.

CHOOSING STEAM

The homeowners considered the situation: old bathroom in need of a serious remodel, a tight budget, and a tight time schedule. They took on the job of being their own general contractor, and along with it, the job of scheduling a number of deadlines that had to mesh perfectly to get the job done within a reasonable amount of time. They scheduled the overall project by mapping out each individual stage to make sure the right steps were taken at the right time.

The first stage of the project was demolition with a twist of reconfiguration. The homeowners wanted to flip-flop the sink and toilet so the toilet wasn't next to the door. To do this, a plumber was brought in to make the necessary plumbing changes.

The old toilet, sink, and vanity were removed. The clunky radiator was also removed, and all plumbing connections were then capped.

Next to go was the old vinyl flooring and warped plywood subfloor, as well as the old shower and tub. Minor repairs were made to the plaster walls where the radiator had been.

CREATIVE HEATING

The homeowners wanted a tile floor (in this case granite with ceramic accents) and decided to have it serve double duty by becoming the heat source. Prior to the tile installation process, an in-floor heat blanket was laid into a new cement subfloor.

The subfloor had been left to harden for a day, and then chiseled so the heat blanket, which was about $3/16$"-thick, would fit under the tile and into the subfloor.

The blanket, a fibrous mat with electrical elements woven into it, was connected to the electrical service through a thermostat. The blanket and remaining exposed subfloor were then covered with a

thick coat of mortar to provide an even base for the floor tile.

A new Americast tub was installed along with the necessary plumbing fixtures, and a shower light was wired directly above the tub. Durock Cement Board, a moisture-resistant cementitious substrate made by USG, was installed around the tub and inside the shower cove.

The new cement board underlayment was screwed to studs using special moisture-resistant screws, and all board seams were finished using mortar and USG's fiberglass mesh tape.

ACCENTING GRANITE

A rich-looking granite tile was selected for the floor and shower/tub combination. But in such a small space it was clear the dark granite would absorb too much light, causing the space to appear much smaller. To break up the dark look, accents and borders of white ceramic tile were mixed with the granite into eye-catching patterns.

Granite can be a challenge to work with. A diamond blade is required to cut it, and its weight calls for a high-performing mortar to secure the tiles. Several of the granite tiles were cut to make the patterns and to fit around plumbing fixtures. All the tiles were back-buttered with mortar and firmly set in place. Once the tiles had set, a dark gray grout was installed.

To finish the job and give it a "period" look, a matching stool and lavatory were selected and accented with brass fixtures. And, a vintage light fixture rescued from an architectural salvage yard provided a rich accent, while shutters were used to control the view to the outside. The new bath was ready to serve its owners well for years to come.

USING THE SHOWER

Typically it takes about 10 minutes to get a steam shower up to speed before it is used. Although the generator's stainless steel tank holds about a half gallon, an average 15-minute session requires only about a quart of water. It is energy-friendly too: one session in the steam will consume only about 13 cents worth of electricity.

Steam generators are sized depending on the enclosure size and material used, according to Keith Raisanen from Finnleo. The shower stall in this installation measures 105 cubic feet, and uses a 6.5 kilowatt generator, a size adequate for most residential applications.

Home steam generators, see page 17, come packaged with controls and steam head which go inside the shower area. Installation is relatively simple, requiring only a pipe wrench, tube cutter, flaring tool, adjustable wrench, and screwdrivers.

If you want to investigate converting a bathroom in your home into a luxury steam spa, suppliers can help you with the planning. For example, Finnleo offers prefabricated modules in four basic configurations, including a 44x44" size that will accommodate two persons, a 83x44" size for four persons, a 83x83"size with five sides for six persons, and a 83x83" size for seven persons. If you like crowds, units for nine persons or eleven persons are also available.

For more information, write:
• Amerec Products, P.O. Box 40569, Bellevue, WA 98015; or call 1-800-331-0349.
• Finnleo Sauna & Steam, 575 E. Cokato St., Cokato, MN, 55321; or call 1-800-346-6536.
• U.S. Gypsum Company, P.O. Box 806278, Chicago, IL 60680-4124.

STEP ONE: TEARING OUT

To reformat the old bathroom in this project, the first step was to tear out the old fixtures. This included the old tub and steam radiator, as well as the old vanity and toilet. Removing the old radiator and providing electric radiant heat in the subfloor would free up much-needed space. The vanity and toilet were removed because the bathroom would be reconfigured. Adding a steam shower is much less complicated if these fixtures can be left in place and if the current heating system is adequate.

1 Once the old radiator was removed, minor wall repairs were necessary to fill holes where the radiator had been.

2 Durock Cement Board was installed in the shower and tub surround. The joints were filled with mortar, taped with a fiberglass mesh tape, and covered with another coat of mortar.

3 Below where the old vinyl floor had been, a cement-based subfloor was installed for strength and moisture resistance.

4 After the new subfloor had set, space for the thermal heat blanket was created with a chisel before laying the heat blanket in place.

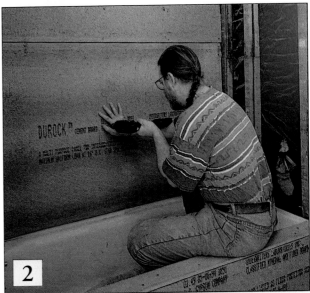

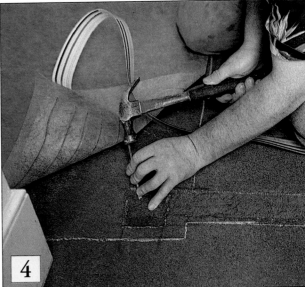

STEP TWO: RESURFACING

The project continues with finishing the connections of the thermal heat blanket and installing tile on the newly prepared surfaces. Proper installation for a moisture-laden steam shower using heavy tiles must include selecting the backer board with care to avoid eventual deterioration of structural members behind the walls and floor. Attention must also be paid to the type of mortar used to attach the tile to the backer board. Thin, pre-cut granite tiles available require a special blade for further cutting.

1 The in-floor heating blanket is hooked up to a wall-mounted control unit after being covered with a protective layer of mortar.

2 USG's Durock acts as a moisture-resistant, protective layer between studs and tile in the steam shower area.

3 The granite and ceramic tiles were installed by first applying mortar with an acrylic additive to provide extra resistance to heat and moisture.

4 Working in a small area at a time, each of the tiles was set with a slight sliding motion and then pressed into place.

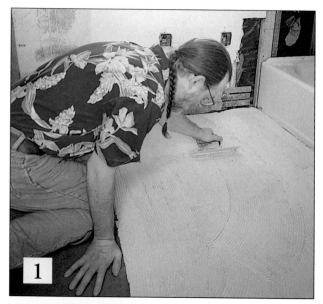

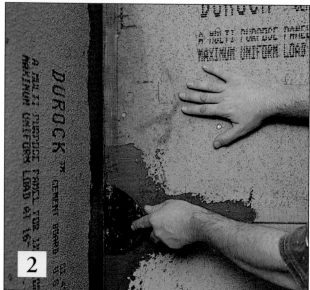

STEP THREE: CONNECTING

New high-tech, compact steam generators provide a continuous, quiet supply of softened steam. There is no noisy turning on and off since the generator never needs to stop to refill the water reservoir. Generators can be placed up to 50′ away, either under a vanity, in a basement, over the ceiling, or in a closet. In this project the generator was located in space available behind the control-side of the steam shower. It draws 6.5 kilowatts, although generators are available in versions that draw from 4.5 to 30 kilowatts.

1 The control unit for the generator is installed in the shower, after cutting the granite tile to provide an opening.

2 Next, wiring from the steam generator is run to the in-shower digital control unit. Controls are available which provide a digital read-out of termperature.

3 The steam generator's brass nozzle is screwed onto the steam exhaust pipe, using pipe tape to seal the joint.

4 To provide water, the steam generator is connected to the home's water supply system using a copper feeder pipe.

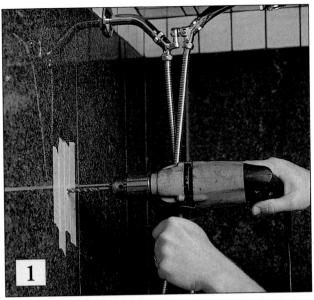

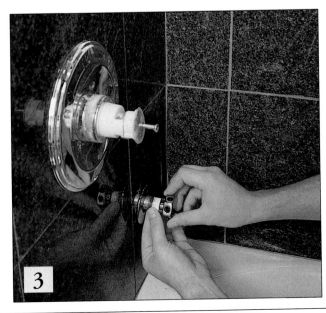

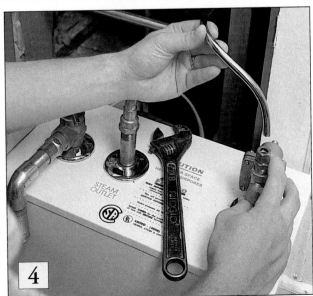

STEP FOUR: FINISHING

Keeping the generated steam inside the bath area is essential. The steam bath doors used here provide a vapor-proof seal, and are available in a wide range of standard and custom sizes and styles, including sliding bypass or standard hinged door versions. Installation of the special doors is no more complicated than installing a traditional shower door unit. An on/off air switch inside the bath allows turning the generator on and off without opening the door and letting steam escape.

1 A brass frame is installed for the new sliding shower doors which replace the plastic shower curtains of the old tub.

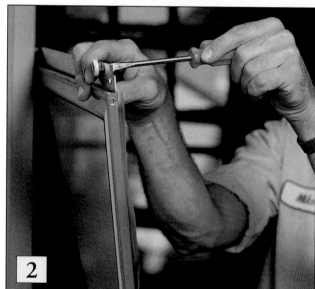

2 Rollers for the custom-fit vapor-proof doors are attached using a Phillips screwdriver. Doors are available in either sliding or hinged versions.

3 The shower doors of safety glass set easily into the frame, and the rollers provide smooth sliding action.

4 Seams between the door frame and tile are sealed with a silicone sealant to keep steam inside the enclosure.

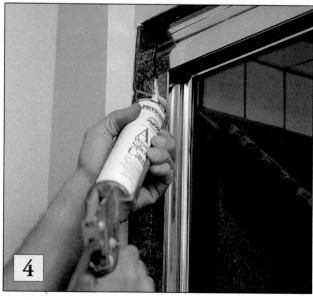

TECH NOTES: INSTALLING A STEAM SHOWER

The very attributes that make a steam shower desirable—high heat and clouds of billowing steam—are what can mess up the infrastructure of a home. When installing a steam shower, special attention must be paid to the materials that go on, and inside, the walls of the bathroom.

Once the tear-out stage of this project was completed, tile guru Mark Milcarek began the process of building out the wall and floor substrate, using materials specially designed to withstand the heat and humidity of a steam shower.

First he tacked a special Pasco liner over the exposed stud walls in the shower stall. This liner creates a vapor-proof seal to prevent steam from seeping into interior wall spaces where it could potentially warp or rot studs, saturate insulation or deteriorate the wiring.

Next he applied the wallboard, using USG's Durock Cement Board. Durock is favored in high-moisture applications for its ability to withstand extremes of humidity and heat without breaking down. It's also an excellent wall substrate for ceramic tile or stone, since it provides an excellent sticking surface for the mastic or mortar used to install the tile.

The humidity of a steam shower, combined with the 5-lb. weight of each granite tile, puts special strain on the setting material, too. Mark Milcarek used a thin-set mortar from USG which was fortified with an acrylic additive to withstand the heat and moisture of steam.

Containing all that steam in an enclosure calls for a special door. This bathroom was fitted with a Finnleo vapor-proof sliding door which uses soft vinyl insulation strips between the tempered glass doors. Once installation of the steam-proof enclosure is completed, the next step is to install the steam generator.

Depending on the manufacturer, the generator can be located 25' to 50' away from the enclosure, allowing several options for concealing the unit. Plumber Joe Blaha mounted the Finnleo steam generator outside the bathroom, against the wall opposite the tub. This allowed easy access to plumbing, and also made it easier to feed a dedicated 240-volt, single-phase line up from the electrical service in the basement.

In this installation, a simple wall timer control switches power on and off to the unit. Finnleo also offers an optional Digi-Temp control panel which is mounted inside the shower. The panel provides a constant digital temperature readout, and also lets the bather control the temperature by turning the unit on or off with the push of a button. Optimal temperature for a steam shower ranges from 100 to 120° F., while the length of shower varies according to individual preferences.

Water reaches the generator through a copper feeder pipe. The generator's stainless steel tank holds about a half-gallon of water which is plenty to provide a steady stream of soothing steam. Steam reaches the shower from the generator through another copper pipe. A decorative steam head inside the shower even includes a special fragrance reservoir, allowing the bather to soak away amid clouds of steam spiced with such scents as mint, pine forest, sandalwood, herbal pine, or eucalyptus.

THE GENERATOR

Here's what makes that soothing steam. The heater element, similar to that in an electric water heater, enters the unit from the left-hand side, directly below the electrical connection box. Water enters through a ⅜" pipe, through an in-line filter (if necessary) and a float-control unit.

This home steam generator, from Finnleo, is UL-listed, and comes with a 60-minute timer, designer wall control plate, and polished chrome steam head.

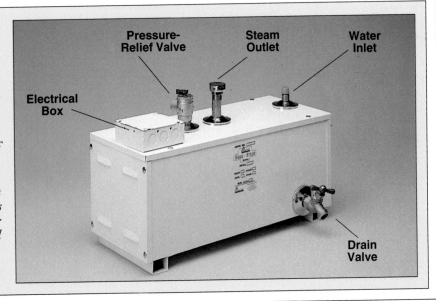

Pressure-Relief Valve · Steam Outlet · Water Inlet · Electrical Box · Drain Valve

WELCOMED WARMTH

*Gas-Fueled Stoves And Fireplaces
Provide The Mood Of Wood Without The Bother*

Does your mood demand a fire? Just reach for that remote. At the touch of a button, your hearth comes to life with spirited, golden flames among wood-cast logs and glowing embers. Is it wood or gas? It's difficult to tell. And that's the beauty of today's gas-fueled stoves, fireplace inserts, and fireplaces.

But beauty is just the beginning. The lion's share of today's gas appliances offer fabulous flames with real firepower, maximizing on America's most used and, in many areas, least expensive fuel. This has led fire-loving homeowners to push gas appliance manufacturers into overtime shifts. And the following, adapted from a new publication called *HEARTHWARMING*, will show you why (see end of article for ordering information):

While gas is not a renewable resource such as wood, it burns cleanly. Natural gas emissions rank below wood and pellet stoves, and well below oil. Gas is far safer to transport than foreign-produced

Gas-fueled see-through fireplaces make a design statement, while adding heat and ambience to three or more rooms of your home.

oil, and is a "Made in USA" fuel, with over 90% of the gas we use each year supplied by North American resources.

If you're not on line with gas, consider a hearth appliance that

It is hard to tell the difference between a gas fire and a wood fire. Peninsula fireplaces, such as this one, provide welcome warmth.

burns propane. Most manufacturers today make both propane and natural gas-burning models, and many can be converted later from propane to natural gas when it becomes available in your area. In the meantime, you'll enjoy the same aesthetic appeal and warmth offered by natural gas appliances.

Common to all gas appliances are gas burner modules and logs made of refractory or ceramic fiber. By reducing the air entering the firebox and dispersing gas through a ce-

ramic burner or a bed of sand or vermiculite, golden flames are made to dance and flicker among the logs, creating a convincing wood-fire look. On some appliances, a blanket of rock wool is spread beneath the logs to create flowing orange and red embers for even more authenticity.

Log sets are ingeniously crafted to duplicate a wide variety of wood species in molds made from actual cordwood. From madrona to driftwood, from birch to oak, the natural color, texture, and grain of charred, burning logs are flawlessly duplicated. A masonry firebox appearance on many models completes the illusion.

The flames themselves are triumphs of engineering. While only blue flame gas appliances once received national testing certification, the American National Standards Institute created new standards that allowed for the development of an authentic looking yellow flame tested and listed by national testing labs such as the American Gas Association, the Canadian Gas Association, and the Canadian and U.S. Underwriters Laboratories.

Once a yellow flame was established by adding flame rods or re-

Above, a beautiful installation using gas for no-fuss fires. Below, some appliances can be vented directly through an outside wall of your home.

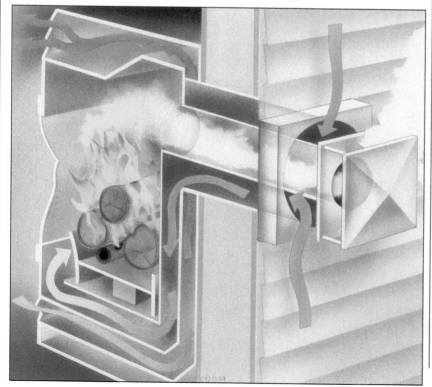

fining the fuel-to-air ratios, manufacturers got to work duplicating the realism of flame movement. Today, you'll find a broad range of innovative designs, from multitiered burners to flames that can be adjusted for height and heat output. On many hearth appliances, flames vary in color and movement, cleverly recreating the delightful diversity of burning wood.

Gas hearth appliances can be tested and certified to decorative, room heater, or wall furnace standards. If fabulous flames are all you're after, decorative appliances are an ideal fit. (Some do produce substantial amounts of heat, but are usually not tested for efficiency.) If you want substantial heat from the fire as well, opt for an appliance listed as a room heater or wall furnace.

While Btu output is a key concern with woodburning hearth products, maximum Btu input is the operative word with gas. Input indicates how much fuel your appliance uses in one hour. Manufacturers often list Btu output too, and by dividing the unit's output by its input, you'll see exactly how efficient a given appliance is.

High-efficiency gas appliances generate more heat output with less fuel input. (In other words, you'll be getting more heat for less money.) Efficiencies for gas heaters can exceed 80%, making them more efficient than central gas furnaces which, even at a 90% efficiency rating, can lose between 20 to 25% of the efficiency through ducting heat loss. High-end Btu outputs are about half of those generated by wood stoves. But the beauty of gas appliances is that the heat is steady, adjustable, and even.

You can choose from two ignition systems with most appliances today. One is a push-button system with a standing pilot, which is a small flame that burns continuously to light the main burner. Most work without electricity, so they continue to provide heat during power outages. Safety devices shut down the fuel supply if the light is ever extinguished. The standing pilot also adds extra heat for easier start-up.

Another popular system is electronic ignition, which connects to wall current and lights the main burner at the touch of a button or remote control. While you'll save on gas between firings, electronic ignition systems can't operate without power.

Safety features to look for include flue spill switches, which prevent cold air downdrafts and shut your stove down if the flue becomes blocked or disconnected. Flue spill switches are required on all appliances listed as room heaters, while high temperature limit switches are offered but not required on many decorative units.

GAS STOVES

Today's gas stoves celebrate the beauty of their flames in elegantly crafted steel, cast iron and soapstone. Styles range from city chic to classic wood stove appeal. They can take the place of an existing wood stove with the addition of a 4″ flexible flue liner or Type B vertical vent inside the stovepipe to vent exhaust gases. Type B vent (a double-wall gas vent pipe) is less expensive than wood stove chimney systems, because gas exhaust only requires a vent that withstands 480° F. over ambient temperature, which is considerably less expensive to manufacture.

For new installations, gas stoves attach to Type B vertical vents.

The cast-iron gas stove, above, radiates substantial heat with unequalled convenience. Gas logs, below, can mimic the look of many species of cordwood.

Freestanding gas stoves that are approved by direct-vent installation can be vented through an outside wall. Since gas exhaust is much lower in temperature than wood, gas stoves often can be placed close to combustible walls without the expense of floor or wall protection.

GAS FIREPLACE INSERTS

Gas inserts, ideal for existing fireplaces, are basically gas stoves without legs or pedestals that fit neatly into masonry or factory-built metal fireplaces, framed by metal panels. A wide range of looks brighten virtually any hearth in winning style. Bay window and extended models are offered, as are flush models for more subtle elegance.

Once the fireplace damper is removed or permanently fixed in an open position, the insert attaches to either a Type B vent or an approved single-wall metal chimney liner. Again, Type B vents offer substantial savings over woodburning chimney systems.

GAS FIREPLACES

For a cheery gas fire virtually anywhere in your home, gas fireplaces can't be beat. Unlike gas fireplace inserts, fireplaces are made to have the surrounding wall constructed around them, so finishing options are up to you. Minimum space requirements make placement even more flexible. Many are direct-vent models, which take in outside combustion air and exhaust gas fire byproducts through exterior walls, without the need for a conventional chimney. Others attach to a vertical Type B vent concealed by the unit's facing. All you'll see is a true hearth look with your choice of brick, tile, stucco, marble, or stone. A variety of mantels is available to finish your installation.

Unvented gas appliances that are extremely efficient are also options in many areas of the country. They offer chimney and vent-free installation and natural gas or propane flexibility. While they can be ideal additions in homes where added air moisture is a must, they may introduce excess moisture into newer, tightly constructed homes.

Distinctive looks and stylish features set today's gas appliances apart. Choose from bay, beveled, and curved glass viewing doors accented by gold, chrome, or polished or antique brass. Surface finishes include colorful, glossy enamel and stove paint in a wide range of shades. Only a certified professional should install your gas stove, insert, or fireplace.

GAS LOGS

If you are not ready to upgrade your inefficient masonry or factory-built metal fireplace to a closed gas hearth system or gas insert, gas logs are a great way to enjoy today's advanced golden flame technology. And liquid petroleum gas log models open this elegant option to even more homes.

Note: To discover more ways to add to or update wood or gas-fired appliances in your home, you can call 1-800-835-4323 for a free copy of a 100-page, full-color publication, aptly titled HEARTHWARMING. This publication provides full coverage of wood heaters; factory-built fireplaces; and cook, masonry, and coal stoves, plus dozens of hearth accessories.

Sophisticated designs have resulted in authentic woodburning appeal difficult to distinguish from the real McCoy. Gas log sets combine support grates, burn systems and several refractory or ceramic fiber logs, cast from actual firewood. Color, bark, texture, knots, even axe marks are all faithfully rendered to mimic nature's originals. If you're a stickler for details, you can even choose wood species available in your area.

Beneath the logs are beds of vermiculite or sand which scatter the flames for lively effect. Glowing embers on some models are achieved by a blanket of rock wool spread over sand. A broad range of sizes allows for placement in virtually any fireplace.

A certified installer can easily turn your fireplace into a gas-friendly focal point of light by permanently opening your damper and bringing your natural gas line to the fireplace. Operation is as easy as lighting a match, flipping a switch, or lifting a hand-held, cordless remote control.

Although some gas log kits provide a fair amount of heat through heat exchangers and blower systems, or radiant, infrared heat reflected off the warmed surfaces of the logs, all are tested and listed as decorative products only (as opposed to heating products).

When not in use, your fireplace will have a more complete, finished look. And for even more realism, you can add fireplace toolsets, firescreens, short-shanked andirons, or glass doors which also help to keep room air from escaping up the chimney. Unvented gas logs are unique products sold in many areas of the country. They are especially valuable additions if your home is moisture deficient.

HOW-TO CLINICS

*Three Short Courses On How To Troubleshoot
And Repair Common Home Maintenance Problems*

FIXING TUB DRAINS

If your tub drain has been acting up lately, take heart. Correcting the problem can be a quick fix, requiring only a screwdriver, pliers, and a few minute's time. A faulty tub drain will manifest itself in one of two ways. It will either not hold water, or will drain too slowly. In either case, a minor adjustment will make all the difference.

Drain Mechanics. Tub drains, generally known as waste-and-overflow drains, are really three-part piping assemblies that join your tub to your home's drainage system. Mounted in the drain opening of your tub will be a drain spud, which will be threaded into a drain shoe below the tub. The

drain shoe, in turn, empties into a tee fitting. The bottom of the tee is connected to the drainage system, and the top end supports a pipe and fitting that extend up to the overflow opening of the tub.

Inside the waste-and-overflow piping will be one of two tripwaste mechanisms. If your tub has a pop-up-style drain plug, the trip mechanism will consist of a large coiled spring, suspended from a lift wire and channel. A hinged pop-up lever (connected to the pop-up plug) will then rest below the spring and can be raised or lowered by a trip knob

The key to keeping a home in good condition—including balky tub drains, deteriorating tile, and damaged wallpaper—is to take care of problems as they occur.

on the overflow plate. If you find only a strainer (screen) in your tub drain, then your overflow will consist of a brass plunger, which slides up and down in a machined cylinder within the drain tee. This plunger is raised or lowered directly against the flow and is also controlled by a lift wire.

Drain Seepage. If your drain allows bath water to seep away when closed, the plunger inside the overflow tube will need to be adjusted downward. (If a spring-loaded pop-up, adjust upward.) To accomplish this, remove the two screws that hold the coverplate to the overflow fitting, grasp the coverplate and pull the entire mechanism up and out of the overflow tube. If yours is a pop-up-style drain, pull the plug and lever out of the drain shoe before removing the trip mechanism.

While some differences among various manufacturers can be expected, you should see a threaded lift wire locked in place by a small brass nut. Loosen this nut and thread the lift wire downward ⅛″ to 3⁄16″. Then tighten the lock nut against the channel and replace the assembly.

Again, if your drain has a pop-up plug, hold the trip knob in the open position and feed the pop-up lever back into the drain shoe.

With the coverplate replaced, test with several gallons of water.

Drain Slowdowns. A drain that drains too slowly may be the result of a clogged line, or it may only need adjustment. Clogged drains are more common in pop-up waste-and-overflows. The usual culprit is the pop-up lever. Over time, the lever will snag enough hair to close the drain almost completely.

Luckily, this problem is easily corrected. Just lift the pop-up and pull the lever from its shoe. Clear the hair accumulation from the

lever and replace it. If you don't find any hair accumulation around the drain's pop-up lever, or if you have a plunger-style mechanism, chances are that the lift wire connection has been stretched through years of use.

The result is a plunger that sits too low in its seat. To raise it, remove the coverplate and trip mechanism, as described above, and loosen the lock nut. Thread the lift wire up slightly, lock the nut and return the mechanism to the overflow tube. Then test out your work.

1 To access the tripwaste mechanism, undo the two screws that hold the overflow-coverplate in place.

2 With the coverplate screws removed, pull the entire mechanism out by its coverplate.

3 Loosen the brass lock nut and thread the plunger down to stop a leak, up to increase flow.

4 To check for hair clogs, grasp the pop-up plug and pull the lever out through the drain opening.

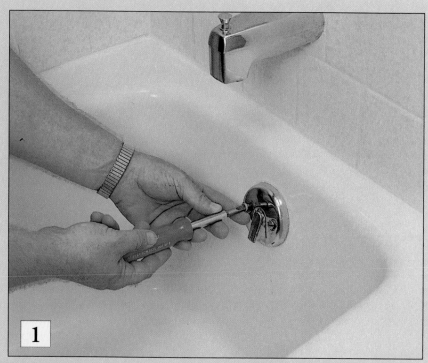

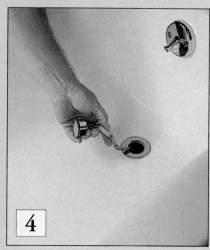

A Retrofit Option. Many new owners of existing homes discover a rubber stopper in the tub in place of a discarded pop-up drain. To remedy this, replacement pop-ups are available, but a toe-operated replacement offers several advantages.

Toe-operated drain stops are easy to use, but more importantly they require no adjustment and are less likely to clog with hair. They can be installed in nearly every brand of waste-and-overflow and cost from $10 to $15. To install a toe-operated stop, you will need to remove all internal parts from the drain and overflow tubes. You can either undo the lift mechanism and use the existing coverplate, or replace the coverplate with a blank model.

You will also need to remove the old drain spud from its drain shoe. This can be done by inserting the handles of a pair of pliers into the cross-piece of the drain spud, threading it out of the shoe from above. Because the spud is likely to be stuck in place, use a wrench to turn the pliers. If you can't break it free initially, heat the drain shoe from below with a propane torch, taking all proper precautions, and try again.

With the old spud out, scrape all old putty and soap from the drain opening. Then press a ½″ roll of plumber's putty around the underside of the spud flange and screw the new spud in place. When all putty is squeezed from the joint and the spud feels snug, stop. As a final step, thread the toe-operated pop-up into its drain spud. Next, open the faucet and test out your handy work.

5 If the lift wire channel is made of plastic, simply thread the lift wire up or down through the channel.

6 To remove an old drain spud, insert handles of pliers into cross-piece and turn the pliers with a wrench.

7 Press putty around the underside of the flange of the new drain spud.

8 Thread the new drain spud into the existing shoe until all putty is squeezed from under the flange.

FIXING CERAMIC TILE

Ceramic tile is an attractive and durable material that is especially popular above bathtubs and shower pans. It is not maintenance-free, however. When tile problems occur, you have two basic choices. You can fix them now for a few dollars, or you can fix them later, for much more.

Once water penetrates the tile grout, wall damage can be extensive. Fortunately, tile maintenance is relatively easy, will cost you less than $20, and will require few tools you probably don't already have.

Tile problems almost always start with damaged grout joints, for a couple of reasons. In today's economy tile installers need to finish jobs fast. However, tile-work resists speed in two ways. The first is that tile mastic cures slowly; the second is that tile grout cures quickly.

The mastic used to attach tile to walls will set in one day, but it takes days longer to cure. Should the spaces between the tiles be grouted too soon, the gases that must escape during curing will force tiny pinholes through the grout.

When cured properly, grout becomes hard and water resistant. A wet cure, where normal drying rate is prolonged, is best. If allowed to dry too quickly, the grout will acquire a soft, chalky surface that absorbs water. When the water is absorbed, the grout will swell, fracture, and fall away. In either case, water will reach the drywall behind the tiles and destroy it.

Damage Control. How can you tell when the ceramic tiles in your

1 Use a carpet knife or grout removal tool to pick away loose or cracked grout.

2 Use a sharp knife or razor scraper to cut the damaged caulk from around the tub. Then clean the joint thoroughly.

3 Use a tub-and-tile cleaner, or homemade solution, to remove soap scum, mildew, or hard water stains.

4 Rinse the cleaning solution and allow to dry. Buff the residue from the tile with a soft cloth.

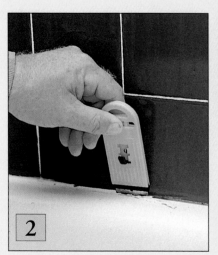

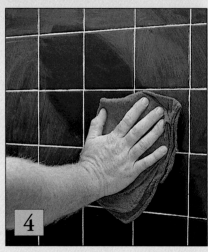

home need attention? First look for discolored grout. Dark spots in the grout signal that water is penetrating, either because of pinhole openings or because the grout is loose. When water penetrates these gaps, molds begin growing in them, retaining more water and further weakening the grout in those areas. If the water has a high mineral content, the dark spots will be accompanied by lighter, yellow/orange discolorations. Should small strips of grout have already fallen out, you will have little time to waste.

When checking in bathrooms, also examine the caulked seams in the corners and where tiles meet the tub. If you discover dark spots or cracks, some do-it-yourself repair is in order.

To bring tiled walls back into shape, the first step is to remove any loose or degraded grout. You can find grout removal tools at the stores, but a simple carpet knife will do the job about as well. Using proper precautions, force its blade into the grout joint in problem areas and remove the grout a few

inches on either side of the discoloration. If you have areas where grout has already fallen out, enlarge these openings until no loose or soft grout remains.

Should the caulk joints around the tub and in the corners be cracked or discolored, the best solution is to remove it all. A sharp knife or razor-type scraper will do the job. Just cutting along each edge of the caulk seam will loosen the caulk so that you will be able to pull it away in strips.

After removing the damaged

5 Mix grout and grout additive to the consistency of toothpaste, then use a rubber float to apply and squeegee off excess.

6 After spreading the grout with a float, use a damp rag to wipe off any excess grout.

7 Apply silicone caulk to the seam between tub and the ceramic tile, using only enough caulk to fill the gap.

8 Smooth the caulk with a finger, using soapy water to keep the caulk from dragging.

caulk and grout, the next step is to clean the entire surface well so any new grout, caulk and sealer can adhere properly. You can use a commercial tub and tile cleaner, or if you want to mix up your own, try a half-cup of household ammonia, plus a half-cup of white vinegar, and a quarter-cup baking soda.

Scrub the tile with this mixture and then rinse it off with clean water. Likely a few grout stains will persist. To clean up these areas, use a toothbrush with either the above-mentioned cleaners or diluted household bleach (use safety precautions and proper ventilation). At the point where the entire surface is clean, allow it to dry and wipe away any residue with a dry cloth.

Grout Replacement. Today grout comes in a variety of forms, from small, pre-mixed tubes, to dry powder. While the small, pre-mix packages may appear to be the most convenient, they are not always the best choice. These often won't match the color you want, even when the color is white.

Dry grout, however, is easy to mix and can be doctored with an additive that retards drying. It also can be tinted to closely match an existing color in your tile, or to create a new color.

If you choose dry mix, buy 1 to 3 lbs. of it, plus some drying-retardant additive. Don't skimp when buying these materials. Start by pouring about two cups of powder into a bucket. Then pour in a small amount of additive and mix with a paint-stirring stick. The goal is to get the mixed grout to the consistency of toothpaste.

---

9 Apply a thin bead of caulk between the tub spout and tiled wall. Then wipe excess away.

10 Apply silicone caulk to faucet trim plate, using a tissue to wipe all but a narrow bead from the trim plate seam.

11 To wet-cure the grout, drape plastic sheeting over tiles and mist with water several times a day for a day or two.

12 Seal each grout joint with clear silicone sealer, then buff with a soft, dry cloth.

9

10

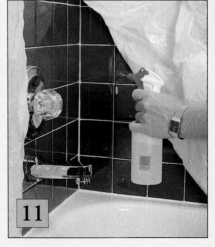

11

12

It is best to use a rubber float to spread the grout over the tiles, sweeping it in several directions to make certain the grout will be forced deeply into the joints. Then use the float like a squeegee to skim off as much of the excess from the tile as possible.

Next, wipe the remaining grout from the tile with a damp cloth, rinsing the cloth often. Then wrap the cloth over a finger and smooth the joints individually. With this accomplished, allow the grout to set for 15 minutes, or until the residue on the tiles turns a powdery white. Then buff the entire surface with a soft, dry cloth.

By mixing the additive in the grout, drying time will be extended substantially, so a wet cure is not absolutely necessary. However, the longer the drying time, the stronger the cure. If you decide to use a wet cure, tape sheet plastic to the walls so that it allows you to easily reach inside. Then mist the tiles with water, using a spray bottle, several times a day for a day or two.

Finishing The Job. There are two types of caulk to choose from, either silicone or latex tub and tile caulk. Latex is much easier to use; however, it doesn't match silicone's elasticity. And since caulk must absorb the natural flexing of floor and walls intact, silicone can be the better choice.

Silicone caulk can be messy if you haven't worked with it before. However, it can be very manageable if you know some basic tricks of the trade: Don't use more than you absolutely need to fill the joint, and don't use more than you can smooth out before it gets tacky. (This is usually a 2′ to 3′ bead.)

When opening the tube, cut the smallest possible opening in the applicator tip and run the tube tip along the seam in an even, angled path, applying consistent pressure on the caulk gun handle. Remember that it is best not to put more caulk in the seam than will be absolutely needed.

To smooth the caulk, draw a finger lightly along the bead so that the caulk is arched against the opposing angles of the walls at roughly 45°. Practice using a light touch; don't press so hard that caulk is forced to the sides of your finger. Have a container of warm, soapy water (dish soap) at hand. If you find that the caulk begins to get tacky, dip your finger into the water regularly to keep things flowing smoothly.

You will need to apply a bead of caulk all around the tub's perimeter where it meets the wall. Also caulk the two vertical corner seams and, if needed, the seam between tub and floor. Also consider caulking the top half of the tub spout and the faucet trim plate.

The spout and trim will require a slightly different technique because the goal is to make the bead all but invisible. First, apply a thin bead in the joint between the tile and trim pieces. Then wipe most of it away with a tissue. You will want the remaining caulk to form a bead less than ¹⁄₁₆″ wide. Continue wiping until only a slight film is left on the surrounding tile. This film can later be buffed out after the caulk dries.

Allow the caulk to cure for 8 hours, then seal each grout seam with clear silicone sealer. This is a very important procedure that takes only a few minutes. After all the seams have been sealed, wipe the entire surface with a soft cloth. For longer-term protection, you may want to consider applying another coat the next time you clean your tiles, and periodically thereafter.

With these steps accomplished, plus a little regular maintenance, your tiled bathroom walls should last a good many years.

Note: The products shown in the photos include grout and additive from Color Tile Manufacturing, Inc., 515 Houston St., Fort Worth, TX 76102; silicone grout sealant from Tile Care Products, Inc., 730 Tower Dr., Hamel, MN 55340, and silicone caulk from Macklinburg Duncan, 4041 N. Santa Fe, Oklahoma City, OK 73118.

FIXING WALLPAPER

For all its decorating charm, wallpaper can eventually crack, bubble, separate, or fall victim to the signatorial scrawls of three-year-olds. However, neat repairs can be made with the simplest of tools and a $2 tube of seam adhesive.

Repairing Blisters. Blisters (or bubbles) in wallpaper are of two types. They may be the result of air trapped under the paper, or they may be caused by a high spot, a particle of dirt or fleck of paint on the wall. You will know the difference by pressing on the spot. You will also approach them differently.

If only an air bubble, injecting a little seam adhesive under the bubble and pressing the air out through the opening will do. You can do this with a knife and the applicator tip of the adhesive tube. However, a diabetic's insulin syringe will do a neat job and will produce an all-but-invisible opening. If you know someone who uses insulin, borrow a few syringes for your tool kit. They can be quite useful.

If you feel a speck of grit under a bubble, your approach will need to be a little more involved. Start by cutting a small slit diagonally across the bubble with a razor knife. Then, lift one edge to determine what is holding the paper away from the wall. If you see a speck of dirt or a grain of sand, pick it free through the single-slit opening.

If you find a more stubborn blemish, such as a paint bubble, cut a second slit diagonally across the first, intersecting it midway. This will allow you to open the four corners and reach in with a putty knife to scrape the surface smooth. With the high spot leveled, apply seam adhesive to the underside of each corner and press the seams together, smoothing the joints and wiping away any excess adhesive in the process.

Repairing Seams. Seams are often the most troublesome aspect of a papering job, especially when apparently good seams lift away from the wall long after the adhesive has dried. Luckily, this is a minor nuisance, and one easily corrected. Simply re-paste the raised edge of the paper with seam adhesive and press the edges back together. Again, be sure to wipe away all excess with a damp sponge.

Cutting and Patching. At times, damage to a small area will be too severe for a simple re-pasting. In these cases, it is usually better to replace the entire strip. When all you have is a small remnant, however, a neat patch job will be barely noticeable, especially when working with vinyl or with paper having distinct linear patterns.

Start by cutting a rough opening an inch or so smaller than the area

1 An insulin syringe is ideal for deflating air bubbles and re-pasting the paper beneath.

2 To remove a high spot from under a paper bubble, cut an X-pattern across it and shave the area smooth with a putty knife.

3 Raised wallpaper seams can be repaired by re-pasting a raised edge with seam adhesive and then pressing it back in place.

4 After re-pasting a seam, smooth the repaired edges and wipe away excess adhesive.

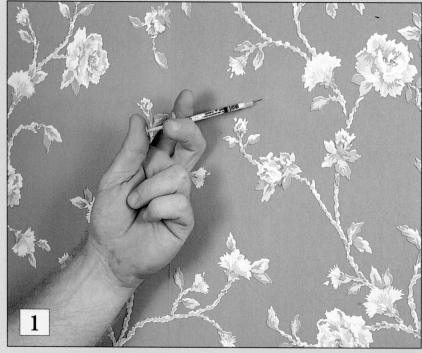

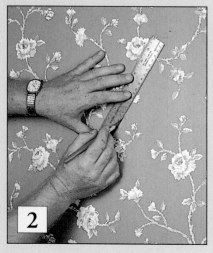

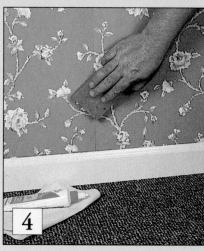

to be replaced. Next, soak the area inside the cut with warm soapy water or with a stripping agent. Then strip the paper off. If the covering has a vinyl surface, just pull the vinyl from its backing and then strip the backing with water. If the damage extends into the drywall, as it does here, you will also need to patch the damaged area with spackling. The best choice for this application will be one of the new no-shrink spacklings on the market. When the spackling dries, sand it smooth.

Taking pains to match the pattern, cut a section of the remnant slightly larger than the finished area. After soaking and booking the remnant, press it to the wall, trying for perfect alignment with the surrounding pattern.

Finally, lay a metal ruler along one side of the patch and cut through both the new and old layers of paper with a razor knife. Then move to the other sides and make butt-cuts on them in like manner. With cuts on all sides made, pull the top layer of excess

away from the cut. Then, lifting the edges of the new patch slightly, reach under and pull the old layer of excess from the wall. This should leave a patch that fits perfectly within the opening and that rests directly on the wall, at the same plane as the surrounding paper.

The last step is to smooth the edges and wipe all excess paste from the seam. If one or more edges will not lay perfectly flat, touch them up with seam adhesive, clean up the excess paste, and consider the repair job done.

5 To remove vinyl or foil papers, peel the outer layer off, then strip any backing remaining with warm, soapy water.

6 Apply a patch slightly larger than the area to be replaced, using conventional pasting and hanging methods.

7 Make a perfectly uniform butt-cut through both the old and new layers of paper surrounding the patch area.

8 After removing any top excess, lift the patch edges slightly and peel the strip of excess from the old layer.

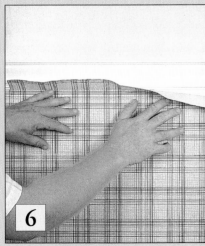

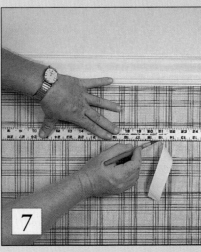

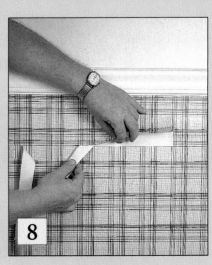

DECK FEVER

*A How-To Primer On Planning, Building,
And Finishing A Deck Of Your Own*

Summer may be the time when "the livin' is easy," but it's also the time that hammers, saws, and power drills spring into action on America's most favorite outdoor project: building a deck.

Wooden decks top the most-wanted project list for several good reasons. A deck can expand outdoor living space, add to a home's value, and be a relatively straightforward building project. When it's done, the final result contributes to the good times of our lives. What more could you ask for?

If you have deck fever, you will appreciate the pages that follow. Here you can learn the basics of how a deck is built, plus how newer tools, metal fasteners, and other materials can make your building project easier.

The popularity of deck building has created a raft of support from those who market tools, lumber, fasteners, and finishes. A good place to get more planning information is from the companies who market these materials, and from the major lumber associations.

The redwood deck with spa, opposite, was designed and built by John Hemingway in Los Altos, California.

The kind of deck you build will depend not only on your budget, but also the space you have. Among the options is the ground-level deck, the simplest way of expanding outdoor living space. It can be

Many builders prefer to put posts on concrete footers instead of burying them, and to use diagonal bracing under joists while decking.

either attached to the home or freestanding, and can be effective in damp or uneven terrain. The raised platform deck is also an excellent way to deal with the problems of sloping sites. Terraced decks likewise conform to difficult sites, while minimizing railings and the cost of long structural posts. If your opportunities are limited, a roof deck might be the answer.

Whatever deck you build, some general principles apply. Today's deck builders are increasingly aban-

doning nails for deck screws. Double hot-dipped galvanized screws can be used, but stainless steel screws are better. If you use nails, they should be hot-dipped zinc-coated or equally protected. To help reduce lumber warping, consider using ring- or spiral-shank nails. For dense or brittle wood, blunt the nail points with a hammer, or even better, drill pilot holes.

Use flat washers under lag screws, under the nut and head of machine bolts, and also under the nut of carriage bolts. Metal connectors available will cut down on the fasteners you need and simplify the job. Check them out at your local supplier, or write to the Simpson Strong-Tie Company at 4637 Chabot Dr., Suite 200, Pleasanton, CA 94588.

Also remember that the ends of boards may not be exactly square. Re-trim the ends, and also bevel the tops of uprights and joist ends at a 30° to 45° angle to provide for drainage to minimize rot.

Most pros suggest applying some kind of protective treatment as soon as possible after the deck is built. If you plan to stain your deck, remember that the wood should be dry. Above all, give safety an absolute top priority.

DECKS WITH A VIEW

Not everyone has the good fortune of having a panoramic view like the owners of the fabulous deck shown at right. But even when the surroundings are less than breathtaking, a beautifully executed and finished wood deck can create an atmosphere of class.

This 708-sq. ft., two-level deck offers a sweeping view of the Pacific Ocean. Laying the deck boards at a 45° angle creates an attractive herringbone pattern, and placing the deck boards of the lower 9x12′ deck at right angles to the 15x40′ upper deck provides additional visual contrast.

An elevated 14x14′ deck next to the northwest corner of the house, near the family room, offers an inviting hot tub. Glass panels anchored to 4x4 posts protect against strong breezes without obstructing the ocean view. The main deck is of 2x4 redwood construction heartwood, an economical, knot-textured garden grade, while the hot tub deck is of clear all-heart redwood.

The photos on pages 32 and 34 through 47 are from the California Redwood Association, an excellent source for deck-building ideas.

DECKS BUILT TO SUIT

Even if your property doesn't seem a first-choice site for a magnificent deck, don't despair. As these photos from the California Redwood Association show, depending on how well you plan, you might have the makings of a one-of-a-kind deck.

The deck at right and below was built on a large lot covered with old oak trees, a site that seemed unusable because of existing rocks and a 45° slope. But Scott Smith of Terra Design Group solved the problem with a 13x50′ redwood and brick deck, complete with lap pool and hot tub. And only two trees were removed to build the structure.

Though without an ocean view, the redwood deck at left dramatically encases an above-ground pool to give the appearance of a custom in-ground installation. The two-tiered deck was enhanced with greenery in redwood fence/planters around the edges. The gray stain used on the redwood matches the color of the house siding.

DECK CONNECTIONS

*Plans On How To Build A Beautiful, Single-
Level Deck Using Metal Connectors*

If there's one thing builders and code officials agree on, it's that metal connectors can simplify and strengthen a deck. The following pages show you how they are used to build a one-level 12x12′ deck.

Even if you plan a more complex deck, the drawings, assembled with the help of experts at Simpson Strong-Tie Co., will help you understand how a deck goes together.

Simpson Strong-Tie makes connectors to help install posts and railings, fasten joints, or fasten your deck to concrete footings; the photos below show only a sampling. Also check the joist hangers shown on page 33, and the deck board ties shown on page 42.

If you already have a deck, turn to page 46 for ideas on how to use metal connectors to help strengthen and restore it structurally.

DJT14 Deck Joist Tie above ties joists to posts. The DPT7 below attaches 4x4 posts to rim joists.

DPT5 above attaches 2x4 posts to rim joists. DRT8 below installs rails without surface nails.

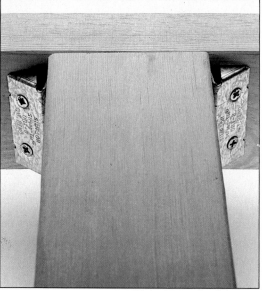

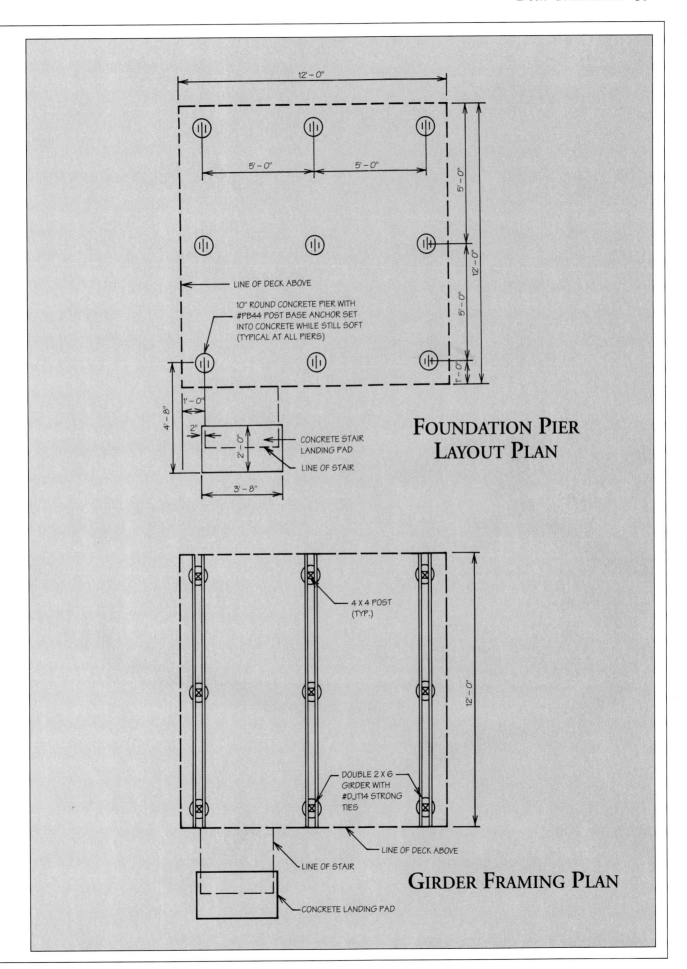

12' - 0"

5' - 0"   5' - 0"

5' - 0"

12' - 0"

5' - 0"

1' - 0"

LINE OF DECK ABOVE

10" ROUND CONCRETE PIER WITH
#PB44 POST BASE ANCHOR SET
INTO CONCRETE WHILE STILL SOFT
(TYPICAL AT ALL PIERS)

4' - 8"

1' - 0"

2"

2' - 0"

CONCRETE STAIR
LANDING PAD

LINE OF STAIR

3' - 8"

FOUNDATION PIER LAYOUT PLAN

4 X 4 POST
(TYP.)

12' - 0"

DOUBLE 2 X 6
GIRDER WITH
#DJT14 STRONG
TIES

LINE OF DECK ABOVE

LINE OF STAIR

GIRDER FRAMING PLAN

CONCRETE LANDING PAD

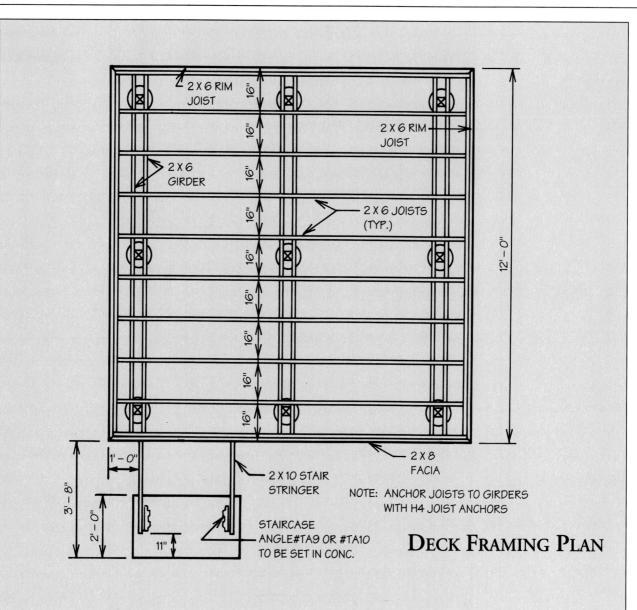

2 X 6 RIM JOIST

16"

2 X 6 RIM JOIST

2 X 6 GIRDER

16"

16"

2 X 6 JOISTS (TYP.)

16"

12' – 0"

16"

16"

16"

16"

2 X 8 FACIA

1' – 0"

2 X 10 STAIR STRINGER

3' – 8"

2' – 0"

11"

STAIRCASE ANGLE#TA9 OR #TA10 TO BE SET IN CONC.

NOTE: ANCHOR JOISTS TO GIRDERS WITH H4 JOIST ANCHORS

DECK FRAMING PLAN

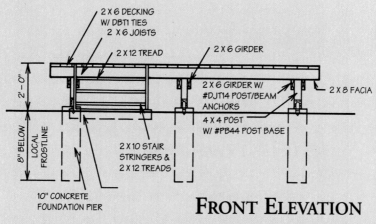

2 X 6 DECKING W/ DBT1 TIES
2 X 6 JOISTS

2 X 12 TREAD

2 X 6 GIRDER

2 X 6 GIRDER W/ #DJT14 POST/BEAM ANCHORS

2 X 8 FACIA

4 X 4 POST W/ #PB44 POST BASE

2' – 0"

8" BELOW LOCAL FROSTLINE

2 X 10 STAIR STRINGERS & 2 X 12 TREADS

10" CONCRETE FOUNDATION PIER

FRONT ELEVATION

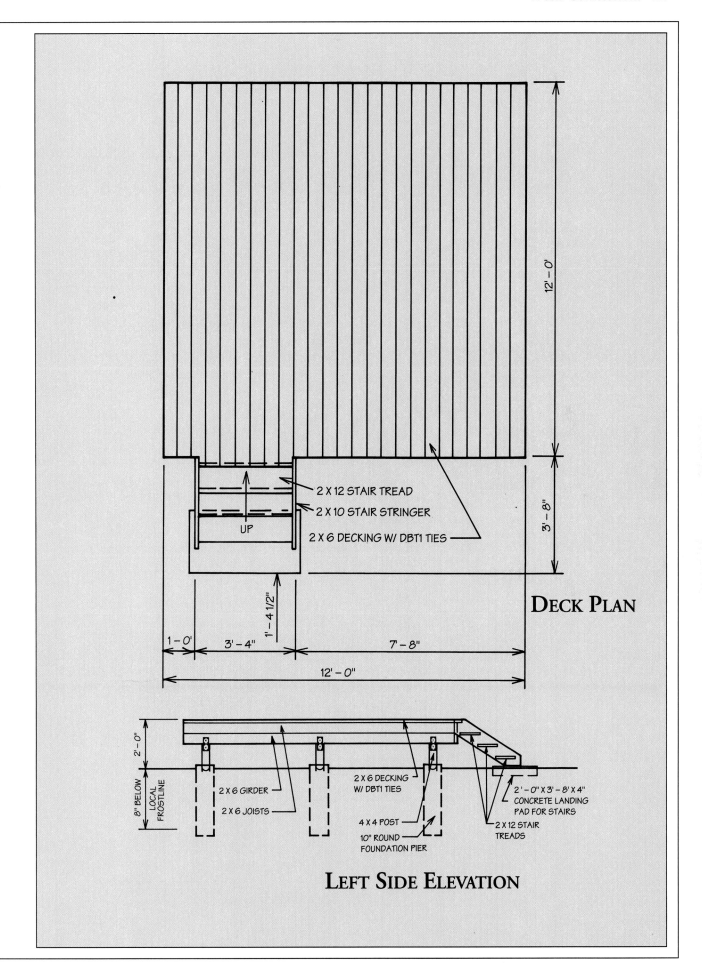

2 X 12 STAIR TREAD

2 X 10 STAIR STRINGER

2 X 6 DECKING W/ DBT1 TIES

UP

12' – 0'

3' – 8"

1' – 4 1/2"

1 – 0'

3' – 4"

7' – 8"

12' – 0"

DECK PLAN

2' – 0"

8" BELOW LOCAL FROSTLINE

2 X 6 GIRDER

2 X 6 JOISTS

2 X 6 DECKING W/ DBT1 TIES

4 X 4 POST

10" ROUND FOUNDATION PIER

2' – 0" X 3' – 8' X 4" CONCRETE LANDING PAD FOR STAIRS

2 X 12 STAIR TREADS

LEFT SIDE ELEVATION

MATERIALS LIST FOR 12x12′ SQUARE DECK

Quantity	Size	Description	Total Length
		LUMBER	
1	4x4x10′	Post, cut for 9 posts	10
6	2x6x12′	Girder	72
4	2x6x12′	Deck & rim joists	48
4	2x8x12′	Fascia	48
25	2x6x12′	Decking	300
		(For Optional Stairs)	
1	2x10x8′	Stair Stringer	8
1	2x6x10′	Stair Riser, cut	10
1	2x12x12′	Stair Tread	12
		CONNECTORS	
16	LUS26	Joist to rim joist hangers	
18	DJT14	Deck joist ties	
20	H4	Joist anchors	
250	DBT1	Deck board ties	
8	A35	Framing anchors for rim joist	
Base Option A: (Precast Pier Blocks, Poured Footings)			
9	ABE44	Post bases (or AB44, ABA44 or BC40 bases)	
Base Option B: (Poured Footings)			
9	PB44	Post bases (or CB44, CBS44, EPB44, EPB44A, LCB44, or PBS44)	
		(For Optional Stairs)	
2	A35	Staircase riser and rim joist corner anchors	
6	TA10	Staircase angles	
		FASTENERS	
	10d	Common galvanized nails for fascia	
	16d	Common galvanized nails for DJT14, ABE44, (or PB44), and rim joist	
	10dx1½″	Common galvanized nails for DBT1, LUS26	
	8dx1½″	Common galvanized nails for H4	
12	⅜″	Lag screws with washers for ledger	
		(For Optional Stairs)	
36	¼x1½″	Lag screws for TA10	
		MISCELLANEOUS	
9		Pre-cast deck piers (For Option A Bases)	
Approx.¼ yard		Concrete for footings and step pad	
2 Gals.		Deck finishing (optional)	

ADD FOR OPTIONAL RAILING

4	2x6x12′	Railing top	48
24	2x2x14′	Balusters and cleats	336
3	*4x4x12′	Posts, cut for 12 railings	36
4	2x4x12′	Railing stringers	48
13	*DPT6	Deck post tie	
48	DRT8	Deck railing tie	

*2x4s may be substituted; use DPT5 for 2x4 posts.

Note: Before building any project, be sure to go over the materials list carefully with your supplier and make adjustments as necessary. Or, when laying out a custom deck different from this 12x12′ version, also consult your lumber dealer, a qualified contractor, or a structural engineer.

Some basic ideas in deck construction include:

• The posts raise the deck above ground.

• The girders attach to the top of posts and provide support to the joists.

• The joists attach perpendicularly between girders and support the deck planking.

For proper support of a deck, consider three different factors: height, distance between support posts, and joist size. Tables available from Simpson Strong-Tie can help determine proper girder and joist sizes based on their spans and the type of wood used. One set of figures is used for western pines and cedars, redwood, and spruces, while another is used for Douglas fir and southern pine.

The CBT1 Deck Board Tie below allows decking without using surface nails.

TECH NOTES: BUILDING THE SINGLE-LEVEL DECK

BEFORE YOU START

Before starting your deck, check with your utility companies to locate any underground utility or sewer lines. If you find that you do have lines in the way, you may wish to relocate your deck. In any case, be sure to stake the locations of any underground lines to prevent any injury or damage.

Check with your local building department to determine code requirements and obtain a building permit. In corrosive environments, such as coastal areas, special protection of building materials may be required. These plans are meant as a guide only. When constructing a deck, always consult with a qualified supplier, contractor, or structural engineer.

LAYING OUT THE DECK

The first step is to mark the position of the lower deck on your house wall, following the deck framing plan. Measure out from your house the depth of your deck and drive a stake to mark each corner.

Construct batter boards 2' each way past the outer corners using 2x4 stakes as shown. The top of the batter boards must be level. Extend chalk lines across the batter boards to outline the deck, keeping them taut

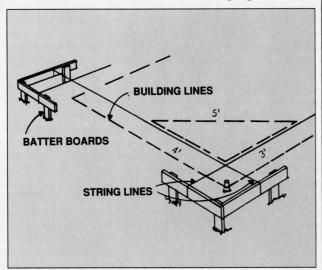

LOCATING DECK POSTS

Now that you have your deck outlined with the chalk lines, you must mark the location for each post. This plan is for a 12x12' deck. For other size decks consult qualified sources for post placement and joist spacing. Following the plan, locate the 4x4 posts and piers and place a stake in the ground to mark each location.

DETERMINING DECK HEIGHT

To determine the height of your deck, you must first measure the height of your house floor above your grade line. Once you have determined this height, you should allow for a 2" to 4" step-down from your house floor to the deck so that water won't enter the house. The remaining dimension will be the height of your post from the bottom of the ledger to the grade line.

INSTALLING THE LEDGER

Wood Frame Construction. First, brace the ledger against the house wall at the desired height. Temporarily nail once at the board's center, then level the board with a carpenter's level, and temporarily nail both ends. Recheck for levelness. Using washers and ⅜" lag bolts that are 2" longer than the thickness of the ledger, se-

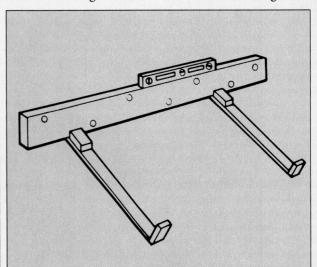

and level. To make sure your deck will be square, make a right angle with the chalk lines, as follows:

Mark the line 4' from where the lines cross. Mark the other line 3' from where the lines cross. Measure the distance diagonally between the marks on both chalk lines. When the distance measures 5' exactly, your deck is square. Repeat the process at the other corner of the deck.

cure the ledger to the existing interior floor framing box joist. Be sure to space the lag bolts no more than 2' apart.

Stucco, Masonry, or Concrete Construction. Brace the ledger against the house wall at the desired height and level the board with a carpenter's level, using makeshift braces for support. For stucco, drill lag screw holes through the ledger into the house floor frame header. For masonry, mark expansion shield holes on the wall and then drill using a masonry bit. Bolt or lag screw the ledger in place. Remove braces, if any, and recheck for levelness.

Using washers and ⅜" lag bolts that are 2" longer than the thickness of the ledger, secure the ledger into expansion shields. Be sure to space the bolts no more than 2' apart.

INSTALLING PIERS AND POSTS

Option A: Pre-cast Pier Blocks with Poured Footings. An easy way to install a single level deck is to use pre-cast pier pads. Follow the manufacturer's directions for installation, including pouring a concrete footing to hold the pier pad firmly in place. The bottom of the footing should be located below the frost line to guard against heaving. The top of each pier should be at least 8" above grade. Install Simpson Strong-Tie post anchors (AB, ABA, ABE or BC) on each pier.

Option B: Poured Footings. Dig post holes 10" in diameter for 4x4 posts. The depth of the hole should be half the height of the post above ground, but not less than 2'. (Check your local building code regulations. They may require that the pier extend to 6" below your local frost line.) The top of each pier must be 8" above grade unless you use posts that are resistant to decay.

Fill each pier hole with concrete. When concrete begins to set (cure), position the post base anchor PB44 as shown on the plan. (Post bases CB, CBS, EPB, EPBA, LCB, PB, or PBS may be used instead of PB44, but these bases must be placed in position *before* filling the hole with concrete.)

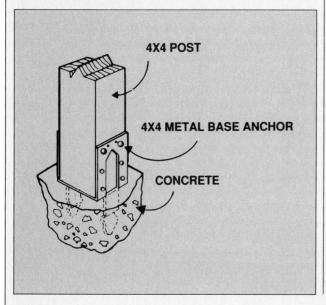

4X4 POST

4X4 METAL BASE ANCHOR

CONCRETE

When setting the posts, start with the lower level post closest to the house. This will serve as the base post for setting the heights of all other posts. It is very important that you measure post heights accurately if you are to successfully achieve a level deck.

Tie a string to a nail that is flush with the top of the ledger board. Extend the other end of the string over the top of the base post and extend over the top of the other posts as they are set. Attach a line level to the string and adjust the line at each post to the proper height. Saw off the excess post height. Plumb and square each post with a level. When posts are square and level, nail them to the post base anchors.

INSTALLING THE GIRDERS

Cut the 2x6s to be used for the girders to the proper lengths following the girder framing plan. (For deck sizes other than this 12x12' deck, check with qualified sources for post, girder, and joist layout.)

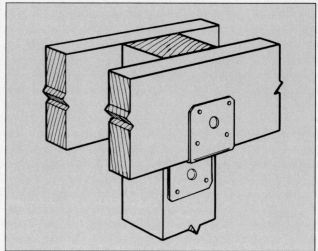

Nail LUS26 joist hangers to the ledger board with galvanized joist hanger nails (10d x 1½"). After this is done, you can proceed by joining your 2x6 girders to the 4x4 posts using Simpson Deck-Tie DJT14 girder/post connections and 16d galvanized nails. Nail one girder per each post side.

INSTALLING JOISTS AND RIM JOISTS

Cut the rim joists to their proper lengths. Attach Simpson Strong-Tie LUS26 joist hangers to the rim joist at diagrammed points. This allows you to set your joists in place and hold them level with no other help. Repeat the process for remaining hangers, spacing them 16" on center.

Set the first joist at each end on the girder and fasten to the girder using Simpson Strong-Tie H4 joist

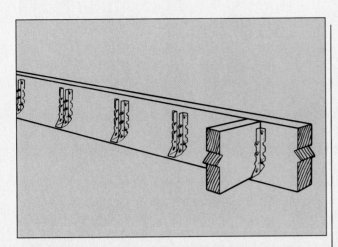

anchors and galvanized 8d x 1½″ nails. Set rim joists in place and nail them to the two intermediate joists.

INSTALLING THE DECKING

Nail the decking in place with great care, since this is the most visible part of your deck. Start the first board along the wall of the house. This board will then serve as the guide for the rest of your decking—place it as square as possible.

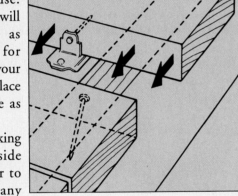

Place decking with bark side up in order to minimize any cupping of the boards, and then fasten with Simpson Deck-Tie DBT1 deck board ties. Instructions on the product carton provide a method which results in no surface nailing to give your deck a beautiful, clean appearance that requires less effort to keep it looking good.

When the decking is in place, snap a chalk line along the outside face of the end joists. Saw the deck boards at the chalk line so they are flush with the end joists. Attach fascia with 10d galvanized common nails.

INSTALLING STAIRS (OPTIONAL)

Step Support Method. Staircase angles (Simpson Strong-Tie TA10) are 10¼″ specially configured step support brackets made of 12-gauge galvanized structural grade steel. They make it easier to build stairs when you want to adjust the angle of the stringers to span the distance from the deck to the ground.

Measure the rise (vertical height) from the top of the grade to the top of the deck. Divide the rise dimension by 7″ or whatever stair rise you prefer (8″ is usually the maximum). This will tell you how many stair risers are required. To determine the total run of the stairs, multiply the number of steps required by 11¼″.

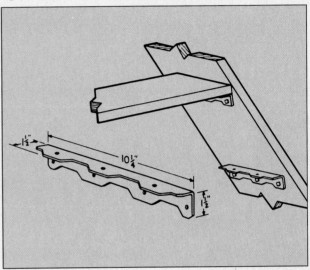

Cut the 2x10 stair stringer to size and fasten it to the deck framing with a Simpson Strong-Tie A35 4½″ framing anchor. Mark the staircase angle support position on both stringers. Staircase angles can be installed either from below the tread or from above it. Use ¼″x1½″ lag screws to fasten staircase angles to stringers and treads.

If there are more than three steps up to your deck, a hand railing should be added to each side of the stairs.

INSTALLING A RAILING (OPTIONAL)

If your deck is more than 24″ above the ground, a railing will be required by most building codes. You may even wish to add a railing to a low deck to enhance its appearance. You will find it easy to use Simpson Deck-Tie post ties (DPT5, DPT6, or DPT7) and railing ties (DRT8) to install railings that are strong and give a professional finished appearance to your deck.

FINISHING YOUR DECK

While Simpson Strong-Tie deck products are galvanized for extra corrosion protection, they may be easily painted if you desire. If you have built your deck of pressure-treated lumber, you may want to let it weather naturally. If you prefer, you can apply a lightly pigmented stain that will offer protection without obscuring the grain of the wood. Whether you paint or stain your deck, follow the manufacturer's instructions.

USING CONNECTORS TO REJUVENATE A DECK

Most wooden decks need some attention every few years. The maintenance required will be dictated by how much traffic your deck endures and on the severity of your winters.

Then, too, some decks are simply not well built. Just a few structural compromises seem to instill a wanderlust, causing a deck to squirm underfoot and to creep away from its moorings.

Shifting Decks. A deck suffering middle-age spread can usually be pulled back together, or at the very least, further deterioration can be prevented.

Some decks seem to want to pull apart because nails were used where screws were needed, or screws were used where bolts were in order.

Another source of trouble is footings that don't reach below winter frost lines, which make them susceptible to frost heave.

Improper water sealing methods also cause a deck to strain against its fasteners. When only the exposed sides of deck planks are treated with sealer, only those sides repel water. The remaining surface area soaks up water like a sponge, causing those areas to swell disproportionately.

This unequal expansion causes two things to happen. First, it causes deck planks to warp upward at their edges, turning them into permanent water troughs. Second, it can cause the entire deck to lift up at its outer corners when it freezes.

When rapid freeze/thaw cycles occur, the problem gets worse. On cold winter days, it is not uncommon to see a deck floating above its supports at the outside corners. Given enough of these cycles, something has to give.

Using Brackets. Galvanized-steel framing brackets can work wonders on a spreading deck. You will find a variety of them in every home center and lumberyard in the nation, and for very little money.

There are three instances where steel brackets can help solve a problem. The first is when a growing separation occurs where the stair stringers join the band joist of the deck. This is a common problem because the deck often rests on frost footings, while the stair sits on a floating concrete slab.

The stair stringer in the photos was nailed from the back side of the band joist. While blind-nailing makes an attractive joint, it is not particularly sturdy. To fix this, a 2x4 scrap was placed on the face of the top stair tread and tapped with a 3-lb. hammer to move the stair back in place. Then a corner bracket was nailed to the stringer and band joist.

When the strength you need is shear-strength, as it is here, codes will require approved bracket nails, which are short but heavy.

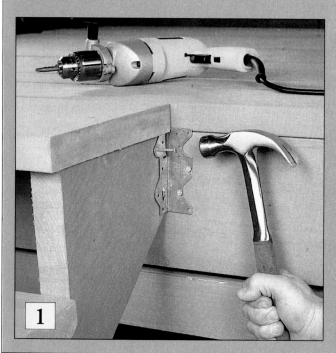

THE PROCEDURE

1 After tapping the stair stringer tightly against the band joist, secure it with corner brackets and bracket nails.

2 Use strap-type brackets to secure railing supports. Then screw through the bracket and post. Metal joist hangers also can be used to secure joists that may be pulling away from the ledger plate.

3 Use lag bolts to bind the ledger and joists to the home's rim joist. Caulk the joint between house and ledger. To reduce ridges that form at the edges of deck planks, you can use an aggressive sander and coarse-grit paper.

Another problem common to many decks is loose railing posts. The best railing supports are those that are actually continuous footing posts. But railings are sometimes afterthoughts, and in the deck shown their 2x4 supports were nailed directly to the band joists.

To fix this, one option is to drill through both members and draw them together with bolts. Another option is to use two strap-type brackets, which are bent and drilled to fit.

Brackets bind with greater surface area than bolts and washers. They are also a good choice if your deck is built so low to the ground that you can't work from beneath. To secure the posts in the deck shown, 5/16x3" lag bolts were driven into pre-drilled holes in the band joist.

This deck had two more structural problems in need of attention. First, the floor joists were pulling away from the ledger plate that is secured to the house. Second, a narrow gap was forming between the ledger and siding. To fix these problems, a sledge hammer and backing board were used to close the gaps as much as possible. Then standard joist hangers and code-worthy nails were used to support the joists at the ledger, and 3/8x5" lag bolts were used to bind the ledger to the siding and rim joist. Holes were pre-drilled to avoid splitting.

If your deck is enclosed, or is too low to permit access from beneath, you'll have to remove several deck planks to gain access from above.

Lumber Problems. Quite often, deck lumber will crack and splinter as it ages, plus expansion and contraction will encourage twisting and cracking. When planks are cracked and worn, the best approach is simply to replace the worst offenders.

If some planks refuse to lay flat, especially at abutting ends, pull nails and drive coated, coarse-thread deck screws into the same holes. Choose screws at least 3" long and countersink the heads.

Where stair treads and deck planks are curled up at the edges, you have two options. With stair treads, the best approach is to replace the treads. But, before you do, check the end grain of each tread. You'll see that the age rings are off-center. Install the treads with the centers of the age rings (grain pattern) arcing up, and ends of the rings pointing down. Then treat both sides of each tread with water-repellent sealer.

With warped deck planks, you might try sanding the ridges down with a belt sander or random-orbit sander and coarse grit paper. Just run the sander along each pair of raised edges until the planks are level again.

As soon as you've reduced the ridges, stain the entire deck with a semi-transparent or solid stain and apply a liberal coating of sealant. If at all possible, crawl under the deck, and using a paint roller, seal the concealed lumber as well.

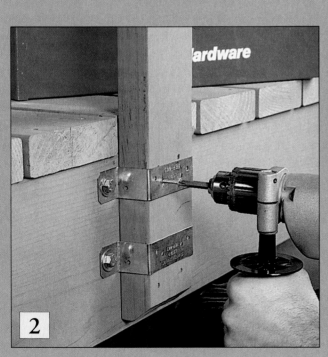

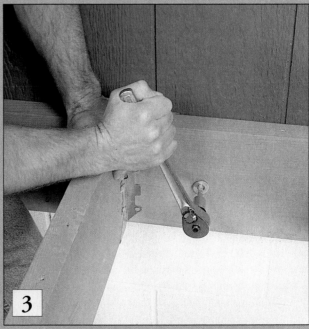

Mitering Help. *This Craftsman miter table extension allows you to make extremely accurate, repetitive crosscut, bevel, and miter cuts for decks and other projects. Costing about $150, the extension attaches to the left side of most 10" stationary tablesaws. From Sears, 3333 Beverly Road, Dept. 903, Hoffman Estates, IL 60179.*

THE HIGH-TECH DECK

*New-Age Tools And Materials Designed
For The Modern Home Deck Builder*

Building decks gets easier every year, thanks to the introduction of new tools and materials from companies who keep engineers at work figuring out a better way. The photos show a sampling; even more will catch your eye when you make that big buying trip for lumber and supplies.

Once you get supplies and tools assembled, keep in mind that many deck-building professionals increasingly prefer placing structural posts on above-ground concrete footers instead of burying them, and also avoid resting stair stringers directly on the ground. Many also use diagonal bracing under joists to hold them evenly while decking the surface.

One controversy about deck building pertains to which side of surface boards should face up. Some builders now say that deck boards should be bark-side up to keep grain from raising. Also keep in mind that a pressure-treated 2x6 can shrink as much as ¼" as it dries, so plan your board spacing accordingly.

Milled Decking. *These pressure-treated 2x6s have a ⅛" milled crown to shed water and prevent rot. A patented profile includes rounded top edges and relief cuts on the back; they're about 10% more expensive than pressure-treated 2x6s. From Supreme Decking, 10125 Richmond Hwy., Box 1458, Lorton, VA 22079.*

Long-Reach Measures. *For deck projects, here are tapes long enough to do the job. This open-reel fiberglass tape from Sears comes in both 100' and 200' versions which are moisture resistant and non-conductive. Their heavy ABS plastic housing further protects the PVC-coated blade. Sears, 3333 Beverly Road, Dept. 903, Hoffman Estates, IL 60179.*

Portable Cutting. *A new benchtop saw like this Craftsman 10" offers a powerful 2½-hp motor, plus a new quick release, self-aligning, pick-off rip fence for easy set-ups. It also has a built-in sawdust collection port, plus on-board accessory storage. From Sears, 3333 Beverly Road, Dept. 903, Hoffman Estates, IL 60179.*

Tough-Job Bits. *New Forstner bits of super-hard, high-speed steel are useful for boring angled pocket holes, tough end-grain holes, and any part of a circular recess in board edges. They come in 16 sizes ranging from ¼" to 2⅛", have ⅜" shanks and a center spur point. From Vermont American, Box 340, Lincolnton, NC 28093.*

Deck Kit. *This kit for deck builders includes all the tool accessories needed to build a wood deck or porch, plus a deck-building guide. It includes a ⅜" Irwin dual auger bit, a Marathon 7¼" silicone-coated circular saw blade, a 50' chalk reel, and more. From American Tool, 8400 Lakeview Pkwy., Suite 400, Kenosha, WI 53142.*

Straight Cuts. *It's easy to make perfect crosscuts with this Cheeter metal saw guide that costs less than $20. It has a calibration window for positioning the saw exactly on the board in seconds. With the saw against the guide, the blade is exactly 10" from your reference mark. From Beckwood Industries, Cheeter Div., 889 Horan Dr., Fenton, MO 63026.*

DO-IT-YOURSELF
PROCEDURES

TRADE SECRETS

*Insider Know-How To Give You
A Head-Start On Home Building Projects*

Carpenter lore abounds with special sayings that can help you remember certain basics. Some include: Measure twice, cut once. Keep your eye on the nail, not on the hammer. Let the tool do the work, not your muscles.

A great project, a great day, and beautiful lumber all add up to a memorable do-it-yourself project. Knowing a few tricks of the trade can help it go a little more smoothly.

Learning all the techniques of the carpenter's trade can take a lifetime. However, if you are a beginning do-it-yourselfer, don't despair. Some of the more important basics can be mastered easily if you keep yourself in a learning mode and ask plenty of questions.

More help is available than ever before for the beginner, from night classes at your local home center to special booklets, brochures, and videos produced especially for the novice by marketers of tools and supplies. The key is to keep your eyes and ears open to available sources of information.

To give yourself a head start on learning the carpenter's tricks of the trade, review the following tips gleaned from conversations with home building professionals, those who strap on a tool belt to go to work. Many of the suggestions on the following pages should be of help to you on future projects.

BUYING LUMBER

The final quality of any project built of wood begins with obtaining good lumber. Be especially wary when you buy lumber in the lumberyard or when you order it to be delivered. The sad truth is that lumberyards and home centers may not treat a do-it-yourselfer as well as a high-volume contractor who is a frequent customer. They know the do-it-yourselfer isn't going to order another large load of lumber again next month, or maybe ever again. So there is a natural temptation to reserve the cream of the crop for the contractor.

When selecting boards in the yard and you only find seconds or left-overs in the pile, be aggressive about asking the supplier to bring out more lumber that hasn't been picked over. If they say that all they have is already out, tell them you will be going someplace else. Lumber is so expensive today that you deserve to get quality stock.

If you order lumber to be delivered, also be very critical when the truck arrives. Before allowing the driver to unload the order, look the wood over as carefully as you can. You won't be able to see it all, but inspect as much as is visible.

If the wood is obviously flawed, refuse to accept it. Later on, after it is unloaded and sorted, if you find that some bad wood was stuck in the middle of the load, toss it into a pickup truck and take it back (contractors do). Usually, if the wood is in sorry shape, you can demand that it be exchanged for good lumber.

MARKING FOR CUTS

Even when framing a house, the goal is to achieve tolerances of as little as ¹⁄₁₆″. If you do sloppy work, little errors will start adding

The best time to deal with bad lumber is when you select it, or at the time that it is delivered. Be picky; you're the one who is paying for it.

up. Before you know it, the floor plan will be off slightly, your fixtures and furnishings won't fit right, and you will be constantly adjusting forever into the future.

Remember that a pencil line has a certain dimension which can be especially critical in finish work, when you are trying to make absolutely precise cuts.

You can sharpen a pencil to a fine point, but even that line may be too thick for precision work. A better way is to draw the line with a utility knife. The knife gives the thinnest possible line. The only thing you have to be careful about is to put the line where you want it. You can erase a pencil line, but not a knife line.

Keep in mind that the saw blade itself also has a thickness. It is far thicker than the line you draw. If you saw straight down the middle

If you need to take an inch or so off a board, try this. Set your combination square, then hold a pencil at its end and run down the board length.

of the line, the blade will overlap it on both sides, and both pieces will be slightly shorter than you wanted. Some carpenters deal with this problem by following the rule: "Leave the line on." Others follow another maxim: "Cut to the line, not through it." They make the saw cut toward the outside edge of the line so that half of the line is still visible after the cut is made.

CUTTING TO LENGTH

If you need to cut lumber to the same length, such as for studs or floor joists, here is a method to save time. To start the job, carefully stack all the boards to be cut so that the pieces are all flush and square at one end. Then measure the top piece and mark the cut line.

Next, set your circular saw so that the blade cuts about ⅛" deeper than the thickness of one board. When you make the cut, the blade will cut into the piece below, leaving a mark that shows where to cut the next board. You will then be able to go right down the stack, without having to measure each piece separately.

When using this method, make sure the saw is cutting a true 90° angle and remeasure after every four pieces or so. You can use a framing square to check that the opposite ends of the pieces stay flush and square.

USING THE HANDSAW

When using a handsaw, some beginners heave and strain on the saw and produce ragged cuts. By contrast, experienced carpenters seem to slice through wood without effort, and each cut they make is even and precise. The challenge is to cut straight.

Even if you start with a good clean line scribed on the surface of

Cutting boards to the same length can be faster if you line up the boards square on one end, then set the saw ⅛" deeper than the top board to give you a cut mark.

the wood, saws seem to resist going in a straight line. But there is a fairly easy solution. Instead of looking at the blade or at the wood being cut, look down the line, just ahead of the blade. It's like keeping your eye on the road while driving. If you look where you are going, instead of where you are, your body and brain tend to automatically head there in a straight line.

You want the cut to be straight on the top surface of the wood, and you also want it to be straight vertically. What helps to accomplish this is to draw a vertical line on the cut end of the piece of wood, as well as a horizontal line on the top. Then, begin the cut with the saw held on the vertical line. As the cut progresses, gradually work the saw back into the normal angle for cutting.

The start is all-important. If you

Drawing a vertical line on the end of a board, as well as on top, can help you keep the cut straight with a handsaw.

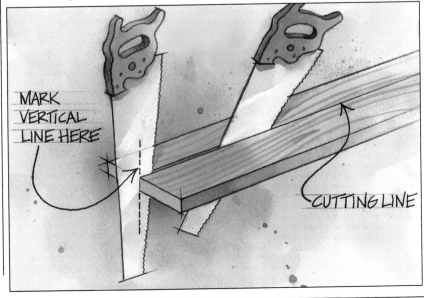

begin with a good vertical cut, you should be able to maintain it. Try to keep your shoulder and elbow in the same plane with the saw blade and edge of cut. This will help keep the cut square and straight.

Another factor in making precise cuts is learning to be consistent. Get into a natural flow and make similar strokes. Get into a comfortable position, lock yourself into it and ride the saw. It should be a steady, rhythmic flow. Apply a slight pressure when you push the saw, then relax when you pull it back. Your cuts will be straighter, and you won't exhaust yourself by constantly fighting the tool.

LEARNING TO TOENAIL

Good hammering basically boils down to good nailing, and good nailing means good construction. It starts with selecting good lumber and choosing the right nail for the job. But there are ways to make sure the nailing you do with your hammer is adequate for the job.

Toenailing is an example. You can use toenailing to pull a warped plank into line. If you are putting down subfloor planks, and one of them is slightly warped, you can toenail into the edge of the warped plank at a very shallow angle. If the plank doesn't split, the nail will pull the plank over.

When done correctly, toenailing is a very flexible, useful technique. The primary purpose of toenailing is to pin together two pieces of lumber that butt against each other—a floor joist to a header, for example. The secret is to angle the nail to take advantage of the holding power of the wood's grain. If a nail goes into a piece of wood from the end so that it is parallel to the grain, it will be easy to pull out. Toenailing prevents this.

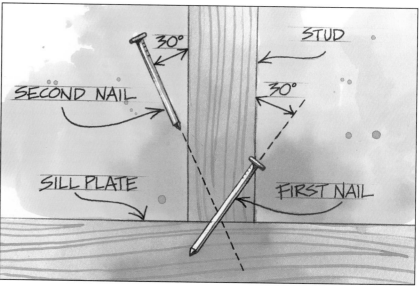

Toenailing techniques can vary. Some pros like to drive three or four nails into a stud, toenailing from both sides at about a 30° angle.

Generally aim to drive the nails in at a 30° angle. This way, the shaft of the nail comes into the header almost at right angles to the grain. The grain grips it and holds it firmly in place by compression. Meanwhile, the head of the nail grabs the joist, so even though the shaft is almost parallel to the grain of the joist, the joist will be firmly attached to the header. If you use three or four nails, toenailed from both sides of the joist, the structure will be quite strong.

Precision toenailing also works well with two pieces of wood running side by side. Two joists may be next to each other, but one might be warped so that it is higher than it should be in the middle. The brute force approach would be to drive a nail down through the warped joist, trying to force it into line with the other joist. This

Toenailing is easier if you first drive a holding nail on one side of the stud. Then drive two nails on the opposite side, remove the holding nail and toenail that side.

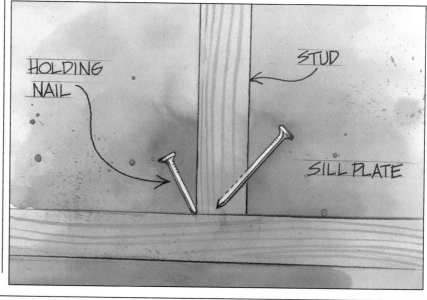

might work, but may not be the best approach.

For example, if you hit the nail too hard, most of the force will be taken by the nail itself, not by the joist. So the nail will go in, but the joist might not move much. A better way to solve the problem is to drive a nail upward, going through the straight joist into the warped joist. You don't have to whack away at the nail, because the nail will pull the warped joist downward. It works because the nail claws its way upward, pulling the joist down as a result.

There are other instances where you can use a nail to draw two pieces of wood together. For example, when nailing partition walls to exterior walls, the top plates will overlap. The obvious way to nail the plates together is to drive a nail down through the plates. But if you nail up at an angle, the nail will pull the two walls together. It's action and reaction—the nail goes in one direction, the top plate goes in the other.

NAILING FOR STRENGTH

There also are tricks you can use to improve your hammer work. Occasionally you need to drive nails in a confined space. One way to give yourself sufficient room for swinging is to bend the nail by hand before hitting it. Then, in effect, you can drive the nail around a corner.

Also, if you are nailing into brittle wood, you can use the old carpenter's trick of blunting the point of the nail. A sharp nail acts as a wedge, driving wood apart. This can cause brittle wood to split. But a blunt nail punches through the wood directly in front of the nail while leaving the surrounding wood intact.

One way to blunt the nail is to

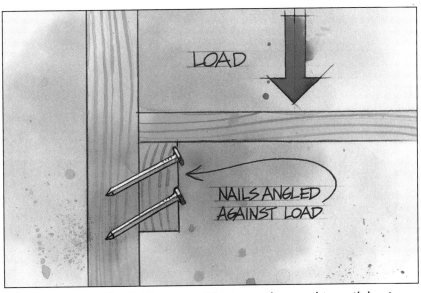

Nail position can affect holding power. This is a good way to drive nails bearing a heavy load. The load force will drive the nails in deeper.

find a nail that is already in the wood. Turn the new nail around, placing it head-to-head with the first nail. Then you can simultaneously hit the point of the new nail while driving the first nail a little deeper into the wood.

A special brittle-wood situation is installing clapboard siding, such as cedar. Hitting a nail into the clapboard can make it split. One way to avoid this is to carry a small power drill, and quickly make a small hole for each nail before driving it in.

If you find that you are missing the nail, try to remind yourself of a couple of things: first, keep your eye on the nail, like a batter keeping his eye on the ball, and second, slow down your swing. You really don't have to swing fast to hit with sufficient force. A slow, deliberate swing will do, and it is much easier to control.

If you're in a situation where swinging room is tight, one solution is to first bend the nail by hand so you can hit the head squarely.

INSTALLING PLYWOOD

Plywood is made of several layers of wood, with the grains running at right angles to each other. But the overall grain of a sheet of plywood runs along the length of the sheet from top to bottom. This fact should be considered, for example, when putting plywood sheathing on the walls of a house.

Often plywood is mistakenly installed *vertically* with its grain running parallel to the grain of the studs. But it's weaker this way than if you install it *horizontally*. You want the plywood to extend horizontally across the studs so that the strength of the plywood's grain will truly help to brace the studs.

Also, if you want to get maximum strength from plywood, keep in mind that plywood sheets will be rigid only if they are nailed down on all four sides. This generally means you will have to install blocking. Also, don't skimp on nails. Space them 4″ apart, maximum, to fully anchor the plywood. In fact, it's best to glue the sheet in place with construction adhesive in addition to nailing it.

KEEPING WATER OUT

Drip caps rank among the unsung heroes of home construction. They are almost invisible, thin strips of sheetmetal used above doors and windows. They serve the vital function of preventing rain or melting snow from leaking into walls, allowing moisture to soak insulation and rot structural members.

Some drip caps are manufactured with a built-in slope. Others come without any slope, and you need to bend them slightly before installing them, otherwise they will catch and hold water instead of shedding it.

Sometimes the drip caps aren't long enough to go over a large win-

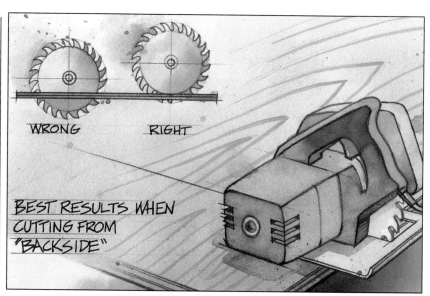

Splintering can be a problem when cutting plywood. Adjusting saw blade depth and learning to cut backside up are two ways to get better results.

dow. In that case, you may need to use two or more sections of drip cap. The sections should overlap each other by 2″, and the overlap should be caulked and nailed.

It's also a good idea to fold the ends of a drip cap by cutting ¼″ slits at each end of the cap and making the sections extend beyond both sides of the door or window frame by ¼″. Then fold the ends of the drip cap down so they hug the sides of the frame for both a neater look and to keep water from entering under the ends of the cap.

After the cap is installed, be sure to lap building paper over the top edge. Then, when installing wall shingles or siding, leave a space of about ¼″ between the bottom of the shingles and the sloped surface of the cap. This space will prevent water from being drawn up under the shingles by capillary action.

Some drip caps need to be bent slightly before installation. Cut and fold down around door or window frames, and caulk between if you use two or more sections.

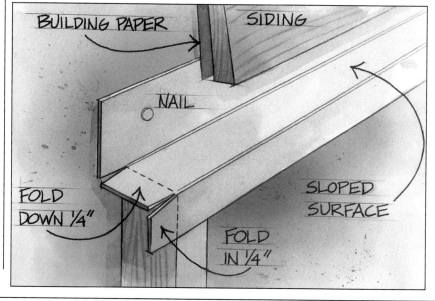

USING UNSEASONED WOOD

Using wood that hasn't been seasoned can sometimes offer advantages—it's frequently cheaper than kiln-dried, store-bought lumber. Also, using it can be emotionally gratifying, especially if it has been cut from trees on your own land. Some builders say it can actually work better than dry wood in certain projects.

Green wood is lumber that has not dried and still contains sap. It twists slightly when it dries, and that can be an advantage for post-and-beam construction. As the wood twists, the tenons and mortises will be pressed tightly together so the structure will become much stronger.

There are some tricks to working with green wood. If the lumber is cut in local sawmills, it often emerges in a variety of irregular sizes. For example, 2x10s can range anywhere from 9½" to 10" in width. If you use these for floor joists, the result will be a very uneven floor unless you take the variations into consideration.

One way to prevent this unevenness is to take all of the joist members, line them up and arrange them from narrowest to widest. Then you can use them in that order, with the joist width progressively increasing to the other end. The floor will slope slightly, but not noticeably, and you won't have dips and rises in the floor.

A controversy exists among carpenters on the best way to position boards used for projects like decks. Some claim it's best to face surface boards heart side up; others claim the opposite. However, many pro's advise positioning green wood *heart side up, heart side out.*

When green wood dries, it tends to cup. That is, if you look at the

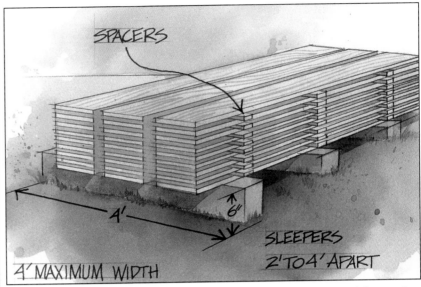

Stacking green wood correctly is important. Stack level, with spacers of dry wood set directly over sleepers positioned 2' to 4' apart.

wood from the end, you'll see that the edges have curled. They curl away from the heart side, the side of the wood that was closest to the center of the tree.

By putting the heart side up when you build a deck, for example, you help prevent the edges of the planks from curling upward, making it hard to walk on. You'll also minimize cupping if you nail the planks down with screw nails or ring-shank nails, which hold much better than regular nails.

Be aware that despite the advantages green wood can offer in some applications, there are times when you should avoid using it. Always use dry wood anywhere you want to avoid gaps; it won't shrink or cup nearly as much as green wood. Trim and other surfaces that you want to stay weather-tight also should be of dry wood.

One way to use irregular lumber as floor joists, for example, is to arrange them by increasing width, and install in that order.

FENCE BUILDERS

*Ideas On How To Build Fences That
Enhance Your Property And Neighborhood*

There are many ways a thoughtfully designed fence can touch your life. Once you sink the posts and set hammer to nail, the results can be transformational, especially when you work with beautiful woods like the redwood shown in the accompanying photographs.

These terrific fence and gate designs were assembled by the California Redwood Association, an excellent source of wood project information (see below for address).

There are a surprising number of fence styles to choose from. You may settle on an existing design or create your own from scratch. You can also modify a basic design into a look that is distinctively yours. If you are working within a limited budget, try a style that uses less lumber or use a more economical grade of redwood and make the best use of standard lumber lengths.

Specialists at the California Redwood Association advise that you start by making a rough sketch of your site, keeping in mind the sun's

Radiant beauty describes this post-and-rail fence of redwood, photo opposite page. For more details on how it was constructed, see the top of page 63.

path. Check the site during the day to note how the shadows fall.

Another tip from the experts: Try to keep spaces as large as possible to avoid a boxed-in feeling. Three-foot gate openings are usually adequate

Half of fence building projects is using your imagination to plan and design the project. The 2x4 wall treatment shown here allows filtration of light and air to a spa and deck.

for one person or a piece of equipment. Four feet will accommodate two people, while ten feet should be enough for vehicles.

Before you build your fence project, check out the local codes and ordinances. Most have height restrictions on boundary or division fencing. Some laws and codes may actually require you to erect fences, for instance, around a swimming pool or open well.

If you have any question about

whose land the fence will be built on, arrange for a survey. Remember that if any part of the fence encroaches on your neighbor's property, you may be asked to move it.

If you decide to build with redwood, it is helpful to know its different grades and characteristics. •*Construction heart* grade contains knots of limited size and works well on or near the ground. Also use it for posts, rails, kickboards, and fence boards. As with all heartwood grades, it is decay and termite resistant. •*Construction common* grade is similar, except it contains sapwood, and it can be used for most above-ground applications, such as fence boards, trellises, and gates. •*Deck heart* and *deck common* grades can be used for fence boards, and deck rails and caps. • *Merchantable heart* and *merchantable* grades allow larger knots and knotholes and can work well for rustic applications.

For more information on building a redwood fence, write to the California Redwood Association at 405 Enfrente Drive, Suite 200, Novato, CA 94949. Or call them at (415) 382-0662. The organization offers several publications of interest to backyard builders.

POST-BOARD-AND-RAIL FENCE

Here is an ideal design for enclosing a backyard or corner lot. The height of the fence effectively screens out street sights and sounds, and the spacing of the boards can be varied to accommodate a specified amount of air flow and privacy. Built of clear grade redwood, the contrasts in the sapwood-heartwood content add color interest to the design.

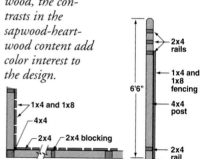

RUSTIC AND FUNCTIONAL

A rustic fence of construction heart redwood defines a property line. The fence is personalized with built-in benches and planters to add extra beauty and liveability to a house and yard. The trellis-shaded fence provides maximum privacy and protection from wind while serving as an attractive support for flowering vines.

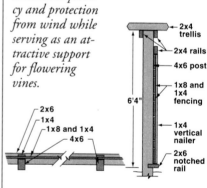

GABLED HILLSIDE FENCE

A series of redwood fence panels are stepped along a sloping site to create a structure of startling originality. Sections are built with construction heart 4x4 posts, 2x4 frames, and 1x2 and 1x6 redwood fencing. Whimsical gabled redwood "roofs" alternate with sections of 1x1 upright boards.

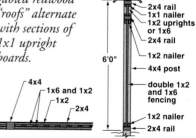

ELEGANT BOUNDARY FENCE

Blending with an existing arbor, this simple post-and-rail style fence offers both security and elegance. Design details such as the kickboard and 2x6 cap rail create visual interest. Custom latticework on the gate is contained by a 2x8 intermediate rail. Fenceboards are alternating 1x4s and 1x6s with 1" spaces.

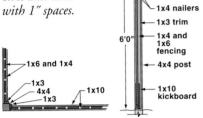

2x6 cap rail

1x4 nailers

1x3 trim

1x4 and 1x6 fencing

4x4 post

6'0"

1x6 and 1x4

1x3
4x4
1x3

1x10

1x10 kickboard

ORIENTAL ENTRY AND FENCE

Posts, rails, and beams of this attractive fence and pergola were constructed from clear all-heart redwood. Fenceboards are 1x6s while the structural members and decorative elements of the pergola are fashioned from larger dimension redwood timbers. Diagonal gate boards soften the impressive entrance.

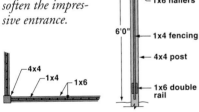

2x6 cap rail

1x6 nailers

6'0"

1x4 fencing

4x4 post

1x6 double rail

4x4
1x4
1x6

SECURITY AND PRIVACY FENCE

A seven-foot-tall fence of construction heart redwood buffers traffic noise on a busy main street. The massive design is a board-on-board "good neighbor" style that looks good from either side. Supporting the 1x12 fenceboards, 2x8 top rails, kick board and cap rail are 6x8 posts. Capitals add a light touch.

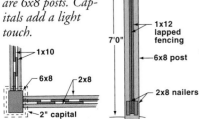

2x10 and 2x8 capital

2x8 cap rail

2x8 nailers

7'0"

1x12 lapped fencing

6x8 post

2x8 nailers

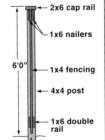

1x10

6x8

2x8

2" capital

INTRICATE POOL-SIDE SCREEN

Visual interest and privacy for a spa are provided by combining two different fence designs. The elegant lattice, built with 2x2s which alternate front to back, creates a decorative and airy screen, while the louvered screen provides privacy and wind protection. Overhead trellises support hanging plants and shade benches, as they complement the built-in planters.

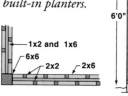

LOUVERED PRIVACY SCREEN

Louvered construction is a sophisticated way to let in light and fresh breezes while maintaining privacy. This all construction heart 8′ redwood garden screen adds visual interest to this backyard garden setting. Louvers require dimensionally stable lumber such as redwood to prevent twisting during the weathering process.

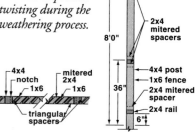

PRIVACY FENCE FOR SPA

The clear all-heart redwood fence allows privacy while permitting air and light to filter through to an 8′ spa and beyond. Redwood decking, planters, and bench complement the ¼x4″ bender board fence.
The 1x2 vertical nailers on both sides of the fencing provide stability and strength.

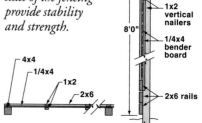

GATES FOR FIRST IMPRESSIONS

A gate is often the first thing the visitor encounters, so it is worth devoting time and careful thought to the impression you want to create. For example, a brightly painted picket gate sends a welcome message to those who approach, while a tall, solid gate proclaims that only those with permission may enter. Some gates are basic and utilitarian, blending with a fence or surrounding landscapes, while others are ornamental and employ hand-forged hardware. Gates framed with a canopy or arbor create a natural and pleasing portal.

Top: This intricately crafted double gate was built using mortise and tenon construction techniques. A pleasing iron arch tops the gate bordered by a lacy, hand-forged wrought iron fence. Materials are clear all-heart vertical grain redwood accented with a hand-forged steel gate handle and mortise lock.

Right: Upper railings of the gate gracefully curve to match the bays of the property line fence. Fence and gate use only quality brass screws. The iron strap gate hinges and other copper and iron hardware and accents are handmade. Alternate sizes of upright fence pickets create design interest.

This magnificent double gate of architectural grade clear all-heart redwood is supported by 6x6 posts topped off with capitals for a stately entrance.

The 5½"-thick door with its graceful arch is identical on both sides. Latticework helps to lighten the massiveness of the gate.

This entrance to a 1930s wood-shingled house has a delicate porthole and arch adding further contrast to the rough-textured fencing.

TECH NOTES: BUILDING THE PERFECT FENCE

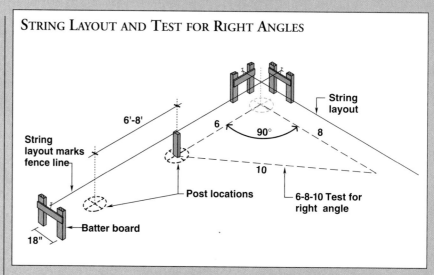

STRING LAYOUT AND TEST FOR RIGHT ANGLES

Fence building is divided into three stages. First, you physically plot the fence by staking out the location of the posts, then you install the posts, and finally you add the rails and the fence boards.

Most people prefer to set all the posts in place and then attach the rails and fencing, especially when posts are being set in concrete. Another approach, however, is to assemble the fence in sections by filling in the rails and fence boards whenever two posts are in place.

To calculate your costs and materials, it is easiest to first determine what it will take to build one fence bay (usually 8′ from post to post), then multiply that by the number of bays required. It is best to add another 8% to your order so you don't run out.

POSTS AND RAILS

The first step in building your fence is to locate the exact course it will take and mark the line with stakes and string. This is the most exacting part of the project, because it establishes the foundation and framework for your fence.

To plot a straight line for your fence, mark the location for each end or corner post with a batter board—two solidly driven stakes 18″ apart and connected by a 1x3. Use the center of the batter board as your point of alignment and drive a nail or cut a notch. Tie a piece of mason's twine or string to the nail of one batter board, draw it taut, and tie it to the nail on the other. If the fence line is particularly long, you will want to support the twine with stakes whenever the twine begins to sag.

Posts are generally spaced 6′ to 8′ apart, depending on the style of

fence. Measure and mark the center locations of all the posts with chalk or a pen. Corner posts will be located directly under the crossing stringlines at the batter boards. Take the string of your plumb line, line it up directly with the first chalk mark. Mark where the point of the plumb bob falls, using a spot of spray paint or a stake stuck into the ground. Paper nailed into the ground can also serve as a marker. Once the center marks for all the posts are indicated, you can untie the string.

If your fence includes 90° right angles, they can be accurately determined by using the 6-8-10 triangle measuring technique shown above. Any multiple of 3-4-5 will work, although larger numbers are easier to measure.

Establish the first fence line as explained above. Then establish the second fence line roughly perpendicular to the first, using another batter board. Measuring from the stake that will form the corner, place a chalk mark 6′ away along the twine that forms the first fence line. Next, put a mark 8′ away from the corner stake on the twine

forming the second fence line.

Finally, measure the distance between the two chalk marks and adjust the second fence line on the batter board until the diagonal measurement between the two marks equals 10′. This gives you an accurate 90° angle.

SET POSTS

Now comes the hardest part of building a fence: digging the holes and setting the posts. For the first step, a post-hole digger is often all you need, but if there are many holes to dig, you may want to consider one-man or two-man power augers. Auger-type diggers are good for rock-free earth, but if you're likely to encounter large stones, a

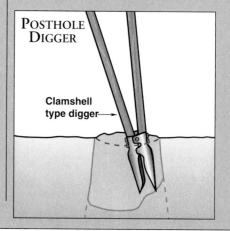

POSTHOLE DIGGER

Clamshell type digger →

POSTHOLE OPTIONS

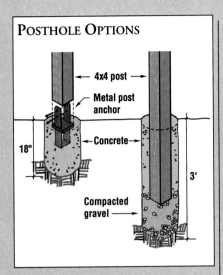

4x4 post

Metal post anchor

Concrete

18"

3'

Compacted gravel

clamshell type is better. A digging bar is also useful for prying rocks and other hard-to-move debris from the hole.

In most cases, your posts will be 4x4s or 6x6s, depending on fence style. Posts can be set directly into the concrete or attached with metal post anchors. Posthole diameter should be at least 3 times the width of the post. Post depth should be ⅓ the above-ground height plus an additional 6″ for the rock or gravel bed (see above). If you experience frost where you live, dig postholes down to a foot below the normal frost line to minimize damage from ground shift due to alternate freezing and thawing of soil.

Once the holes are dug and all loose dirt is removed, make a drain bed at the bottom of each hole by

shoveling in about 6″ of gravel. Working carefully, set the posts, making sure that each one is plumb and kept from moving with braces staked to the ground (see drawing at right). To make sure all posts are in alignment, reattach the twine to the batter boards and move the tie points so the twine runs along the outside of the posts.

You will also want to adjust posts for height at this time by anchoring a string on top of one post, drawing it taut and anchoring it to the top of the next. Then, running a level along the string, move the second post until it is in alignment.

When pouring concrete post footings, make the concrete thick enough so that you can solidly pack it into the hole. Ready-mixed concrete is preferable for most applications; however, if you elect to mix your own, use a mixture of 2 parts cement, 3 parts sand, and 5 parts gravel. Allow the concrete to set for at least 2 days before you begin attaching the rails.

ADD RAILS

Once the posts are set, the hardest part is over, and it's time to start giving form to your fence by adding the rails. Start by marking and cutting the top rails so that they will span from one post to the next of each 6′ or 8′ bay, then nail

SETTING POSTS

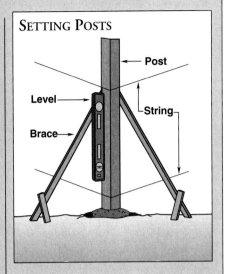

Post

Level

Brace

String

them in place. Once the top of the frame is tied together, go back and mark and cut the bottom rails and nail them into place.

There are different ways to join the rails to the posts (see drawings below left). Top rails can be mitered, butted, or notched and bolted, while bottom rails can be toe-nailed, fastened with a block or metal brace, or inset into the post by cutting a dado or a notch.

ATTACH FENCE BOARDS

This is easily the most satisfying part of the project as you see your fence take on its final form. The process is also more fun because your most exacting tasks are done. All you need to do is to work out a basic procedure and repeat it until the fence is complete. Time will fly by as you fall into a rhythm of working.

Though there are many different fence styles, they tend to fall into two general categories: nail-on and inset. Neither installation is difficult. However, nail-on is a bit easier and faster, while the inset style requires more attention and care in construction, more framing work, and more materials.

RAIL ATTACHMENTS

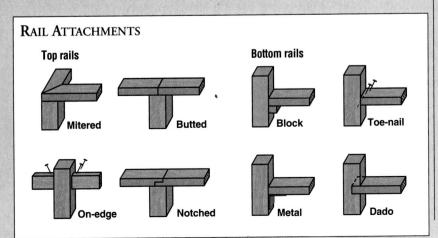

Top rails

Mitered

Butted

On-edge

Notched

Bottom rails

Block

Toe-nail

Metal

Dado

NAIL-ON FENCING STYLES

Nail-on fence styles are easier to build because they require fewer steps. Also, you don't need to precut the boards to length unless you prefer to do so. You can simply nail the boards at random height and trim them later, using a chalkline to mark your cutting line.

To make sure your fence boards are raised an even distance from the ground, determine the bottom fence line by tacking your string across several bays at a time, making sure it's level. Then, starting at the end, corner or gate post, use the string as your baseline and begin nailing up your fence boards. If your fence is designed with spaces between the boards, use a block of wood as a spacer that you can move from one board to the next.

Every few feet, it is a good idea to use a level on the vertical edge of the last board you've mounted to make sure it's plumb. If you notice that you're falling out of plumb, you can make minor adjustments over the next few boards.

Trim all the boards at once after attaching them to the rails. Use a chalkline to make your trim line.

INSET FENCING STYLES

An inset-style fence takes more time and additional framing materials, but results in a fence with clean, graceful lines that will please your neighbors. Both sides have an equally finished look.

Start by determining the height and width of several bays. If you discover discrepancies between one bay and another, you may want to measure them all to make sure that boards will be properly cut to fit. Next, check each bay with a framing square.

If anything is out of square, you will need to make minor adjust-

ments when installing the boards for that bay.

Precut the fence boards to proper length. Now measure and mark the nailing strip positions on each side of the fence and install the outer strips first to give the boards something to rest against as you nail them in place. Toenail the boards to the frame, checking occasionally to make sure that edges are in plumb. Then toenail the other set of nailing strips into position. If your fence design calls for horizontal or diagonal fencing, attach vertical framing strips at the posts. Use the same material as the nailers.

You can use any of the various rail attachment techniques when joining the nailer and framing strips at the corners (see drawings, page 67).

NAILS AND FASTENERS

When working with redwood, it's important to use only aluminum alloy, stainless steel, or double *hot-dipped* galvanized fasteners. Inferior hardware is likely to corrode and cause unsightly stains when it comes into contact with moisture. As a guide, select 16d common nails for the frame, 8d or 10d box nails for the fence boards, and 6d or 8d finish nails for the fine trim.

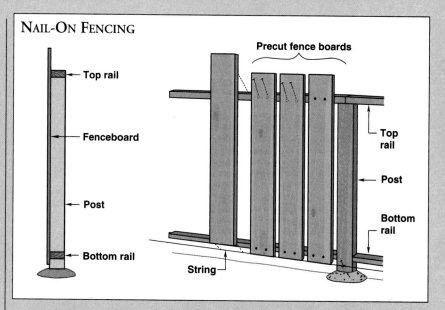

NAIL-ON FENCING

Top rail
Fenceboard
Post
Bottom rail
Precut fence boards
Top rail
Post
Bottom rail
String

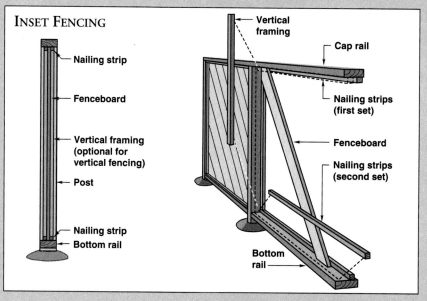

INSET FENCING

Nailing strip
Fenceboard
Vertical framing (optional for vertical fencing)
Post
Nailing strip
Bottom rail
Vertical framing
Cap rail
Nailing strips (first set)
Fenceboard
Nailing strips (second set)
Bottom rail

CRAFTING A PERFECT GATE

There's something deeply satisfying about a gate that opens easily, swings freely, and closes securely with a re-assuring click. Building such a gate requires you to exercise care and craftsmanship in each of the five steps of gate construction: setting the gate posts, building the frame, adding fencing boards, hanging the gate and installing the latch.

Gate posts should be set deeper than fence line posts—about ⅓ their *total* length—and anchored in concrete. Posts also must be carefully plumbed so that their inside faces are exactly parallel.

GATE FRAME & BRACE

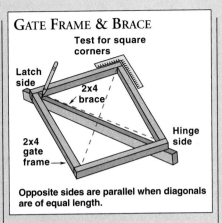

Test for square corners

Latch side

2x4 brace

2x4 gate frame

Hinge side

Opposite sides are parallel when diagonals are of equal length.

HINGES & LATCHES

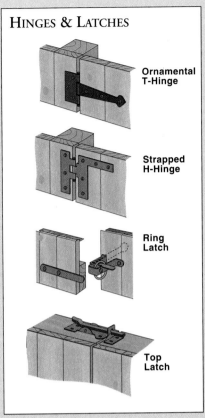

Ornamental T-Hinge

Strapped H-Hinge

Ring Latch

Top Latch

GATE ELEVATION

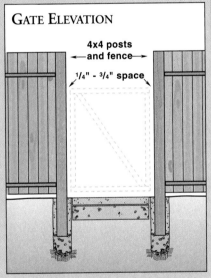

4x4 posts and fence

¼" - ¾" space

When measuring the opening, make sure to allow for clearances on the hinge and latch side of the gates (see above). For gates with standard 2x4 framing and 4x4 posts, leave a ½″ to ¾″ space between the latch post and the gate frame. On the hinge side, it will depend on the hardware you use. About ¼″ is usually sufficient.

Once the posts are set, begin assembling the frame. Cut the pieces to length and assemble them on a flat surface, making certain that the gate frame is in square (see above). Use a carpenter's square to check

the corners and then measure the diagonals. When the diagonals are equal, the sides of your gate are parallel and the frame forms a true rectangle. Use wood screws and a good exterior wood glue instead of nails for added strength.

To measure the brace, lay the frame down on top of the 2x4 bracing member and mark your cut lines. The easiest cut is a single, angled cut so that the brace will run from hinge side bottom to latch side top. Cut the 2x4 just outside your marks so the brace will have a tight fit, and attach the brace to the frame with nails or screws.

Now add the boards, starting from the side where the hinge will go. If the last piece is not flush with the frame edge, either space the boards slightly or plane a little from each board until they fit. Then drill your pilot holes and fasten the hinges to the gate. There are a large variety of hinges and latches to choose from (the drawings, above right, show the most common).

At this point you are ready to hang the gate, but before you do, you will want to check the fit by moving the gate in position and trimming any areas that are too tight to provide ample clearance. Now prop the fitted gate into the opening using blocks to support it, or have a helper hold it in position, and mark the hinge and screw hole

positions on the post. Once the holes are drilled, replace the gate, and attach the hinges to the post.

Finally, mount the latch assembly on the gate and post, using screws a little longer than usual to help the latch withstand the punishment it will take through years of use.

HANGING THE GATE

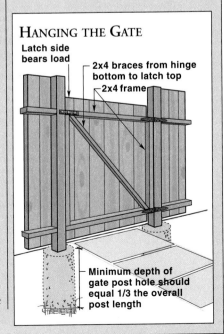

Latch side bears load

2x4 braces from hinge bottom to latch top

2x4 frame

Minimum depth of gate post hole should equal 1/3 the overall post length

MARBLE THRESHOLD

*An Easy Way To Handle The Transition
Between Different Flooring Materials*

Most homes have more than one type of flooring, often for maintenance reasons. Wall-to-wall carpeting usually ends at the kitchen, the bathroom, or entryways where, typically, a utilitarian metal strip serves as a connector to ceramic tile, vinyl, or hardwood flooring. A more attractive alternative is a marble threshold.

Sometimes called saddles, marble thresholds have been around for years and can still be used to accent, instead of conceal, the transi-

tion break between dissimilar flooring materials. And while thresholds of years past were made of genuine marble, the cultured marble available now is inexpensive, durable, and easy to work with. You'll find a variety of colors, widths, thicknesses, and profiles to match just about every flooring configuration.

The photos show a 2″ threshold that cost under $7. Even adding $15 to $20 for marble-mortar and a latex additive, the cost is still low, especially when you consider that a

single bag of mortar will do every threshold in your home.

This bathroom doorway installation connects hardwood to resilient vinyl. The first step was removing an existing metal strip and trimming the new threshold to fit the opening. Thresholds are sold in lengths that are common to standard door widths, but you probably will still need to trim them a little. A hacksaw will do the job.

With the threshold sized to fit the jamb, it was set in place to de-

1

termine the best positioning. Because thresholds are wider than metal strips, placement often requires trimming back some of the existing floor covering. Ideally, a narrow threshold should be just visible under a closed door. In this installation about 1″ of vinyl was trimmed to make a perfect fit.

With the excess flooring removed, the two floor surfaces were taped off with 2″ masking tape just to limit the mess. This step, of course, is more critical when working against carpeting.

Next, the mortar was mixed to the consistency of toothpaste and troweled onto the floor between the two strips of tape. Then the threshold was set on top of the mortar and pressed down so that any excess mortar would squeeze out the sides. With the threshold set, the tape was pulled up and each joint was wiped clean with a damp sponge.

And, finally, after the mortar had set for several hours, a thin bead of latex tub-and-tile caulk was applied between the newly trimmed vinyl and the threshold. The caulk will keep the vinyl edge from lifting up with years of cleaning, while the mortar creates a neat, clean joint against the hardwood floor requiring no further treatment on that side of the threshold.

Note: For more information on using a marble threshold, you can write to Thornton Tile and Marble, 612 South 9th Street, Murray, KY 42071-3097, or call (502) 753-5719.

THE PROCEDURE

1 Use a straightedge and sharp utility knife to trim away any excess vinyl.

2 Then apply masking tape to the floor on each side of the saddle position and apply marble mortar strengthened with latex additive.

3 Press the threshold into the mortar and lift the tape to remove excess mortar. Wipe each joint with a damp sponge.

4 Next, apply a neat bead of latex caulk to the seam between the vinyl flooring and the threshold; wipe with a clean sponge.

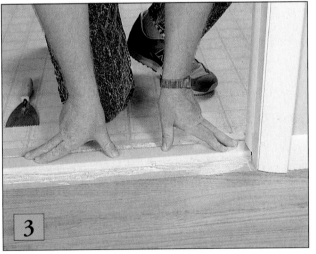

3

2

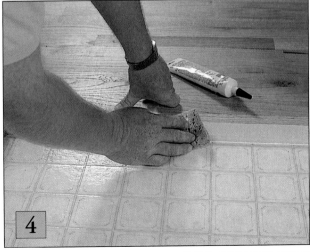

4

MECHANIZED SANDING

*Break-Through Sanding Options
Offer Better Results With Less Elbow Grease*

Hand sanding has its place, no doubt about it. But take a stroll through a well-equipped tool store and you'll see that tool inventors and manufacturers have made major breakthroughs in a variety of ways to make sanding more pleasant and productive, no matter if you are putting the final touches on a piece of fine furniture or finishing the trim on a new window.

Motorized sanders have been around almost since the invention of electricity. But within the last decade, new sanding tools have broken through new barriers of performance, efficiency, and user comfort. From tiny third-sheet palm sanders to new orbital wonder-workers, nearly all offer built-in or optional accessories that respect your concern for keeping the home workshop environment clear of air-borne dust.

The most recent innovation in sanding technology is a new down-sized drum sander which brings production-shop technology to your own workshop, no matter how small it is. Until recently, power-fed

The 16-32, photo opposite, evolved from re-engineering larger drum sanders popular with production shops.

surface sanders were relatively scarce in the home workshop. First, they were bulky machines that required a generous amount of valuable space. Second, their price tags ran well over a thousand dollars.

A new category of workshop tool, this 80-lb. Performax benchtop drum sander is offering do-it-yourselfers useful capabilities beyond surfacing in either the home workshop or on the job site.

But now an improved benchtop version has become available which costs around $800 and is compact enough to fit into a small shop where space is at a premium.

The machine attracts crowds at woodworking shows mainly because it can make sanding of flat surfaces almost a push-button operation. Hooked to either a shop vacuum or central dust collection system, it also can be used to occasionally do the work of a thickness

planer to bring rough stock down to workable dimensions.

This new category of shop tool is represented in the marketplace by the Performax 16-32 from Performax Products, Burnsville, Minnesota. Inventor and president Gary Green points out that the sander offers the same open-throat design of several of the firm's larger drum sanders now popular in production workshops. The 16-32 designation refers to the new machine's 16"-wide sanding drum that is suspended from one end. This 5"-diameter extruded aluminum drum allows sanding a 32"-wide panel in just two passes, and is really the heart of the machine.

The unit's drum is wrapped with a 3"x 92" abrasive strip in your choice of grit in a spiral pattern. A patented spring-loaded abrasive take-up fastener keeps the strip flat and tight to the drum, eliminates the need for adhesives, and also makes it easy to change the abrasive strip or reverse it to prolong service life. The changing of strips takes only a minute. The self-cooling drum dissipates any heat build-up so it won't warp, stretch the abrasive strip, or burn the wood being sanded.

Here's how it works. A film-backed abrasive conveyor belt riding over a steel conveyor bed feeds the stock under the sanding drum, which is driven by a directly coupled 1-hp motor. A separate, high-torque gear motor powers the conveyor and can be adjusted to feed rates from 0 to 10' per minute. The sanding drum is raised or lowered by a turn of a height adjustment handle to adjust for the thickness of the material sanded, while tension rollers keep stock from slipping on the conveyor to produce an even finish.

According to Gary Green, home workshop owners like the versatility of the new scaled-down production-shop drum sander. Among the capabilities of the 16-32 are these hands-free operations:

• Abrasive planing to surface rough boards instead of using a thickness planer.

• Dimensioning parts to a uniform thickness of within .010".

• Sanding stock from as little as 1/64" thick to as much as 3" thick.

• Sanding pieces as short as 2¼", and as wide as twice the width of the drum (32").

• Quick-changing of the abrasive strip to move progressively from coarse to very fine grits to give projects a professional-quality surface.

Woodworking enthusiasts who have experimented with the new sander say it works a little slower than a thickness planer in dimensioning stock, taking off from 1/32" to 1/16" per pass. However, they agree that the abrasive planing tool works well for surfacing and finishing wood carrying knots, burls, cross grain, or reverse grain, as well as for removing cups or crowns.

Wood turners find it handy for leveling out blanks for safe and easy turning. They also use it to bring pieces to a uniform thickness for glue-ups so there won't be any voids between the seams when they are exposed after turning.

Craft workers find they can easily sand small parts safely in a hands-free, dustless environment. That includes short scrollsaw and bandsaw cut-outs as thin as 1/16", saving tedious saw mark cleanup on delicate parts. Even narrow, thin wood strips used for wood baskets and Shaker boxes can be easily dimensioned and sanded.

Cabinetmakers find they can use the machine for sanding large panels, as well as stile-and-rail material for door stock and face frames, to a consistent thickness. They also find it useful to edge-sand stock up to 3" thick, instead of using a jointer which can result in chipping, tearing, or sniping.

Furniture restorers find the drum sander useful on solid wood surfaces, such as table tops, to remove old finishes, flatten cups or crowns, and sand it smooth. They report it can make veneer repairs easier since it helps them bring veneer to a precise thickness to match grain and color.

So how do you operate it? After you have set up the benchtop sander, hooked it into a dust collection system, and run through a few pre-operational checks, you are ready to install an abrasive strip with your choice of grit (see How The Strips Are Attached, next page). Then you set the depth of cut, using the hand crank and the adjustment gauge, start up the drum and the conveyor, and set the feed rate.

After switching on the dust collector, you are ready to feed pieces through the sander. To feed stock through, you simply rest and hold the board on the conveyor table, allowing the conveyor belt to carry the stock to the drum. While the board is being sanded, you step to the outfeed side of the machine to receive and control the board as it exits from the back side of the sanding drum.

Keys to success, explains Warren Weber, Performax tech specialist,

SELECTING ABRASIVE GRITS

Various grit sizes available on continuous rolls and their common applications are listed below. On larger drum sanders with two drums, a coarser grit often will be used on the front drum and a finer grit on the rear drum.

GRIT*	COMMON APPLICATION
36 Grit	Abrasive planing, surfacing rough-sawn boards, maximum stock removal, glue removal.
60 Grit	Surfacing and dimensioning boards, trueing warped boards.
80 Grit	Surfacing, light dimensioning, removing planer ripples.
100 Grit	Light surfacing, removing planer ripples.
120 Grit	Light surfacing, minimal stock removal.
150 Grit	Finish sanding, minimal stock removal.
180 Grit	Finish sanding only, not for stock removal.
220 Grit	Finish sanding only, not for stock removal.

Success with drum sanders can depend on using quality abrasives. Performax Products recommends using 3"-wide continuous rolls which are cloth backed, aluminum oxide, resin bond, open coat, X weight.

The 16-32 drum sander is a hit with woodworkers who say it takes the work out of finishing. Changing its abrasive strip on the drum takes only a few minutes of time.

include setting the proper depth of cut, along with selecting the proper feed rate of the conveyor. When sanding with grits finer than 80, he says a good procedure is to turn the machine off and raise the conveyor table so the drum just contacts the workpiece and still can be rotated by hand. When using grits coarser than 80, you can raise the conveyor table slightly more. The proper setting will depend on several variables, including 1) abrasive type and grit, 2) width and hardness of the workpiece, and 3) feed rate setting of the conveyor belt.

The variable feed rate control of the conveyor belt adjusts the load on the machine; a faster feed rate allows faster sanding but fewer revolutions of the drum per inch of sanding. A slower feed rate provides more revolutions of the drum per inch of sanding to allow a greater depth of cut and smoother sanding. Warren suggests to begin experimenting with the feed rate set at about 40% to 50% of maximum.

The best feed rate will also depend on a combination of factors, including type of stock, grit and depth of cut used, and whether the stock is fed directly in line with the conveyor bed or at an angle. The feed rate should be slowed if you hear the drum motor lugging down, if the conveyor belt is slipping, or if a ripple effect is observed on the stock.

If the finish is smooth and the machine is not overworking, you can experiment with a faster feed rate. A faster feed rate is also indicated if the stock begins to show burn marks. With cherry, hard maple or other hardwoods, using a shallower depth of cut will also help minimize burn marks.

As with any sanding operation, Warren says the idea is to begin with a coarse grit, based on the roughness of the stock and the amount of stock to be removed, then progressively work toward fin-

er grits (see chart). Grits 24, 36, 60, and 80 are primarily used for stock removal, while grits 100 through 220 are usually used to remove the scratch pattern from the previous grit used. For best results, he suggests not to skip more than one grit grade when progressing through a sanding sequence.

For fine work, such as furniture, it's best not to skip any grit grades at all. In general, Warren notes that premium quality abrasives, such as silicon carbide and film-backed abrasives, will produce a better finish. However, grits that are too fine can sometimes burnish the wood and leave a glossy surface which will not accept stains evenly. This varies by the type of wood. Oak, for example, is susceptible to burnishing because of its open pores.

The real beauty of the new benchtop, power-fed drum sanders like the Performax 16-32 is how easy it is to attach and change abrasive strips. It's a one-minute job, simplified by the fact that the drum design eliminates the need for using any adhesives. The strips can be bought in either 35′ or 52-yard lengths.

The strips do not have to be premeasured. As explained on page 77, the end of the roll is first tapered and attached to a clip-type fastener on the outboard side of the drum, then it is wrapped around the drum and a second taper is made to fit a patented take-up fastener on the inboard side of the drum.

Operating the machine is not difficult. But getting the best results from it, says Warren, will come through experimenting with different abrasives, as well as adjustments, to fit the particular job at hand. Following on the next page is a checklist of useful tips which can help improve performance of most any drum sander, large or small.

Tech Notes: Tips For Harnessing Drum Sanders

Below are suggestions from the factory to help get the most from a sander like the Performax 16-32:

■ **Dust Collection.** Woodworkers report they can get 100% of the dust collected when hooked up directly to the 2½" hose of a shop vacuum. When connecting to a centralized dust collector drawing from a number of tools, remember that straight pipe will not restrict airflow as much as flexible tubing. Also, Ys and elbows will restrict airflow less than Ts.

■ **Multiple-Piece Sanding Runs.** When abrasive planing or thickness sanding a run of similar pieces that you want to have the same thickness, it is best to sand all the pieces at the same time. This way you will be able to determine the thickness of the thinnest piece and process all pieces to that same thickness. Be aware that the sander will remove cups and crowns in the workpiece; consider this when measuring and processing stock to the same thickness.

■ **Multiple Pieces Together.** When sanding multiple pieces simultaneously, it helps to stagger (step) the pieces across the width of the conveyor belt. This provides better contact with the tension rollers. Try to only process multiple pieces of similar thickness. If there is a significant thickness difference, the thinner pieces can slip on the conveyor belt as they may not contact the tension rollers. Also, when pieces thicker than ¾" are being sanded, they should be longer than the minimum normally recommended to prevent tipping of the stock.

■ **Edge Sanding.** When edge sanding, the drum sander will mimic the opposite edge of the stock which is laying on the conveyor belt. Because of this, it is important for the stock edge to have been ripped at the proper angle to the face before the sanding process. When edge sanding stock that is less than ¾" wide, or more than 2" high, it is good procedure to stack and clamp several pieces together to prevent them from slipping or tipping on the conveyor belt.

■ **Sanding Imperfect Stock.** When sanding stock with a cup or crown, place the crown up. This will stabilize the stock to help prevent tipping or rocking during the sanding process. (After the crown has been removed and the top is flat, turn the stock over and sand the opposite side.) To avoid personal injury, take special care when sanding stock that is twisted, bowed, or otherwise varies in thickness from end to end. If possible, support such stock as it is being sanded to keep it from slipping or tipping. Use extra roller stands, help from another person, or hand pressure on the stock, to help minimize potentially hazardous situations.

■ **Face Frames & Raised Panel Doors.** It is very important to have the proper abrasive contact when doing this type of sanding. If the machine is set to take an excessive depth of cut, the result can be a gouge or dip as the drum goes from sanding the rails at full width to sanding just a few inches of width on the stiles. To prevent this problem, for example, make sure that when using abrasives finer than 80 grit the drum just contacts the wood but can still be rotated by hand. If there is room, angling the stock on the conveyor belt can also help. Slowing the conveyor feed when coming to a rail in the stock can help prevent a dip or gouge. This allows the abrasive to work the wider width with less effort, and to achieve better consistency of the finished surface.

■ **Stock Feeding Angle.** Some pieces, because of their dimensions, need to be fed into the machine at a 90° angle (perpendicular to the drums). However, even a slight offset angle of the stock will provide for more effective stock removal. The optimum feeding angle for stock removal is about 60°. Angling the workpiece for stock removal provides other advantages, such as less loading of certain areas of the drums due to glue lines or mineral streaks in the stock, more uniform wear of abrasive strips, potentially faster feed rates, and lighter loads on the motor. To get the best final finish, however, feed the stock through so it will be sanded in line with the grain of the wood on the final one or two passes.

■ **Cleaning Abrasive Strips.** Regularly clean the abrasive strips on the drums with commercially available cleaning sticks, following the manufacturer's directions. When cleaning, also brush the stick crumbs from the drum while it is still rotating. It's important to wear tight-fitting clothes and keep alert during this operation to avoid injury. Cloth-backed abrasives can be cleaned by soaking in paint thinner or mineral spirits for 20 minutes to 1 hour, then using a brush to remove any buildup or burns. Dry the strips completely before reuse. Using safety precautions, you may be able to remove buildups from burns by holding Plexiglas on edge over a rotating drum.

■ **Stretching Abrasive Grit Life.** When sanding metal or solid surface, MDF or particle board, a silicon carbide abrasive may last longer than aluminum oxide and also allow a more uniform finish. Abrasive life can also be increased by removing the abrasive strip from the drum and reversing it. To do this, remove the strip and use what was the trailing end as the starting end on the left (outboard) side of the drum. Reversing the strip will provide a fresh set of cutting edges.

■ **Keeping The Machine Clean.** For best results, make cleaning the machine a regular workshop procedure. Allowing excess buildup of dust and debris can adversely affect performance through the loading of the abrasives, slippage on the conveyor table, and/or the accumulation of material inside the drum which can throw off its center of balance. Leave the dust collector on when cleaning dust from the drum. Also brush the conveyor belt after cleaning operations. If not cleaned, the conveyor may allow stock to slip during sanding.

HOW THE STRIPS ARE ATTACHED

The 3″-wide abrasive strips attach easily to the drum of the 16-32 as follows:

1. The tapered end of the strip is inserted in a slot at the outboard end of the drum by raising a take-up fastener and pushing the strip end in so that it occupies the entire slot width. Release the take-up fastener to secure the one end of the strip, then wrap the strip around the drum.

The tapered cut of the strip end should be lined up with the edge of the drum. The strip is wrapped in a spiral fashion by rotating the drum with the left hand while guiding the strip with the right hand. As the strip is wrapped, the strip edges should butt against, but not overlap, each other.

2. The trailing end of the strip is marked at the point where it crosses the inboard end of the drum. From this point, a taper is cut, similar to the one used on the starting edge of the strip. (The resulting taper on the remaining roll can be used as the taper for the starting edge of the next strip to be cut.) With the trailing edge of the strip cut, the drum is rewrapped and the tapered end is inserted through the slot in the inboard end of the drum and into the inboard take-up fastener.

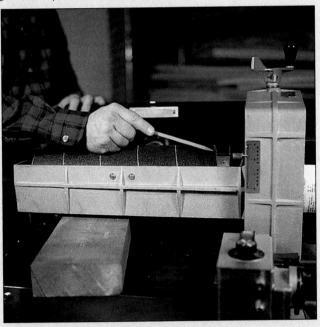

The strip spirals the drum, using patented end fasteners.

3. After the strip end is inserted, the take-up fastener is released to retain the abrasive strip in position tightly against the drum. The fastener is designed to automatically take up any slack caused by stretching of the abrasive strip. It is important to position the abrasive strip in the slot with sufficient room between the inside of the slot and the tapered end of the strip to allow it to be pulled into the drum as needed. Not leaving enough space between the strip and the inside of the slot will sometimes prevent the take-up fastener from operating properly during sanding.

4. The abrasive strip may stretch enough in use to allow the take-up fastener to reach its lowest position so it no longer is able to maintain tension on the strip. If, and when this occurs, it is necessary to reset the take-up fastener by raising it, pushing the strip end into the slot, and then releasing the fastener.

A sandpaper cleaning stick may be used to remove deposits and help extend the life of the abrasive. To do this, a cleaning stick is held against the rotating drum and moved along the drum surface, taking proper precautions. Once you are done cleaning, a shop brush can be used to remove any remaining cleaning stick crumbs from the drum.

POWER SANDING OPTIONS

New Gear That Can Make Sanding Jobs Easier,
Healthier, And More Productive

Inventors and manufacturers have been working overtime to make sanding jobs easier for the home do-it-yourselfer. Besides the new scaled-down surface sander shown on the previous pages, the power tools shown here are just a sampling of ways to make sanding jobs easier. Each has the capabilities to help you get the job done faster, better, and with less of the free-floating dust that has been associated with sanding in the past.

Those watching the sales of these tools report that improvements in such standbys as the basic pad sander, belt sander, and belt/disc sander are providing home workshop owners good reasons to upgrade. Sales numbers confirm that those updating their sanding arsenals are also favoring the new compact palm-grip sanders, random-orbit sanders, and oscillating sanders for their ability to prepare surfaces for fine finishes.

The oscillating sander is a good example of innovative engineering to help you take the drudgery out of sanding curved surfaces by hand. It can make quick work of sanding rough edges on items like scroll-sawn items so you can quickly get on to painting or finishing. Its dual-action spindle, driven by a cam-activated, direct-drive transmission system, doesn't burn the workpiece and also reduces buildup on sandpaper.

Engineers haven't forgotten favorites like the belt/disc sander shown on the opposite page either. This updated workhorse rapidly delivers project pieces well sanded, sharpened, or deburred and ready for the next step. Its 6"-deep throat provides easy access to the inside surfaces of intricate scroll work and lettering. Tool sellers call this tool a sander, but many workshop owners dub it their "belt grinder," and find so many uses for it that it could be voted first place in the jack-of-all-trades category. Besides sanding, it's also handy for touching up tool edges, such as chisels, drawknives, or other dulled edges, including saw blades.

Which to buy first? The best advice is to do some research, then talk with other shop owners who already have what you are considering. Using the voice of experience can help you confirm your decisions and help you get the most from your tool-buying dollars.

This Craftsman ½-hp oscillating spindle sander is perfect for sanding curves on projects such as craftwork, fireplace mantels, window valances, or other decorative accents. The sander's spindle oscillates at 60 times a minute through a 20x20" Melamine table top. You can get drums or abrasive sleeves for it in ¾", 1", 2", and 3" sizes to fit the tool's ½" spindle. The sander sells for about $150.

Belt/disc sanders like this one use a 2x42" belt operating at 3,100 feet per minute. Look for a spring-loaded tension/tracking mechanism that makes belt replacement quick and easy, as well as an ample cast-iron table that tilts to 90°. The 8" sanding disc on this unit operates at 3,450 rpm, and uses a cast-aluminum table tilting to 45°.

Palm grip sanders, sometimes called block sanders, can generate an ultra-smooth surface using just one hand. These handy sanders typically use ¼-sheets of sandpaper and most often are available with a dust collection system. When testing these out, look for one that comfortably fits your hand and transmits low vibrations.

Belt sanders can vary in size from 3x18" to 4x24". The 3"-wide models generally will be 3x24" or 3x21" sizes. The 3x24" models will typically have sanding areas from 4¾" to 5¼" long. Power can vary from ½- to 1¼-hp, like the one shown here, and most will have dust collection systems.

Random-orbit sanders produce swirl-free finishes. Both 5" and 6" models are available with auxiliary handles, variable speed, dust extraction, and other options. More powerful models can remove material nearly as fast as a belt sander and are excellent workhorses for a variety of jobs, including roughing, finishing, or polishing.

SANDING BY HAND

*Insight On How To Make Hand Sanding An
Enjoyable, Rewarding Experience*

While there's more ammunition than ever for sanding wood projects, some woodworkers like Hugh Foster point out that there is still a place for hand sanding, not only for parts that are difficult to reach with power sanders, but also for reasons which might not be all that obvious. Here's what he has to say:

"Anyone who has created projects of wood eventually gets to the stage that calls for sanding. I've tried to improve my sanding skills over the years. And I've found there are some things you can learn about yourself while performing this necessary task.

I used to hate to sand, and I often spent more time trying to get out of sanding than I would have spent just getting on with the job. For instance, I thought I would learn to scrape. I bought all kinds of scrapers, scraper burnishers, and the like. I have scraper planes, free-iron scrapers, hook scrapers, scrapers of all sizes and shapes; some with curved edges, others with flat edges; thin scrapers for maximum flexing, thicker ones for heavy duty work.

I have learned to sharpen them with a file, perfect them with a stone, and burnish a nice hook onto them. I have built scraping planes, and I have bought scrapers like the old Stanley #80. I have used them with some measure of success now and again. But, all-in-all, scraping has not been the answer, at least for me.

Power sanders are fine, and I have a full array in my workshop. But then one day it occurred to me that in some respects I was not taking advantage of the more intangible benefits of folding over that sheet of sandpaper, physically taking it in my hand, and simply working with the organic nature of wood. That flash of enlightenment on many occasions has resulted in a new personal fulfillment in my workshop. What I'm talking about is not tied into some mystic religion, but has more to do with a physical exercise.

For example, I read somewhere that a simple way to meditate is to count to two (one-two, one-two, one-two), concentrating only on the counting. The counting helps clear the mind, and 20 minutes worth is claimed to be equivalent to a two-hour nap. I decided to apply that rhythm of counting to the job of sanding by hand. And I found that it brought the task into a new dimension.

If you try it yourself, using a comfortable rhythm, you will find

that you can mentally lose yourself in your work. I found that the trick is simply this: You select a piece of sandpaper, and you rub with it, keeping your mind on what you are doing. Because it is an organic material, the wood responds and soon you can change to a finer grit of sandpaper. After you have sanded through several grits, your project will be ready for a finish.

Chances are good that as you proceed the sanding will bring the surface of the wood to a glass-smooth state, its grain more beautiful than you imagined possible, and you will have generated a strong feeling of accomplishment in yourself. If you think this sounds boring, consider that no task is inherently boring, especially if you keep focused on what you are doing, and if the result is something useful.

Hand sanding can be relaxing. You will find that you can sand by hand almost instinctively. I use my fingers to check my progress even more than with my eyes, freeing up my mind to enjoy the process. I often can leave the shop after a couple of hours of hand sanding more relaxed than when I began. More important, by becoming more relaxed, I find I can give 100 percent attention to the more dangerous operations in my workshop, such as sawing, planing, or routing.

Still another reason not to give up on hand sanding has to do with organizing your work day. You will find it is an ideal job when you want to avoid creating noise in your neighborhood when you first enter the shop just after sunrise in the morning, or after the 10 o'clock news at night. Power sanding has a lot going for it, but, for me, hand sanding still has its place."—Hugh Foster.

HELP FOR MOVING METAL

In many home workshops, shaping and smoothing are not confined to wood alone. A variety of projects can require working with metal, whether to sharpen or modify tools, prepare surfaces before and after welding, or touch-up rough cuts. To handle projects constructed with both wood and metal, or metal alone, the tools below can expand the capabilities of your shop and help you do professional work.

Shop Workhorse. *One of the most verstile tools available for sharpening, smoothing, and leveling, this 8" Craftsman bench grinder is a workhorse of a tool. The grinder has a 1-hp, 7-amp motor that turns 3,450 rpm, and a cast-iron base with rubber feet to reduce vibration. It exhausts dust away from the user and, for safety, it has dual lights and amber eyeshields. It comes with a dressing wheel.*

Big Muscle. *A favorite among metal workers, this 7" right-angle Craftsman grinder has a three-position handle that mounts on both sides and top of the grinding head to boost both control and comfort. The heavy-duty 3-hp motor has ball and sleeve bearings, and turns a no-load speed of 6,000 rpm. It comes with a ⅝" spindle, with lock, to accept a variety of sanding and grinding discs.*

WIRING PROJECTS

How To Troubleshoot And Correct
Home Electrical Problems

Professional electricians will tell you that working with electricity requires definite skill. It's not so much that doing the work is physically difficult, but that it must be done correctly and safely. On the subject of electricity, there is no room for mistakes.

If, as home do-it-yourselfer you are not 100% sure of what you are doing when working with electricity, the best bet is to consult a professional to avoid problems and also make certain that you will not put yourself or others in danger. Beginning do-it-yourselfers can get tripped up in several stages of an electrical project, such as in planning out the circuits, buying new materials, installing boxes, using ground wires, or in buying, pulling, and cutting wires.

Remember that the book containing the National Electrical Code is a big one, and the final authority on what you do falls into the hands of your local electrical inspector. Unless you are wiring a new home, a new addition, or a

Besides cutting and stripping wires, the repair tool shown opposite can be used for crimping terminals, plus cutting and rethreading bolts and screws.

lake cabin that you built yourself, chances are good that the average do-it-yourselfer's wiring projects will be on a much smaller scale. Home electrical projects come in two categories for an electrician,

Home wiring projects require specific know-how and an understanding of safety procedures. If you are not 100% certain of how to proceed with projects, seek out competent help.

what is called "new work" and what is called "rewire." "Rewire" is doing work on existing systems, and this is often the type of wiring work done by non-professionals.

If you live in a house that is over 20 years old, chances can be good that you will have up to three "generations" of wiring in the structure. It is possible that as many as three separate owners may have tampered with the wiring to some degree. As a result, there may be as many as a

dozen problems already in the electrical system that would catch the eye of an inspector, ranging from simple things like loose fixtures to serious, dangerous situations like bare wires hanging in the air.

Here are some typical code violations you might find in an older structure, according to some experienced electricians:

Wires. You might find mixed wire sizes in a circuit. This is permissible only if the added wire is larger; i.e., 12-gauge wire added to a circuit of 14-gauge wire. You can always go to larger-size electrical wire in a circuit, but never to a smaller wire.

For example, if you have a circuit of 12-gauge wire protected by a 20-amp circuit breaker, you should never add smaller 14-gauge wire to that circuit. It will be too small for the intended load. Also, circuits should not contain wire that doesn't have proper insulation and/or which is not UL listed.

Connections. You might find improper connections, such as twisted wire covered with tape, or splices in open air (not enclosed inside of a box). Wire nuts should be used to make connections, and they should be inside an acceptable junction box.

You might also find improper terminal connections, either on electrical devices or in your service panel. Some service panel terminals may accept two wires, but usually only one wire should be clamped under a terminal screw. Wire should be wrapped clockwise around a terminal screw so that the screw snugs down on the wire as the screw is tightened.

Switches. Here most problems are with three-way switches (two switches controlling a light fixture) or four-way switches (three or more switches controlling a light fixture). If they have been installed by a homeowner, it is possible that they may be connected incorrectly. These can be confusing to connect, and it is best to go by good diagrams (see end of article). If switches are installed upside-down, correct them; they may cause a problem in an emergency.

Fixtures. Sometimes you will find fixtures that have been incorrectly installed without an electrical box behind them. Also multiple light fixtures should be wired in *parallel*; i.e., with the black wire from one fixture connected to the black wire of the next fixture. If hooked up incorrectly in *series*, you will get less light from the bulbs.

Circuits. Overloaded circuits can result from under-sized wiring, too big of a load, or too large of a fuse for the circuit (i.e., a 30-amp fuse or breaker in a 15-amp circuit using 14-gauge wire). Overloads are definite fire hazards. Not enough receptacles for the equipment used can also lead to the use of multiple-headed extension cords or "octopuses" which are common causes of electrical fires.

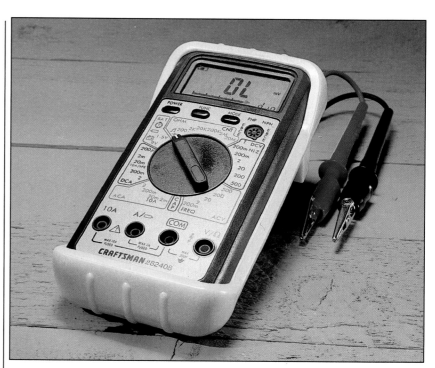

Versatile multitesters like this one will digitally read out either AC or DC voltage.

TROUBLESHOOTING PROBLEMS

According to electrical component suppliers, the electrical requirements for the average home have almost tripled since 1955. In 1940, for example, the average home used 30 electrical appliances while today's home uses about 80.

Homes over 20 years old often require complete rewiring. Even a number of newer homes need either rewiring, or expanded wiring systems (including new circuits) to handle major appliances.

If your home's wiring system has any of the symptoms listed below, the individual circuits may be overloaded and/or the wiring of these circuits may be inadequate:

Blown fuses or tripped circuit breakers. When fuses blow and circuit breakers trip frequently, it indicates an overloaded circuit, and/or that the power drain from appliances is greater than the circuit can handle. Short circuiting in appliances or wiring could also be the problem.

Lights dim or flicker. This problem can be caused by too many appliances on one circuit, or by too large of a power drain on the circuit when turning on specific appliances. (It may also be caused by electrical storms or by voltage drops at the power plant.)

Appliances with heating coils tend to warm up slowly. Inadequate wiring may be indicated by slow warm-up of electric space heaters, hot plates, and similar appliances requiring high power.

Television picture shrinks. If the image on your TV is smaller than the picture tube area, the circuit could be overloaded with too many appliances or extension cords. If it occurs only occasionally, it is probably caused by heavy current requirements of appliances starting up on the same circuit.

Air conditioners work at less than full capacity. The heavy power needs of air conditioner compressors can require more line voltage than circuits provide. With large air conditioning units, separate circuits may be needed.

Remember that circuit breakers and fuses act as the first line of defense when an electrical failure occurs. When a fuse blows or a circuit breaker trips, it indicates that something is wrong within the circuit, and replacing the fuse or resetting the circuit breaker should not be done until the cause is determined. Ignoring this condition could cause a fire hazard, draw excessive power to run up your electric bill, or make appliances run below optimum levels, possibly damaging motors and compressors.

Circuit failures can stem from problems at the main panel, as outlined below. **Caution:** Do not work on a fused or breaker panel unless you are familiar with electrical safety procedures and are confident of your abilities.

Loose connection in a fused panel. After turning off the power, remove the fuses. A loose screw may be found in one of the fuse sockets. If the bottom of the fuse is blackened, discolored or pitted, a loose connection is at fault.

Loose connection in a circuit breaker panel. After turning power off, remove cover from panel.

Warning: The connections where the main wires enter the panel are HOT. Inspect the panel for darkened or pitted marks on the bus or circuit breakers. Also check the wires connected to the circuit breakers for signs of excessive heat.

Fuse poorly seated. Although the fuse window shows no indication of burn-out and the bottom is not pitted or discolored, the fuse may not be contacting the bottom of the receptacle. Remove the fuse and replace with one of adequate length to make contact.

If there is an unused branch space in the existing panel, it may be possible to move the branch wire from the damaged fuse or circuit breaker to the unused space and install a new fuse or circuit breaker. If there are no unused spaces, the entire panel may need to be replaced. If so, consider having an electrician install a larger service to better meet future electrical needs.

Caution: To avoid overloaded circuits, never insert a fuse in the panel which has a higher amperage rating than the rating on the wire for the circuit. Also never use a penny or tin foil in a service panel instead of a fuse.

If power to a circuit is cut off by a fuse or circuit breaker in the main panel, the cause is a short circuit. If a fuse is blown, the fuse window appears discolored and the metal strip running across the inside of the window is broken. This indicates a short circuit caused by either two bare wires touching, or a hot lead grounding out to a metal object somewhere in the circuit.

Circuits protected by cartridge fuses will give no visible indication that a short circuit has taken place. Circuits protected by circuit breakers can be identified by the handle of the tripped circuit breaker being in the "tripped" or "off" position.

The method for identifying the cause of a short circuit is the same for fuses or circuit breakers. Disconnect all lights and appliances on the circuit with the blown fuse or tripped circuit breaker. Then replace the blown fuse or turn on the tripped circuit breaker. If the fuse blows or the circuit breaker trips with all appliances unplugged from the circuit, the short is in the circuit wiring itself and the wiring must be repaired or replaced.

If the circuit is good, reconnect each light and appliance on that circuit, one at a time. **Warning:** Use extreme caution when reconnecting lights and appliances. Do not connect suspiciously frayed cords to outlets. When you turn on the faulty light or appliance, the fuse will blow or the breaker will trip again. Carefully check appliances for bare cords, broken light sockets, or damaged plugs before replugging back into the circuit.

CAUTION: MAKE SAFETY YOUR TOP PRIORITY

• When in doubt about any electrical wiring problem, consult an electrician. Always use caution when working with electricity.

• Before proceeding with any electrical work, make sure the main disconnect on the service entrance panel is at the "off" position, or pull the main fuses if the panel is the cartridge fuse type.

• When working on individual receptacles or light switches, also turn off the circuit breaker for the circuit you will be working on, and test the receptacle with a test light before handling bare wires.

• Never stand on a wet or damp floor when working at the service panel. Wear rubber gloves and stand on a rubber mat for added safety.

If one particular fuse blows several times, shut off all wall switches and appliances on that circuit, and remove all line cords from the sockets. Remove the fuse and screw a 100-watt light bulb into the fuse receptacle. If the bulb lights with all appliances unplugged from the circuit, a short exists within the circuit. If it doesn't light, connect each of the appliances, lamps, and line cords one at a time. If the bulb lights at the fuse panel and the appliance fails to work, you've located the short. Remove the bulb from the panel before disconnecting the faulty appliance.

Most circuit failures are caused by overloads. Electricity in home wiring flows under pressure, much like water moves under pressure in a plumbing system. The electrical pressure is known as **voltage**. The flow of electricity is called **amperage**. Wire of a specific size may have too great a resistance to handle the current required of it.

If one circuit repeatedly fails, there may be a short in the circuit or there may be too many heavy appliances on that circuit. If removing some of the appliances from the circuit does not eliminate the overload, an individual circuit must be added for the appliance with the heaviest current drain.

Fused circuits can be corrected to handle temporary overloads by using a time delay fuse of either 15 or 20 amp. This type of fuse will handle temporary power drains from the start-up of appliance motors. Many electric motors need nearly three times the normal line current for initial starting. Circuit breakers are designed to automatically handle temporary overloads.

A fish tape like this one can be helpful in pulling wires through existing walls.

PLANNING WIRING PROJECTS

Experienced electricians say that the average do-it-yourselfer should be able to handle projects involving the replacement of outlets, switches, or fixtures. Replacement equipment is often available in blister packs with instructions.

However, additions to existing circuits or adding new circuits require specific know-how and most likely a permit, and if you are not willing or don't have the time to make sure you will be doing it right without question, contact a professional electrician. Likewise any work on the service panel, unless you absolutely know what you

are doing, should be handled by a professional. If proper safety precautions are used, beginners should be able to handle #1 in the chart shown below. However, an experienced do-it-yourselfer could handle #1, #2, and possibly #3 and #4 if thorough study and advice from competent sources are used.

The best bet always is to do your homework before you start. Call the local electrical inspector to verify local laws. In many states it is illegal for someone to work on the electrical system of another's home without a license. If you take out the permit yourself, some states require that you also do the work yourself.

Besides the tools you probably already have, a minimum tool kit for electrical work might look something like this: a straight-shanked screwdriver, lineman's pliers with flat jaws and wire cutter, Channel-

---

ELECTRICAL PROJECT RATING
(From Easy To Difficult)

#1—-One-to-one replacement.
#2—-Adding to existing circuits.
#3—-Adding new circuits.
#4—-Multiples of the above.

lock-type pliers, needle-nose pliers, and a neon test light. If you plan to do much wiring, consider buying such tools as a wire stripper, screw-hole tap, larger straight-shank screwdriver, small electrician's pliers, a 6″ Crescent-type wrench, a volt-ohm meter or clip-on amp tester, and a fish tape to use when pulling wires.

You may need special supplies, such as custom plate covers, three- or four-way switches, special electrical boxes or outlets for appliances. If you can't find them, check with a wholesale house that sells electrical supplies; they may sell to you for cash. If they don't carry what you need, they may be able to direct you to a source. You can also ask an electrical contractor if he either has what you need or will get it for you.

Remember that only one wire should be placed under any terminal screw. To achieve this, use pigtails when connecting more than one wire to one terminal. Loop one wire (the same size as the largest wire in the box) under the screw. Connect other wires to this pigtail with a wire nut.

Keep in mind that electricity can be dangerous. If questions arise, seek competent help through qualified sources. Always shut off the current at the main switch on the service panel. Turning off switches and circuit breakers may not be enough. For example, switches may be fed from fixtures, and neutral wires may be shared by more than one circuit. In some cases you can get shocked by white wires assumed to be neutral, but which are really hot wires being used for switching purposes. You can also get a shock from white neutral wires if you interrupt their path to ground.

Put safety first and never guess. Make certain that your body is not grounded when working on electrical systems. Basic protective gear for hands, eyes, and ears is always in order. Always assume the wires are hot.

Check, doublecheck, and triple-check your work before, during, and after your project. Wiring can be tested while the current is off with a continuity tester, either a volt-ohm meter or signal device. Neon test lights can be used to check whether wires, outlets, or switches are live.

If you need to hire an electrician, first try to get recommendations from friends, neighbors, and relatives who have had work done. The electrician they suggest may not be the low bidder, but at least you will have an idea of his professional ability. If you start from scratch, get formal written proposals from at least two, preferably more, electrical contractors. Look for a fair shake, rather than a bargain. Often the low-bid contractor may not be a bargain in the long run.

Electrical contractors have an obligation to point out hazards that they see which should be repaired, even though you may not want to have the work done right away. If you have questions about your own electrical projects, or projects you plan to have hired done, call your local electrical code officials or power company. It is their job to make sure the wiring in your community is done correctly and safely.

Note: Although it is expensive to buy, the National Electrical Code book should be available in your area; check with your electrical code officials on where you can get a copy. Another comprehensive reference is **Richter's Practical Electrical Wiring** *which has over 640 pages and 460 illustrations. The 15th edition is available for $39.95 plus $4.75 for shipping and handling from Park Publishing, Inc., 350 Main St., P.O. Box 387, Somerset, WI 54025. Other smaller starter references include* **Wiring Simplified** *from Park Publishing, a 175-page digest-size paperback which covers the 1993 code changes (about $5.50) and* **Step By Step Guide Book On Home Wiring**, *P.O. Box 2583, Salt Lake City, Utah 84110 (about $3). The last two books are often available where electrical supplies are sold.*

CHECKING OUT CIRCUIT LOADS

To doublecheck loads on a specific circuit, total the number of watts used for appliances and lights on that circuit at the same time. Appliance wattage rates are usually on the nameplate at the back of an appliance, or on the motor. After adding up the total, divide the total by 120 volts to calculate amps.

For example, if the total exceeds 1,800 watts for a circuit with a 15-amp fuse, or exceeds 2,400 watts for a circuit with a 20-amp fuse, the circuit is overloaded. One or more appliances may be plugged into another circuit to avoid an overload, as long as new overloads are not created. If overloads remain, the solution is to add an additional circuit.

Tip: When calculating circuit loads, you may find appliance plates give amps rather than watts. To convert into watts, multiply amps by voltage (120 or 240). If horsepower is given on motors, multiply horsepower by 746 to find watts.

TECH NOTES: SPLITTING A RECEPTACLE

If you are of advanced skills, here is a project that will allow you to control a single receptacle from the room's entryway switch. Many receptacles are designed to be split by breaking the connecting tab between the brass terminal screws, and diverting the hot side of the circuit through a switch loop.

Cable Routing. You will often be able to conceal new switch-loop cable behind baseboards. Carefully prying the baseboard from the wall should reveal a ¾" gap between the drywall and the floor. You can use this gap as a concealed raceway.

The space behind the baseboard will also allow easy access to the stud spaces containing the electrical boxes. Start by turning off the power and cutting a notch in the drywall below the existing receptacle box. Then remove the receptacle and slide a fish tape through one of the box openings. Fish the tape down to the notched opening and pull the cable into the box.

Next, determine the new switch location and cut an opening in the drywall to accept a plastic cut-in box. Bring the new cable into this stud space and pull it through the box opening. Tuck the cable run into the gap between the drywall and floor, and staple it in place before carefully replacing the baseboard.

Receptacle Wiring. After breaking the tab between the brass terminals, reconnect the receptacle with insulated pigtail wires. Start by joining all white wires in a twist connector and running a white pigtail to a silver screw terminal on the receptacle. Follow by joining all black wires with two pigtails. Connect one pigtail to a brass screw terminal on the receptacle and the other to the black wire from the switch loop. Then fasten the white wire from the switch loop to the remaining brass screw terminal on the receptacle. Finish by joining all ground wires with a pigtail to the green terminal on the receptacle.

Switch Wiring. To wire the wall switch, fasten the black switch-loop wire to one terminal and the white wire to the other terminal. Both switch wires will now be hot, so code the white wire on each end.

1 The diagram assumes the use of plastic boxes. Use a fish tape to pull new cable into the existing plastic receptacle box.

2 Break the tab between the brass terminals of the receptacle. Reconnect the receptacle by using insulated pigtail wires.

3 Before installing the new box for the switch, bring the cable into it. Then press the box into the opening and fasten.

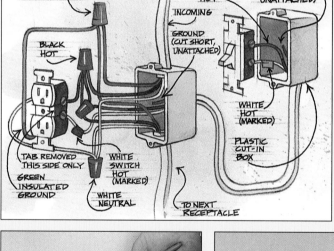

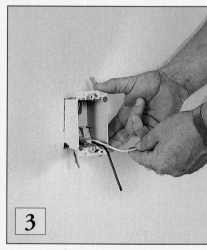

CLAMP HEAVEN

*New Technology Turns Project Clamping
Into A One-Handed Operation*

Conventional wisdom has it that it's tough to improve on a good thing, or that if something works you're better off leaving well enough alone. Tell that to the people who design, manufacture, and sell clamps, and they will say you have another think coming.

An example. A few years ago, when Joe Sorensen decided to build a new boat, he quickly ran into a common woodworkers' problem. Clamping projects usually required three hands to tighten and adjust the clamp.

Joe, then a freelance artist and now manager of research and development for American Tool Companies, searched for a one-handed clamp that would allow him to do the job himself. Finding that such a clamp did not exist, he projected that many others ran into the same problem of trying to hold pieces together while adjusting a clamp. So he and a tool-and-die-maker friend invented what has since become known as the Quick-Grip Bar Clamp and revolutionized the design of clamps used around the home and workshop.

Rather than requiring two hands for adjustments, the clamp they developed could be tightened by simply squeezing a pistol-grip-type handle. A click of the handle's trigger provided quick release for rapid readjustment.

The idea spawned a whole new category of clamping products now offered along with the company's

All because he wanted to build a boat, Joe Sorenson happened on an idea that sparked a new generation of clamps. The original Quick-Grip clamp is now available in several variations.

family of Vise-Grip tools. The original Vise-Grip locking pliers was patented by the late William Peterson, a blacksmith who learned his trade in Denmark and founded the company in 1924.

Besides using a hardened steel bar, the new-style clamps now come off the factory lines with handle and jaws made of a lightweight, durable high-tech resin. The jaws are tipped with pliable plastic pads to protect wood and other soft materials. "Something we focused on in the development of the clamp was simplicity," Joe says, "especially being able to use it with one hand. And the addition of soft pads allows clamping onto highly finished surfaces without scratching them."

His new clamp idea spawned a variety of related products and accessories that can be adapted for many different clamping jobs. Within the first few years of its introduction, Quick-Grip clamps were available in five different sizes, with jaw openings from 150mm to 910-mm.

How They Work. The clamp is adjusted by just squeezing its unique pistol grip handle. This simple procedure takes the place of the tedious tightening of screws on traditional clamps and allows both one-handed operation and quick adjustment. Because the clamp can't be overtightened, the risk of marring associated with metal screw clamps is eliminated. With only one finger on the quick-release trigger, the bar can be slid into proper position. Once the clamping operation is done, the clamp is released by merely applying pressure again on the trigger.

The soft, pliable pads that come with the clamp provide as much as three times more clamping surface than traditional bar clamps. They also eliminate the need to find wood blocks to protect the work, or to hold the blocks in place while adjusting the clamps. The pads also slide off the jaws so that you can use optional corner brackets and corner pads to assemble projects such as drawers and cases. A hollow in the corner bracket allows drilling while the material is clamped. If the regular pads aren't enough, the company also offers full-face pads which are an inch deeper to provide more clamping surface.

Since the first new-style clamp was introduced, the idea has been adapted to mini-bar clamps for hobbyists, then hold-down clamps, plus spreader clamps and accessories for the serious do-it-yourselfer. Later, the company also developed a special version of the bar clamp for welding, as well as applying their new technology to spring clamps.

Welding. For use in welding applications, Joe and American Tool engineers worked up a clamp with heat-treated carbon steel jaws. A unique feature of the tool is its copper-plated pads with horizontal and vertical grooves on the surface which allow easy clamping of round stock and angle iron.

Spring Clamps. High-tech resin was used in a design for spring clamps that better fits the user's hand. Quick-Grip's spring clamps are now available in three sizes (25, 50, and 75mm) and are put to work in woodworking, instrument repair, auto body work, upholstery repair, studio photography, boat projects, and other applications.

Spreader and Hold-down Clamps. Do-it-yourselfers are finding two adaptations of the original clamp especially useful—spreader clamps

ONE-HANDED CLAMPING

1 The original Quick-Grip bar clamp is useful for either indoor or outdoor do-it-yourself projects. Its pistol-grip action adjusts and tightens with one hand.

2 The bar clamps all feature a throat depth of $3\frac{1}{4}''$ and come in five different lengths, with maximum joint adjustments from 0″ to either 6″, 12″, 18″, 24″, or 36″.

3 Regular pads on the jaws of the bar clamps measure $1\frac{1}{2}''$ x $2\frac{1}{4}''$ and can be removed for replacement with special full-face pads that are 1″ deeper, or with mini-pads that measure $1\frac{1}{16}''$ x $1\frac{11}{16}''$.

4 Either the regular or full-face pads also can be replaced with corner pad kits. The 90° corner bracket fits on the handle side of the clamp and the corner pad goes on the jaw at the other end.

and hold-down clamps. As the accompanying photos show, the spreader clamps combine the features of the original clamp with one difference. By reversing the direction of the fixed jaw and movable body, it becomes a spreader which applies controlled outward pressure to push surfaces apart or to secure work. Besides being useful for do-it-yourself projects, it has caught on with woodworkers, furniture manufacturers and restorers, and cabinet and door installers.

The hold-down clamp version is designed like the original, except instead of a fixed jaw at the end of the bar it uses a flange that the bar slips through. The flange and a retaining ring are mounted below a stationary or portable workbench, or even a sawhorse.

Once mounted, you can rotate the clamping pad 360° to securely hold the work to the surface with fast, one-hand locking action. Separate mounting kits are available so you can have them mounted in several places for use with just one clamp. You simply remove the clevis pin, pull the clamp out, and reposition it in an alternate location.

Note: For more information on the one-handed clamping system, you can write American Tool Companies, Inc., 8400 LakeView Parkway, Kenosha, WI 53142, or call (414) 947-2440. The company's customer service department can be reached by phone at 800-767-6297 or by fax at 800-767-6897.

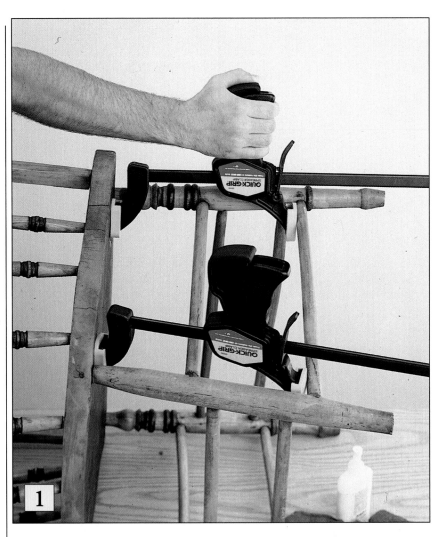

ADAPTING A GOOD IDEA

1 Following on the heels of the original one-hand clamps, the idea was adapted to push instead of pull with Quick-Grip Spreader Clamps.

2 The original spreader clamps, useful in wood-working and furniture restora-tion, ranged from 7¼″ to 27½″. The new version, shown, has a jaw that extends to a full 50″. Corner brackets and pads can be used on the spreaders for assem-bling drawers or cases.

3 Another adaptation is the hold-down clamp which comes with hardware for mount-ing underneath one or more benchtops. Once mounted, you can rotate the clamping pad 360° for routing, sanding, carving, or other benchtop operations.

TIPS ON USING ONE-HANDED CLAMPS

The Quick-Grip bar clamps are designed to hold two workpieces together while performing temporary op-erations. To avoid serious personal injury when us-ing, follow these rules:

• Always wear safety goggles to protect your eyes.

• Position clamps properly, assuring sufficient pad surface contact, correct clamping angle, adequate working space, etc.

• Store clamps by clamping them in a rack, not in a drawer.

• Use clamps with pads to avoid marring the work.

• Discard any clamp that has a bent frame or a bent spindle.

• Do not use a wrench, pipe, hammer, or pliers to gain extra tightening. A wrench should be used only on those clamps especially designed for tightening with a wrench.

• Keep all moving parts lightly oiled and clean. However, make sure there is no dirt or oil on any part that will come in contact with the work.

• Never use a clamp for hoisting work. Special lift-ing clamps are made for this purpose.

• Avoid using extra-large clamps just for the sake of their large throats; instead use deep-throat clamps.

• Never use clamps as devices for lifting, pulling, or transporting.

• Always remove clamps as soon as the required job is finished. Clamps serve only as temporary devices for holding work securely in place.

QUICK-RELEASE CLAMPING

*How To Take Advantage Of Re-Engineered
Clamping Systems For Home Projects*

Clamping is getting a whole lot easier, thanks to designers who have gone back to the drawing board to incorporate quick-release features into a variety of clamps used around the home workshop.

As the photos here show, a complete array of new-age clamps are now available to save you set-up time by engaging or disengaging the spindle at the push of a button or the flick of the wrist. All of the user-friendly clamps shown, available through Sears outlets, are living proof that with an innovative spirit you can indeed improve on a good thing.

1 Even the C-clamp has been updated for easier, faster use. This Craftsman quick-release version allows quick setting and releasing of the spindle when clamping and unclamping a workpiece. The die-cast aluminum frame is lightweight and its I-beam design allows the clamp to lie flat for stability. The clamp's spindle opening accepts workpieces up to 6″ thick, while its plastic jaw pads help protect from marring. The time-saving clamp comes in a 3″ version for about $12, a 4″ for about $14, and a 6″ for about $17.

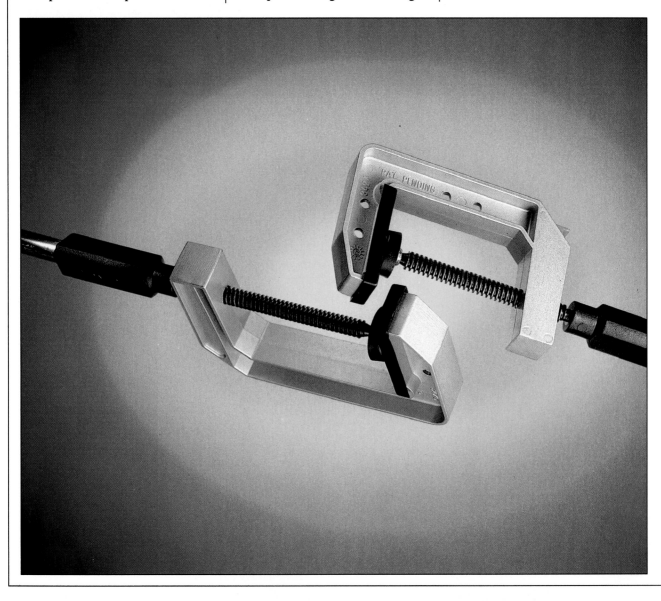

2 This Craftsman 90° Clamp provides a 90° joint for the assembly of picture frames and cabinets, as well as for setting up for welds in metal-working projects. The die-cast aluminum frame is lightweight and its steel jaws are V-grooved to hold tubing. The clamp's quick-release button allows instant adjusting of the spindle to the desired position. Pressure against the workpiece is fine-tuned using the spindle handle. The clamp, which can be mounted to a workbench to accept workpieces up to 2½″ wide, costs about $30.

3 This new-style band clamp has two quick adjust/release levers just forward of the handle to help in securing a variety of projects, including chairs, picture frames, and other irregularly shaped workpieces. The wrap-around nylon strap is channeled through three plastic corner braces to secure custom picture frames and other projects requiring true corners. Once the belt is snug around the project, it is tightened using the fine-tune spindle handle. The Craftsman Band Clamp sells for around $25.

4 Quick-release engineering is also available in drill press vises. This Craftsman vise offers four positions to handle most benchtop operations and can be mounted either over the bench, horizontally in front of the bench, or at 90° or 45° in front of the bench. By pushing its quick-release button the spindle is released to drive the jaws to the workpiece. The spindle handle secures the work and provides fine-tuning adjustment. The vise's jaws, 4″ wide and 1¾″ high, accept work up to 4″ thick. It mounts easily to most drill presses and sells for about $20.

Do-It-Yourself
PROBLEM-SOLVERS

PROJECT AMMUNITION

Helpful How-To Tips, Tricks, And Suggestions
For The Resourceful Homeowner

Years ago, especially through hard times like the Great Depression, good how-to hints were worth their weight in gold. They often helped families survive while keeping outlays of hard-earned cash to a minimum. In many cases good hints even helped them get by without spending any money while still keeping the home fixed up, the car running, or the kids in shoes.

Times have changed, and a quarter saved here or there makes less of a difference today to the average homeowner. But good handy hints are still as valuable as ever; they can save you time, help you make sure that something stays fixed, or simply solve nagging problems in everyday life. And, if a good hint saves your hard-earned cash, so much the better.

Handy hints today go by a good half-dozen of aliases, including useful tips, valuable suggestions, helpful techniques, problem-solvers, slick tricks, or other labels.

Whatever you call them, a good hint basically is a bit of information that helps you get things done in a way not possible if you didn't possess that nugget of knowledge. They provide valuable ammunition to help you pursue the art of resourcefulness—perhaps the best reason of all to find and use hints.

The acid test of a good hint is how well it actually works. The best handy-hint spotters are those who have tried and failed. If you've attempted to solve a problem several ways without success, and then discovered the one way to make it work, you are able to appreciate the value of that bit of information.

The hints presented here are words to the wise, discovered through trial and error by experimenting do-it-yourselfers. You can put them to use for yourself starting right now; each one has the potential to make your projects go a little better.

SHOP PSYCHIATRIST
If part of your goal of having a home shop is to relieve stress from your everyday work, consider a wood lathe. Powering up that wood lathe after a hard day at the office can be as relieving as a whole week's vacation.

DON'T PUSH IT
If you own lower-priced, homeowner-quality power tools, don't try to make them do more than they are designed for. Don't, for example, make a ¼″ drill work all afternoon sanding the bottom of a boat with a 6″ sanding disk. Let the tool run at its rated speed, and don't let it get hot. Pressing hard on a finishing sander can make it sand faster, but it also can destroy the tool. The weight of the sander itself is enough to do a good sanding job.

BUYING USED TOOLS
Beware of buying equipment which needs machine shop work. If you are not equipped to handle the machining at home, you may find the cost of repair more than the cost of a new tool. Also watch for broken small parts; some may not be readily available.

VERSATILE HAND TOOL
Consider buying a commercial beekeeper's hive tool for use around the shop. The tool serves as an extension of your right hand and can be used for scraping, cutting, driving and pulling nails, and prying off tight lids.

SELECTING HAMMERS
A good way to check a hickory hammer handle is to look at the bottom end of the handle. One with vertical grain (straight up and down) will be stronger than one with slashed grain (slanted to the side).

FREE STORAGE
You can use plastic milk, water, or detergent jugs for small parts storage by cutting out a section opposite the handle. The contents can be easily marked by using a hot glue gun to fasten a sample of the parts you put inside, such as nails, bolts, or screws. Also, by cutting off

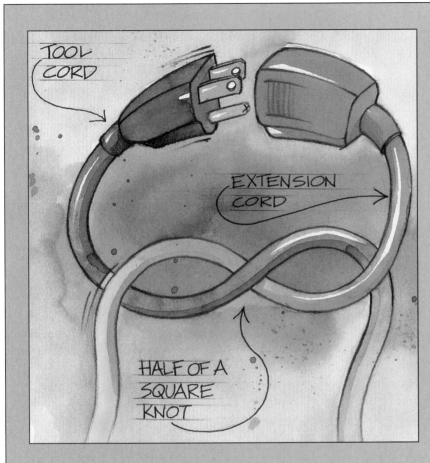

TOOL CORD

EXTENSION CORD

HALF OF A SQUARE KNOT

CORD CONNECTIONS
To keep tools from disconnecting from extension cords, try this: Before joining the cords, first make half of a square knot, like tying your shoes before you make the bow. Then plug the cord ends together. For sufficient power, avoid using undersized cords that can cause voltage drop, tool overheating, and power loss. A 25' 16-ga. cord can handle up to 7-amps, a 50' cord up to 5 amps.

the top of many styles, you can make free emergency funnels.

USING TREATED WOOD
When working with pressure treated wood, wear goggles and avoid prolonged or frequent inhalation of sawdust. Wash up before eating, drinking, or using tobacco. Wash work clothes separately from other loads. Also, don't use treated wood for cutting boards or counter tops and don't burn in open fires or in stoves, fireplaces, or boilers because toxic chemicals may be produced as part of the smoke and ashes.

HANDLING TAPE
To store masking tape for long periods, put inside a plastic bag and keep in the refrigerator. When using tapes that are not in a dispenser, do this: After tearing off what you need, fold a short section of the end under against the sticky side. That way you won't have to search for the end with your thumbnail the next time you want to use it.

COFFEE CAN HELP
To store molding, dowel stock, and the like neatly off of the floor in your shop, use two empty 3-lb. coffee cans. Nail one (with the bottom left in it) 6" or so from the floor. Then nail another with both ends cut out about two feet above the first can. Since the top can is an open cylinder, you can slide pieces of material down through it and into the bottom can.

BUILDING BENCHES
Several guidelines exist to determine the best workbench height. If you are of average height, these include making the bench either 34" high, or as high as the top of your hip pockets, or as high as your knuckles. Adjust as necessary.

Tip: If you make benches the same height as your main shop saw, they can be used as outboard support when cutting large pieces.

SHARP TOOL STORAGE
To protect cutting edges of chisels and similar sharp tools, build a rack which permits storing them vertically, with their tips or blades pressed into a square of foam rubber or styrofoam. The material keeps the blades from banging against each other, and also minimizes danger to the hands and fingers from sharp edges.

WRENCH & CLAMP STORAGE
Do you have a large collection of adjustable wrenches, odd-shaped C-clamps, or screw clamps? You can store them neatly side by side

just by tightening up their jaws to the edge or lip of a shelf. They will take up very little room and will always be easy to spot and use. Ceiling joists can also be used to get them out of the way.

BUYING NEW TOOLS

Buy the best shop tools you can afford. Fine quality tools are a joy to work with, but there are also other reasons to buy top quality. It is cheaper to buy the right one the first time than to break and replace inferior models. You are also less likely to get hurt with first quality tools.

CREATURE COMFORTS

A good deal of shop work involves planning and designing of the projects. Outfitting your shop with plenty of paper, drawing tools, tape, and planning aids, plus a desk lamp and a comfortable stool, will in-

crease your enjoyment of those shop projects.

TOOL SAMPLING

A good way to sample tools is to take a woodworking class. It can give you an opportunity to learn about what you like and don't like. Conversations with instructors or others in the class can provide sources of tools and comments about the various brands to help you find a bargain and/or avoid a lemon. Also visit other people's shops when you can and ask the tool owners how well their tools have worked for them.

STRING DISPENSERS

To keep a ball of string or twine from rolling about the shop, put it under an ordinary flower pot. Pull the free end of the twine through the drain hole in the bottom of the pot. If you want a small ball of

string handy for miscellaneous tie-ups, using a large coffee can as a holder will keep it from rolling around the shop. Just punch a small hole in the plastic top, feed the string through and close the lid. The ball will unwind inside and stay put.

HOMEMADE TOOL RACK

Organize miscellaneous tools by making a handy rack with a section of angle iron about 2″ long. First drill holes in one side of the angle to accommodate the tools you want to store on it. Then drill a couple of holes for screws to hang the angle on the side of your bench. Use hefty screws and round the corners of the angle for safety.

UNDERBENCH TOOL BOARDS

Keep an area open under workbenches for slide-in storage of simple tool boards made of pegboard

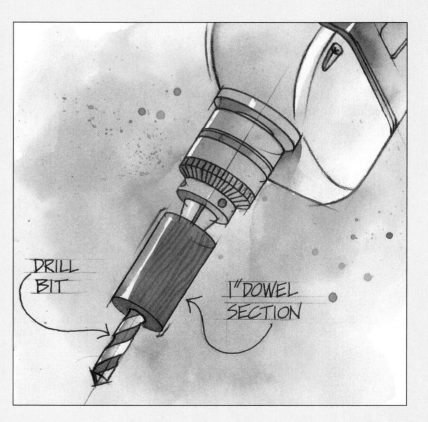

DOWEL DEPTH STOP
If you don't have a depth stop for drill bits and you need to drill blind holes of a certain depth in wood or metal, make your own. Use tape around the drill bit at the right depth. Or drill a hole through the center of a 1″ dowel section, using the bit you're planning to use for the work. Make the length of the exposed bit the depth of the hole.

DRILL BIT

1″ DOWEL SECTION

and dimension lumber. Organize types of tools on individual toolboards. Used at the bench, slide them out only part way; for out-of-shop projects, carry what you need to the job site.

SAWDUST SYSTEMS

Make adaptations so your shop vacuum can be hooked directly up to power tools or to a permanent vacuum line in your shop. Also modify sawdust-producing tools with special exhausts which direct sawdust or chips into collection boxes.

COLLECTOR ADVANTAGES

Besides allowing you to keep a sawdust collector in one spot, a properly built-in central duct system can do a better job of collecting dust at each tool. If you have only one or two major machines, the advantage of a central duct system might be questionable. But if you have three or more major tools, you'll enjoy the convenience.

STORING HAND PLANES

Instead of storing planes in the tool box or a regular shelf, consider using a hanging shoe bag. It has pockets that work well for the purpose. You can hang the bag on your shop door or wall. It will accommodate most commonly used planes, including small block planes, and prevents blade dulling.

DRILLING STRAIGHT

To drill straighter holes, use a small bubble level epoxied onto the top of your drill. By reading the small level, you can drill straight horizontal holes easily anywhere you can keep the level in view.

NATURAL SHOP LIGHT

Projects go much better if you can see what you're doing. When setting up lighting in your shop, consider lining the perimeter of your shop with fluorescent lights. Make full use of any natural light; you may want to reposition your bench to be next to an available window.

SORTING OUT BOLTS

No one likes to dump out a coffee can full of various bolts, nuts, and washers to find the right one. Avoid this by keeping small fasteners and bolts in salvaged cake and cookie pans. You can see what you need in a hurry. You also can make special shelves to house these flat, open storage tins.

LUMBER STACK BASE

If you have some old tires around, you can put them to use as a base to stack lumber. Lay them flat on the shop floor and put the lumber on top of them. They will keep the wood off of the floor, away from

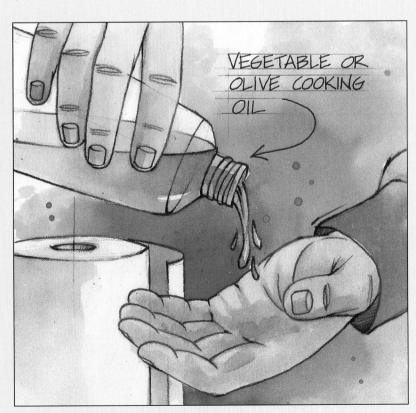

HANDY CLEANER
Engine grime can be difficult to wash off. If you don't have a hand cleaner available, your kitchen cupboard probably contains a solution. Reach for either a vegetable or olive cooking oil and spread a dab over your hands, wiping off with a paper towel. Cooking oils will also help remove oil-based paints, without the risk of exposure to harsh solvents.

dampness. Also, the air that circulates under the lumber will help keep the wood from collecting moisture.

STORING HAND FILES

Protect the teeth of files not in use by hanging them in a rack or by keeping them in a drawer with wooden divisions. Files should always be kept free of water or grease which can make them less effective. It's a good idea to wrap a file in a cloth to protect it when carried in a tool box. Keep file teeth clean by using a file card or a wire file brush to clear the grooves.

USING HAND FILES

For best results, try to match the file to the specific metal you're working on. Soft metals need a keen file used with light pressure. A hard metal requires a file with duller teeth to keep them from bit-ing too deeply and breaking off under pressure. Hard plastics need a file with high, sharp teeth. Soft plastics, which file in shreds, are best worked with shear tooth files.

GLUE DRYING TIME

To avoid machining glued-up wood too soon and getting sunken glue joints, first let glue and wood dry for a minimum of three days at room temperature.

METAL CLEAN-UP

When working on buildings, you can waste a lot of time cleaning up old nails or other metal pieces such as steel siding clippings, etc. Speed up the process by fabricating your own simple electromagnetic clean-up device. Most auto scrap dealers have clutch magnets from junked car air conditioners. These can be hooked to a 12v battery on a car, pickup, or lawn mower. Move the magnet around with a rope, handle, or a unit with wheels.

TOUGHER SANDING DISCS

Sanding discs used in portable power drills wear out fast because of their floppy nature. Here's a trick: Cement two together, back to back. This stiffens them sufficiently to minimize wrinkling and tearing. Two sanding discs cemented together should outlast four or six discs used separately.

ON-OFF REMINDER

The noise from simultaneous operation of more than one machine or tool in your shop can make it hard to tell if one is on or off. To help determine which tools are on, put strips of white paint on all moving parts of each machine—on shafts, belts, chains, blades, etc. The moving strips will give you a visual warning.

HOLE CLEAN-OUT
Steel chips on tables in a workshop can imbed themselves in wood surfaces and also be tracked out of the shop by shoes onto carpets. A solution is to use a large magnet inside a plastic bag to catch metal chips when boring holes in metal. To pull the chips off the bag, simply turn the bag inside out; they will stay in the bag for transfer to the garbage bin.

NYLON SOLUTION

A most useful material around the home is old, worn-out nylons. The foot can be used as a handy paint strainer, or attach a knee-high length to the clothes washer discharge to strain out pipe-clogging lint. Or, cut strips for tying plants like tomatoes to stakes. Cut across the leg for double bands, or snip for single-layer strips. Nylon strips can even be used to attach tools to pegboard by threading through the holes.

POWER SANDING

Consider using cloth-backed, instead of paper-backed, sandpaper with a power sander. It will be more flexible and stronger. Use at least two grades, progressing from coarser to finer.

DRILLING PROPELLER

It is irritating when shavings pile up around a drilled hole, making it hard to see what you're doing. To prevent this, punch the point of the bit through a 4″ strip of masking tape, then draw the tape up the bit so it will clear the work. Fold the strip lengthwise to bring the sticky sides together. The masking tape "wings" act as a fan to keep your work surface cleared of shavings.

BEESWAX SOLUTION

If you have a hammer with a wooden handle, you can also use the old carpenter's trick of boring a ¼″ hole an inch deep into the butt of the handle and fill it with beeswax. When nailing tough wood, you can stick each nail into the hole to lubricate it to help avoid splits.

LADDER GEAR APRON

When working on projects requiring a ladder, a good way to keep small parts and supplies handy is to attach a nail apron to the upper part of the ladder. Tie it so you won't trip on it when climbing.

INK SPOT REMOVERS

If you've crushed a ballpoint pen in your shirt pocket and gotten it all over, reach for an aerosol can of hair spray. Just spray on and the ink will become easy to wipe off. It will also help you get ink from your hands as well. Quik 'N Brite removes ink stains from felt tip pens; wet the fabric before applying the cleaner to the fabric and allow it to soak in overnight. Repeated applications may be necessary, but you can save the item.

DRILLING PIPE

To make drilling larger-diameter pipe on the drill press easier, use a piece of ⅛″- or ¼″-thick by ¾″-wide aluminum stock the length of the drill press table. Run the stock

NYLON STOCKING

RUBBER BAND

PARTS FINDER
Once a small part is lost, you can waste a lot of time looking for it. To find it quickly, put a nylon stocking over the end of your shop vacuum hose and fasten it tightly with a rubber band. Turn on the vac and play it over the area where the part was lost. If the part is there, it will be sucked up and held against the nylon by the suction.

through the pipe and clamp it to the table. You can substitute, depending on what you have available. The arrangement lets you drill any size hole you need, either vertically or horizontally, without the pipe slipping or twisting.

SILICONE WIRE GUIDE

Wires that keep falling out of their routing on vehicles and trailers have a tendency to get torn off. Metal clips work, but silicone sealer is another solution. Put a dab where you want the wire to run, then push the wire into the dab. Tape the wire lightly so it stays put while the silicone cures.

HARD-TO-REACH SCREWS

When working in congested quarters where a regular screwdriver won't fit, try using a flexible-drive auto carburetor adjusting tool. The flex drive will work even at a 90°

angle, and the large handle lets you get a better grip on tight screws.

RECYCLING NAILED BEAMS

Use wood-splitting wedges to separate large nailed-together beams or headers. Put lumber on edge and, with pry bars or wrecking bars, start splitting apart. When two pieces are separated enough at one end, insert a wedge. Keep moving the bars toward the end, adding wedges as the split opens up.

GLUE CONTAINERS

Avoid using coffee cans for glues; use plastic containers instead. Glues with a pH lower than 7 will absorb iron from the can and react to leave black glue lines. Sharp chisels and paint scrapers are excellent tools for scraping away excess glue after the wood is slightly dry. When using chisels, make sure your free hand is out of the way in case of a slip.

NO-TIP SHOP VAC

If you have a shop vacuum with the hose coming out of the top side, it probably tips over more often than you want. A solution is to use a length of elastic, the kind used for sewing clothing. Tie one end onto a caster support, then pull the hose towards the floor and tie the other end about halfway up the hose. It helps move the vac along while you pull on the hose, reducing tipovers.

NAIL-PULLING STRESS

To reduce stress when using a hammer to pull nails, use a block of scrap wood as a fulcrum under the hammer head; the block gives added height for easier pulling. You can also use the head of a second hammer. For a specialized nail pulling hammer, you can even weld a short shaft stub crosswise to the front of the hammer to function as a fulcrum.

TWO-CAN CLEAN-UP
Try this system when cleaning brushes used with oil-based paints. Find two cans with plastic lids, one small can like peanuts are sold in, and one larger like a 2-lb. coffee can. Pour a small amount of turpentine or solvent in the small can to clean the brush. Pour the used solvent into the larger can after each cleaning. Allow the solvent in the large can to settle out so you can reuse the clear solvent which results. Dispose of solvents properly to avoid both fires and environmental damage.

CLEAN SOLVENT

SEDIMENT

PARTS RECOVERY

When working on a vehicle or major tools, it's inevitable that at least one small part will drop onto the floor and vanish forever. Line an old cookie tin with newspaper, and set it under the area where you are working. If a part drops, as it inevitably will, the newspaper softens its fall and it will generally stay on the paper.

EASY-GOING VISE

To protect a part clamped in a vise, you can wrap it in a fold of leather scrap. It is much less expensive to do this than to buy a set of brass jaws for your vise. An old belt, or a section cut from a worn-out pair of shoes, are both good sources for leather with no out-of-pocket cost.

DISASSEMBLY PHOTOS

If you plan to refurbish a used shop tool, take some photos before you start and as you go. The photos will save you hassle later during reassembly. Use a number of different angles, and take close-ups of areas where you think you might have some questions later. The more complex the machine, the more photos you should take. Also, sketches and notes can be especially helpful for small, complex subassemblies.

SHOP INSULATING

A warm-weather shop needs about R5 insulation in the ceiling or roof to relieve summer heat and minimize winter condensation. But a heated shop should be well insulated, including foundation, sidewalls, and ceiling. Insulate sidewalls at least to R13 and the ceiling to R20. Also consider venting the attic area if it is closed off; it will be cooler in summer and/or easier to heat in winter.

SAWDUST CLEAN-OUTS

Excessive dust in a collector drum or filter bag will restrict air flow and cut performance. Empty collector drums when half full and closed style filter bags when a quarter full. (A drum-mounted filter bag can be run until the drum is full, but shake the bag at least once for every 4 hours of use.) Take care of air leaks into the system right away. Wash and dry the collector's filter bag once or twice a year to restore filter efficiency.

STORING PAINT

Just before closing paint cans for storage, slide a rubber band (or draw a line with a felt tip pen) around the can at the level of the remaining paint. You will know at a glance how much paint is left in the stored can. Also write the date and room in which it was used to find the right can for later touch-ups.

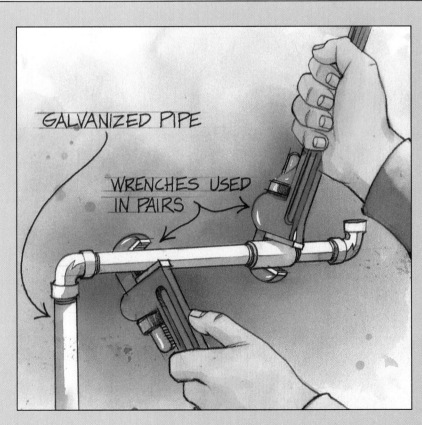

PLUMBING ADVICE
When replacing sections of old galvanized pipe, use two smaller pipe wrenches to avoid twisting and jarring the rest of the pipes. Avoid banging and excess pressure or you may cause more leaks in joints down the line. Whenever pipe leaks develop, always inspect the rest of the piping. An entire section may need replacing, especially if water pressure is low. When joining pipe, some pros use Teflon tape first, followed by pipe compound.

STRANGE NOISES

*A Mini-Guide To Help
The Do-It-Yourself Noise Detective*

Moaning, groaning, scratching, shrieking, rattling, gnawing, thumping, squeaking, crackling, sizzling, whirring. A certain pattern of noise is part of your home's personality, perfectly normal and predictable. However, the same noises that seem perfectly normal to one homeowner can keep an overnight guest wide-eyed and awake wondering if a prowler is slashing the screens. The stranger's mind hasn't adjusted to the home's sound patterns and keeps trying to figure out the source of it all.

Strange, unfamiliar noises in your own house often are detectable only at night, in the absence of daytime din. They might be there all the while, but the quiet of the night draws your attention to them. There can be a sporadic nature to when they occur. They may sometimes last all one night and be completely absent on another night, or they may be closely intermittent, coming and going within an hour's time. Some particularly disturbing noises are those that suggest the presence of spirits or ghosts of past inhabitants; it's these kinds of noises that can leave you puzzled, frustrated, exasperated, and even angry until the source is discovered.

Fortunately, most all strange noises in a house are the natural result of living in a structure subject to the antics of wind and weather and filled with mechanical systems. Their source may be as natural as

Strange noises emanating from a furnace can be caused by simple misadjustments of the blower system.

wooden beams or metal windows contracting when the temperature drops after the sun goes down.

Other possible causes may be as simple as a bird fluttering in the chimney, wind whistling through a screen, or a shingle flapping on the roof. Those moaning and groaning sounds, suggestive of lost souls in torment, often can be traced to overgrown tree branches rubbing on overhead utility wires in the wind. In fact, tree surgeons—those who are often called to trim such branches—report that the most unearthly noises can come from, not the electrical wires, but the telephone or cable tv wires. These wires are usually lower than the power wires, and they often are anchored to the fascia board along the eaves of the roof.

A tree branch rubbing on such a wire can produce ghastly sounds. Imagine a wire attached to the center of a snare drum stretched tight and rubbed with a rosined violin bow—definitely not music to your ears.

As benign as most strange new noises are, it's wise not to ignore them, particularly if they come from your home's mechanical systems. Just like a good car mechanic depends on his ears to help diagnose a problem, noises in a home may signal that something is wrong and needs attention, repair, or replacement.

The sample listings that follow concentrate on common sources of strange noises to give you a headstart in your own detective work. By tracking down the sources and causes, you will sleep better at night, and may even get the jump on sidestepping an impending mechanical failure or preventing other damage to your home.

RATTLING FURNACE

Furnaces sometimes make unfamiliar noises when operating. In fact, the noisiness of forced-air furnaces can cause one to think replacement is due when the cause may be a simple mechanical problem with the motor or fan within the blower system. Sometimes simple adjustments and/or replacing a part will solve the problem.

If your furnace is sounding off, first turn off the power to the furnace, remove the access panels, and make a careful examination of the blower area. Using a flashlight if necessary, check to see that the drive belt between the furnace motor and the blower is not cracked, has proper tension, and is in proper alignment.

Also check the pulley on the motor. See if it is loose on the shaft, has worn grooves, or if it is dirty. Retighten any loose setscrews. If worn or dirty, remove the belt and clean the pulley and sand down its interior sides. Likewise, check the pulley on the blower fan. Spin the blower to check for sound which may be caused by something inside. If the fan is rubbing against the housing, it needs adjustment and the best bet is to call a technician. Push and pull on the blower pulley to check for end-play. If the end-play is excessive, the shaft collars need to be adjusted in or out.

Note that a blower that needs oil can also make noises. Follow the instructions in your owner's manual to oil the unit. Sometimes oilless bearings can wear out and need replacement. To check to see if the motor is making the noise, remove the belt and run the motor. The motor may simply need oiling, but motor bearings may still make noise. If so, decide if you can live with the noise or if you want to re-place the motor. Also be aware that a dirty furnace filter can sometimes also cause noise; clean the filter as recommended.

Important: If the burner of your gas furnace makes an unusual noise, the gas input amount may not be correct, or the burner may be getting too much primary air. In either case, contact a service technician. Also contact a technician immediately if the walls or windows in your home sweat excessively. This may mean that your furnace may not be getting enough ventilation or that the flue pipe may be blocked.

CLUNKING WATER PIPES

Plumbing supply pipes can whistle, bang, hum, or chatter whenever water is used or water is turned off. Most of these problems are fixable. Modern plastic plumbing lines are noisier than older galvanized pipes. However, if the water lines hum excessively, the cause may be vibration or blocked piping. Whistling and chattering are often caused by faulty faucet washers or spindles. Loud hammering of pipes can result when faucets are closed, or when the flow of water to clothes washers or dishwashers is abruptly stopped. The solution often is installing air chambers in the system, or "recharging" existing air chambers.

If the pipes produce a humming sound, check to see if the cause is vibration. If it is, you may be able to solve the problem by installing padding between the pipe and wall. (If pipes hum because they are old and blocked, replacement may be the only solution.) If the noise results only when one faucet is used, the problem may be a broken or damaged washer or a damaged washer seat. If the noise is a hum or honking when the toilet is used, the problem may be a faulty inlet valve or one clogged by debris.

Loud banging that occurs when faucets are shut off quickly is called water hammer. First check to see that pipes are securely fastened inside the hangers which hold them. If your home does not have air chambers which provide a cushion of air in the system, one large air chamber can be installed on the main water line, or smaller individual chambers can be installed behind each fixture.

If your home already has a water chamber in the system, it may be water-logged. This means the section of pipe which normally should have air in it to act as a "cushion" has become filled with water. To correct this problem, turn off the main water shutoff and open all the faucets to drain the system. Leave the faucets open halfway. Close the faucets on the lower level and turn on the water. As the faucets begin to run on the lower level, turn them off and flush any toilets. Do the same on the next level and then on the third level, if you have one. This should automatically replace the water in the air chamber with air.

Keep in mind that noises which may at first appear to be coming from the plumbing system may also be caused by splashing in toilet tanks, boilers with dirty water, or from water heaters (see the other entries).

GURGLING TOILET

Toilets which make excessive gurgling or splashing sounds, or which whine or clunk during the flush cycle, likely have defective parts or need adjustment. While such noises seldom comprise an emergency situation, they can signal a problem that is running up your water bill. Fortunately most toilet noise problems can be isolated and repaired, regardless of the age of the toilet or its components.

If the inlet valve or ballcock assembly closes with a loud noise (known as water hammer), it may be caused by water pressure which is too high. You can try reducing the pressure reaching the valve by partially closing the water supply valve next to the toilet (also see Clunking Pipe, page 107). However, if the water supply is restricted too much a whining sound may result. Normally keep the water supply valve as far open as possible.

If the toilet still whines, check for corrosion debris at the water supply valve, and ballcock or inlet valve, inside the tank. Worn-out ballcock or inlet valves can also cause excessive noise. Replace washers, if possible, or the entire unit. If the toilet's fill cycle is long or noisy, it may be caused by a partially plugged valve inlet or supply line. You can try to clean out the inlet passage of a newer-style inlet valve with a knitting needle or a straightened coat hanger. (Tip: If you replace the brass rod that makes up the float arm, try to keep it the same length as the old one. If it is cut too long, it can cause the inlet valve to honk like a river barge coming through your bathroom.)

A splashing sound can be caused by the refill tube either pointing straight down the overflow pipe, or spraying water directly into the tank. Either problem can be corrected by repositioning the refill tube so water coming out of it hits the inside wall of the overflow pipe. Also, when installing or replacing water supply stop valves, ballcock assemblies, or inlet valve units, be sure to clear any debris from the water line before final assembly. (Instructions that come with replacement inlet valve units will tell how to accomplish this by removing their upper assembly.)

CLICKING HUMIDIFIER

Some noise will naturally be produced with anything that moves air. However, if the central humidifier on your forced-air furnace makes an unusual sound, there may be specific causes which can be corrected. Turn off the electricity at the fuse box or breaker panel or unplug the unit. Then close the saddle valve which feeds water to the humidifier and remove any drain tubing so the unit can be taken apart and inspected.

To check the humidifier, remove the lower unit by unfastening latches and pour out any remaining water. If the humidifier was installed using a plenum stiffener, check it to make sure it is fastened securely to the plenum and that all the screws are tight. Then make sure the humidifier is installed securely to the plenum stiffener. Next check to see that any setscrew in the hub of the media wheel motor shaft is tight. If it is loose, tighten it. Also check to see that the media wheel (the part that holds the pad) is still round. If it isn't, it must be reshaped or replaced. Check the alignment of the wheel, and also make sure there are no bent blades in the blower or the motor fan.

If the noise persists, it may be due to the rough edges that were created when the ductwork was cut to mount the humidifier. If these edges are rough, straighten them. Also check the water pressure to the humidifier. If it's too high, it may cause a vibration noise in the water line between the humidifier and the saddle valve used to tap into a water pipe. This can be remedied by cutting down the flow of water at the saddle valve or by fastening the water line to a ceiling joist or wall.

Tip: To check to see if the noise may be coming from the motor, remove the media wheel, then reassemble and turn on the unit. If the motor is causing the noise, install a replacement or call a technician to do the job.

POUNDING CLOTHES WASHER

If your clothes washer shakes and vibrates when in use, first check to see that the load is balanced, and not bunched up on one side. Make sure that the front legs are not loose, that any shipping straps are completely removed, that the washer is level, and the floor is solid.

Generally, the rear legs of a clothes washer are self-leveling. To level a clothes washer, use a carpenter's level to see that it is level front to back and side to side.

If the washer is not level, determine which side of the washer should be raised or lowered. Prop up the front of the washer and adjust the front legs by turning them in or out (loosen the lock nut to turn the legs in). Then tighten the lock nuts against the base of the washer.

To readjust the rear leveling legs, tilt the washer forward to raise the back about an inch, and then set it back down on the floor. The floor beneath the clothes washer should be level, with no more than a 2″ slope under the washer. The floor should also be strong enough to support the weight of the filled washer, about 315 lbs. or so, depending on the model of clothes washer that you have.

BUZZING REFRIGERATORS

Modern refrigerators, designed to operate as economically as possible, use high-efficiency compressors which run faster and will have a relatively higher pitch, pulsating sound while operating. However, if the compressor simply clicks on and buzzes, it may indicate that the compressor is defective and that a call to a service technician is in order.

If your refrigerator vibrates or rattles, it may be because it is not resting solidly on the floor. If the floor is weak or uneven, the roller screws or front leveling legs may need adjusting. Keep in mind that the foam insulation used in modern refrigerators today has excellent insulating capabilities; however it does

not provide the high level of sound insulation provided by the less efficient fiberglass insulation once used by manufacturers.

Other noises may be normal and do not require a service call. For example, the freezer fan (which circulates cold air to cool the refrigerator and the freezer compartment), as well as the outside condenser fan, will produce a whirring sound, or a sound like rushing air. The flow of refrigerant through the freezer cooling coil can sound like boiling water or a gurgling. Water dropping on the defrost heater can cause sizzling, hissing or popping sounds during the defrost cycle. If the refrigerator has an ice maker, the water valve will buzz when the ice maker fills with water.

GROANING DISHWASHER

If your dishwasher produces excessive noise, first make sure the dishes are loaded properly (see your owner's manual) and see that the unit is level. Strange noises can also be caused by hard objects which have fallen into the pump openings in the bottom of the unit. These may include debris such as fruit pits, measuring spoons, or bottle caps.

To clean out any miscellaneous debris, make sure the machine has cooled down, then remove the bolt above the spray arm. Remove any objects from in and around the pump openings, and replace the spray arm and bolt. (Note: It is important not to let small metallic items, such as pot handle screws, fall into the pump openings since they may cause serious damage to the pump parts.)

POPPING WATER HEATER

Water heaters sometimes make unusual noises which, besides rumbling, may include sizzling, popping, crackling, and pounding.

First, be aware that certain noises from a water heater may be normal, such as the expansion and contraction of metal parts during periods of heat-up and cool-down. Also sizzling and popping may be caused within the burner area by normal condensation during heating and cooling periods. Sediment build-up on the tank bottom may also create various noises (and if left in the tank, may cause premature tank failure).

If your water heater is making crackling, sizzling, or popping nois-

Clothes washers that vibrate may not be level. To check this, use a carpenter's level, and also make sure that the floor is solid.

es, check the heater to determine if the cause is a leak or normal condensation. In some cases the temperature-pressure (TP) relief valve may be dripping because the water supply system has pressure reducing valves, check valves, or back-flow preventers. When these devices are not equipped with an internal bypass and no other measures are taken, they can cause the water system to be closed so it does not allow for the expansion of heated water. In this case the TP valve will drip to relieve the excess pressure. The solution is to call a technician to install a by-pass and/or an expansion tank to relieve the pressure from thermal expansion.

In some cases, the cause of a leaking TP valve may be that the water heater temperature is set too high; in other cases, because the TP valve is bad. Too high of a temperature setting can also cause pounding and rumbling or a surging sound in the heater.

Tank sediment build-up can cause water heater noises as water droplets get under the sediment and flash into steam when heated. Drain the tank to clean; if the problem remains, contact a technician for a professional cleaning. Similar sounds can be caused in electric water heaters because of scale-encrusted heating elements; in this case, the elements can be replaced. Sediment build-up can be reduced by regularly draining a few quarts of water every month from the drain valve at the lower front of the tank.

The temperature-pressure relief valve should be manually operated at least once a year. Check your owner's manual for recommended procedure. Make sure no one is in front of or around the outlet of the discharge line, and that extremely hot water manually discharged will not cause damage. (If, after manually operating the valve, it continues to release water, close the cold water inlet to the heater, following draining instructions in your manual, and contact a technician to replace the TP valve.)

SQUEAKING FLOOR

Floor or stair squeaks are common in homes and usually are caused by floor components rubbing against each other. Squeaks can be caused by floor materials which have dried out and become loose or separated. They may also be caused by loose X-bridging between the joists, gaps between the joists and subflooring, or plumbing pipes or ducts rubbing against the joists.

First try to pinpoint the area of the squeak and see if the problem can be fixed from below the floor or stairs. Check to see if the squeak may be caused by the X-bridging lumber which is used between the joists visible in the basement. You may be able to correct this by cutting away wood where the X's cross with a hand saw. Check and readjust any loose pipes or pipe hangers in that area. If there is a gap between the joist and subflooring, try driving in wedge-shaped shims above the joist. The squeak may be caused by separation of the subfloor and floorboards. In this case, you can try driving screws through the subfloor, into the boards above, to draw the two together. (Make sure the screws reach only about halfway into floorboards.) If this doesn't work, you can try using concealed nailing from above or lubricating the squeak area.

When driving nails through hardwood flooring, first drill pilot holes slightly smaller than the nail size to avoid splitting. Start the pi-lot hole at the edge of the board and angle it down and towards the center of the board. When refastening stair treads to risers from the top side, drive flooring nails at an angle towards each other. In either case, you can use a nailset to avoid marring board surfaces, and wood putty to cover the nail holes.

In some cases you may be able to stop the squeak by using powdered graphite, available at auto parts or hardware stores. Spray the graphite into visible cracks in the area of the squeak. This may lubricate the parts rubbing together enough to stop the noise. Another option on stairs is to reinforce the tread/riser joints with wooden blocks, using construction adhesive and wood screws.

THUMPING ATTIC

Strange noises from attics often can be caused by wildlife pests. If so, it is best to respond to problems as quickly as possible. The longer you wait, the more difficult it will be to change an animal's behavior. The suggestions below are non-chemical methods of dealing with wildlife pests. For more tips on specific problems, contact your local extension service office or an experienced nursery person. Wildlife removal services may also be available in your area to help you deal with wildlife pests humanely; check the Yellow Pages.

For bats, repair all cracks or holes in the home. Bats navigate through use of a type of radar system, sending out signals that bounce back if there is an impediment ahead. Trapped in your home, a bat searches for an opening. You can speed its exit by leaving the largest hole available open for several days. After the bats have left the area in the evening, close up the final

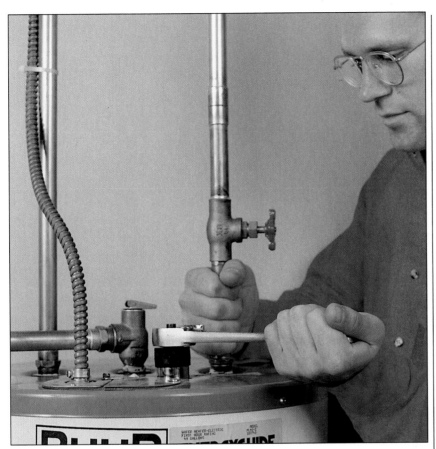

A noisy water heater can result from a number of causes. Regular draining can help stave off noise caused by sediment build-up in the tank.

controlled drafts which limit air supply. The build-up is highly flammable and may ignite.

The average chimney fire has a duration of five minutes or less. Unfortunately, not much can be done during a chimney fire except call the fire department. Extinguish the original fire, if possible. (Some experts suggest dumping large amounts of coarse salt on the fire, then holding a wet blanket over the hearth opening of a fireplace to keep air from entering the chimney.) Do not run water into the hot chimney since this may crack the flue liner or bricks. The fire department will inspect your home to make sure it is okay. Do not use the fireplace or stove after a chimney fire until it has been inspected by a chimney expert.

To minimize the risk of chimney fires, do not use a fireplace or stove for the burning of large amounts of paper scraps or wrappings, corrugated boxes, wood shavings, Christmas trees or wood which contains flammable adhesives, such as plywood or paneling. These materials can burn at temperatures high enough to make chimney damage likely. As a general rule, don't use more than three or four full-sized logs in your fireplace or other wood-burning device, and have the chimney inspected and cleaned regularly. Chemical cleaners can be used to help inhibit soot build-up. (Common rock salt thrown into the chimney will not do the job.) Consider hiring a professional chimney sweep to do the job.

opening, but don't do this in early summer when young may be trapped inside the home.

For mice and rats, use traps or glue boards. Keep household areas clean and free of food particles. Protect other possible food sources. Repair cracks or holes in the foundation, screens, or other areas where mice and rats may enter the home.

For squirrels, use live traps. Repair all holes in screens, attic and eave areas, and the foundation of the home. Also trim the branches of trees that provide squirrels access to the roof.

For pigeons, use sticking substances such as Tanglefoot where pigeons are likely to roost. Use "porcupine" wire such as Nixalite or Cat Claw to prevent birds from roosting. Deal quickly with a problem of woodpeckers on the siding of your home or other buildings.

Harass birds with water spray. String reflective tape along wall; hang nylon netting from eaves to wall to protect damaged area, and use metal flashing or hardware cloth to protect area from continued damage. Check for, and eliminate, insect problems.

ROARING CHIMNEY

A loud roaring sound coming from a chimney is likely a fire caused by an overheated fireplace or a wood stove. Chimney fires can be frightening, and temperatures inside the chimney may reach up to as high as 3,000° F., creating a tremendous updraft which causes the roar. They are often the result of building a fire that is too large or too hot. Another cause is an internal fire in the chimney resulting from an accumulation of soot and tar inside of the chimney, often accelerated by the use of "high efficiency" stoves with

WINDOW SOLUTIONS

*Sash Kits Make Window Replacement
An Easy, Half-Hour Do-It-Yourself Project*

Maintaining the charm of older homes usually means dealing with old windows. Many homes built in decades past have their original double-hung windows which present modern-day problems. They leak air, adding to heating and cooling costs, and often are painted shut, simply won't open, or have sash that fit too loosely in the frame.

In addition, older windows are usually single-pane and fortified with unattractive aluminum storm and screen combinations. Both design elements also make them difficult to clean. In general, they are often a major headache for homeowners.

But, thanks to new technology, all these problems can be corrected without spending a fortune and without having to rip out all the existing window framing in your home. The solution is found in sash replacement kits now available.

Sash replacement kits allow you to replace the sash (the glass and the frame that surrounds the glass)

Sash kits allow the frames and trim to remain intact for an easy, cost-effective upgrade that offers the best of modern window technology.

and the jamb liners of drafty or deteriorating double-hung windows without disturbing their existing frames. Marvin Windows, a leading manufacturer of sash replacement kits, reports that with the kits you

Although the sash in many old double-hung windows are worn out, the frames and trim are still in good shape. In such cases, sash replacement kits are a logical and economical solution.

only pay for what you need—the sash and the jamb liners—not the entire window.

With sash kits, you can work wonders for a room full of old, drafty double hungs. You can make a dull, chilly breakfast nook cozy and inviting again. You can add a traditional style with authentic divided lites. Or you can use the kits to preserve and upgrade unusual sizes and designs from years past— at less expense than ever before.

Using the kits can save you up to 30% on the cost of the new window replacements, plus you save the labor costs of hiring a professional to do the installation. If you are even moderately skilled, you can do the job yourself.

Another factor that makes the kits a good choice is that they can be installed from inside of the home, so you don't have to wait for perfect weather.

One sash replacement takes less than an hour, so several can be done in one day. Replacing all of the windows in your home might take you only a weekend or so. Or you might choose to do one or two replacements on a series of Saturdays.

Installation is quick and easy (see following two pages) because the existing frame stays intact. The result is an energy-efficient window with a sash that fits tightly in the frame for improved comfort and energy conservation.

The kits are ideal for windows that have beautiful existing millwork or window frames that are square and sound. You gain all the benefits of new windows, including attractive, efficient units that add value to your home. You can expect *(Continued on page 116)*

TECH NOTES: UPDATING WINDOWS THE EASY WAY

Sash replacements are ideal for double-hung windows with worn-out sash that do not operate smoothly, won't shut tight, have been nailed or painted shut, or simply look old and worn. As long as the frame is solid and in good condition, the sash can be replaced without disturbing the frame or the original trim.

The E-Z Tilt Pac kit from Marvin Windows can be installed in about an hour. The kit comes with two energy-efficient wood sash and all the hardware you need to install them. All work can be done from the inside of the room, without having to remove plaster, siding, or outside trim. Manufacturers will prime either or both sides of the sash, and also offer cladding on their sash replacement kits which provides an extremely durable exterior that resists fading and weathering, so upkeep is minimized. Here are the basic installation steps:

1 When buying made-to-order sash kits, it is important to carefully measure the inside width and height of the frame, plus the angle of the sill. If you need screens, also measure the distances inside the exterior casing.

2 First, carefully remove the inside casing from the old window. A utility knife can be used to free up joints that have been painted shut. It pays to be careful since the inside casing will be reinstalled later.

3 The old casing on the window is removed with the help of prybars and screwdrivers. The bottom sash is lifted out, then the top sash is slid down.

4 If the old double-hung window has a weight-and-pulley system, the old cords are cut on both sides; they won't be needed. Next, the old top sash is taken out.

5 The next step is to prepare the frame by nailing metal brackets down on both sides of the window. Then new stops and foam gaskets are installed and new jamb liners are snapped into place.

6 A new stop is installed at the top, then the new sash is installed; first the top unit, then the lower unit. The last step is to replace the original casing. Both of the new sash will slide up and down effortlessly and will tilt into the room for easy glass cleaning.

One of the best things about sash replacements is that jambs can be left intact, without risking damage to walls, especially those of plaster. Enough standard options let you preserve your home's character while gaining modern features.

to recover just about 100% of your window replacement investment, especially if you upgrade with wood sash which offer higher energy-use savings compared to vinyl or aluminum replacements.

While the kits allow windows to look original, they incorporate the best technical improvements manufacturers have increasingly put to use since the first energy crisis and escalating energy costs. Insulating glass comes standard with options like Northern or Southern Low E coating, with or without Argon gas, which gives greater insulating value. The spacers between glass panes are improved as well. Manufacturers like Marvin have switched to U-shaped spacers which are less conductive than traditional aluminum spacers, to reduce transfer of heat and cold. The new spacers also help reduce condensation on the windows by keeping the glass warmer on the edges, where condensation usually first occurs.

Sash replacement kits run roughly about 20% to 30% less than the cost of an entire new window. But the real savings comes with the cost of labor. Labor to install an entire new window is significantly higher than a sash replacement, creating a big bonus for do-it-yourselfers.

Another bonus you will also appreciate is the easy-to-clean feature of updated windows. For example, with the E-Z Tilt Pac sash replacement kits sold by Marvin Windows, both sashes tilt into the room for cleaning, eliminating the need for ladders and nice weather just to keep your windows sparkling.

From homeowners to historic preservation projects, there is an attraction to sash replacement kits because the look of the original windows is maintained. And because they do not alter the existing frame, trim, or other woodwork around the window, no special fix-up is necessary once you have all the sash installed. No plaster, siding, or outside trim is removed. The result is an extraordinary savings of time, labor, and money.

The kits are especially ideal if you are renovating a home and need to keep within historic preservation guidelines set by city, state, and national historical societies. Manufacturers will work with you to make sure the sash replacement you use meets the guidelines and are accurate replications of the original units.

Combination storm and screen or screen only are both optional with Marvin sash kits. Half-inch insulating glass is standard for wood units, while ¾″ insulation glass is standard for clad units. Bare wood is standard, but you can order sash primed on the interior and/or exterior. Exterior finishes available include white, Bahama brown, pebble gray, or medium bronze, or 50 other optional colors. A wide variety of sash sizes is available: widths of 16, 20, 24, 26, 28, 30, 32, 36, and 40″, and heights in 2″ increments from 12″ to 36″ per sash.

The preceding pages have shown the steps involved in installing a sash replacement kit. If you are building a new home or want to completely replace the windows in your home, more options are available than ever before; check pages 117 to 119 for some real-life examples.

Note: For more information on using sash replacement kits, or new windows, you can write Marvin Windows & Doors at 2020 Silver Bell Rd., Ste. 15, St. Paul, MN 55122, or call them at 1-800-263-6161 or (612) 452-3039 to locate your nearest dealer. Besides a colorful booklet on their E-Z Tilt Pac sash replacement kit, they also have booklets on made-to-order windows and doors, divided windows and doors, and window and door home improvement ideas.

USING WINDOWS FOR EFFECT

When searching for ways to update windows, look for a supplier that offers a choice of just the right sizes, for an easy fit, and a look that will perfectly match your plan. Subtle touches like crafted millwork and brass hardware can make a big difference in the overall effect.

Fortunately, with either sash replacements or new windows, manufacturers such as Marvin Windows have fine-tuned the process of "made-to-order." Even if you are not concerned about historical accuracy, the made-to-order process allows options to be factory applied, so the new windows match your originals. You not only avoid that "home center" look, but you make sure you get the exact size to avoid unnecessary fitting problems.

Quality window manufacturers offer many of the same features and options on sash replacement kits that are offered on their replacement windows, including choices of accessories and finishes and traditional accessories, such as divided

New windows can be grouped together and look as good from the outside as the inside, clearly demonstrated by the elegant home above. For an inside look, see top photo, page 119.

lites. Divided lites can be ordered to match the existing windows' pattern, size, and muntin width.

By ordering factory-applied accessories and options, you can save labor and cost at installation time. For example, ordering replacement sash primed at the factory can cut your installation time significantly.

If you are considering window replacements, the photos show how they can be used as tools to achieve a balance of shapes and patterns to improve the way your home looks. Creative use of windows can give your building or remodeling project a crowning touch of class.

THE SKY'S THE LIMIT

On this page: *Creative daylight describes a new trend for stacking windows for multiple openings, as shown at left. Windows can also be used to create special nooks, lower left, for reading, thinking, or just getting away from it all. Simulated divided lites of wood muntins, below, can offer an original look in a stylish kitchen.*

Opposite page: *This homeowner's hideaway on a lake in Montana, top photo, uses windows to reflect the elegance of an osprey's wings. Using bow windows, below left, can create a special focal point while transoms above enhance the effect. French-style sliding patio doors, below right, add a touch of Old World charm while serving a functional purpose.*

CARPENTER'S PENCIL

Handy Formulas To Help Do-It-Yourself Builders
Estimate Materials And Supplies

Most modern lumberyards and home centers have estimators and computer programs to work up materials lists for building projects. But, if you are planning a project from scratch and would like to roughly figure out the costs, you can use these handy rules of thumb. Framing lumber, such as for wall studs, floor or ceiling joists, and roof rafters is often priced per 1,000 board feet in larger quantities. One board foot is equal to a nominal 1″ board that is 12″ square (or 144 cubic inches before it is processed to final dimensions). For example, a 1x12 that is 6′ long is considered to be 6 board feet, while a 2x6 board that is 6′ long also equals 6 board feet. Good building!

Roof Sheathing. To figure how many 4x8′ sheets you will need for roof sheathing, multiply the length of the ridge by the length of the rafter, and divide by 32. For example, if the ridge is 60′ long and the rafters are 20′ long, multiply 60 by 20 to get 1,200. Then divide by 32 to get 37.5. Rounding up, you will need 38 sheets to cover one pitch of the roof. To figure the number of sheets for both pitches, double the length of the rafters, then multiply by the length of the ridge. For example, multiply 40 (double the 20′ rafters) by 60 (the length of the ridge) to get 2,400. Divide this number by 32 and the result is 75.

Ceiling Joists. In most cases the total number of ceiling joists will be equal to the number of floor joists required. The only exception occurs when a different number of stairways lead into the attic than lead into the basement. Adjust the total by using the rule of thumb that each stair opening will require three extra joists.

Wall Studs. Estimating the number of vertical studs you will need to build a wall is fairly easy. If the studs will be spaced the normal 16″ on center, figure 1½ studs for each linear foot of the wall. If the wall is 20′ long, for example, order 30 studs. This number of studs should be enough for the regular studs in the wall, as well as the double studs in the corners and around walls, and for the short studs under windows.

Roof Rafters. *To figure how many rafters you will need, multiply the length of the ridge by .75, add 1, then multiply by 2. For example, if the ridge is 60' long, multiply 60 by .75 to get 45. Add 1 for a total of 46 rafters spaced 16" on center. This is the number of rafters that will go on one side of the ridge. Double it, and you get 92, the number needed for the entire roof.*

Wall Sheathing. *Figuring the number of 4x8' sheets of sheathing is similar to figuring subflooring sheets. Calculate the total wall area, subtract the total area of all windows and doors, and then divide by 32. When calculating the wall area, remember that the wall sheathing will cover the headers and sills at the ends of the floors, so include them in your calculations.*

Subflooring. *To figure the number of 4x8' sheets of plywood or other sub-flooring material, first calculate the total floor area. If the house measures 30' x 60', for example, the area will be 1,800 square feet. From this, subtract the size of any stairwells or other openings. If you will have a single stairwell with an opening of 4' by 9', subtract 36 square feet (4 x 9) from 1,800 to get 1,764 square feet. Next, use this formula: Number of 4x8' sheets equals the floor area divided by 32. In the example above, you would divide 1,764 by 32 to get 55.13, or 56 sheets needed. If the structure has measurements not divisible by 4, you will have an extra waste factor to consider.*

Floor Joists (Clear Span). *If the joists will extend from one side of the foundation to the other and are 16" on center, multiply the length of the wall by .75 and add 1. For example, if the wall is to be 24' long, multiplying 24 by .75 gives you a figure of 18. Then adding 1, the result is a grand total of 19 joists needed.*

Floor Joists (Beam Supported). *If the joists will extend from the sides of the foundation to overlap over a beam support in the middle of the span, multiply double the wall length by .75 and add 1. For example, if the wall is 24' long, you double the length to get 48. Then multiply 48 by .75 to get 36. Add 1 and the total number needed is 37 joists. If there will be stair openings in the floor, add an extra 3 joists per opening.*

Roof Shingles. *To figure the amount of asphalt shingles needed, find the total square footage of the roof and divide by 100. That figure will be the number of squares needed. Add about 10% to allow for spoilage and cutting margins. One square of shingles is enough to cover 100 square feet of net roof surface, but depends on the exposure of the shingle used. For example, a 12" x 36" shingle has 3 square foot, but if only 5" is exposed to the weather, its actual coverage is only 1.25 sq. ft. (5" x 36" divided by 144" per sq. ft.). So it will require 80 such shingles (240 sq. ft.) to make a square (80 x 1.25 = 100 sq. ft.).*

Wallboard Materials. *Standard gypsum boards are 4' wide and 8, 10, 12, or 14' long. To figure the number of boards, divide total square footage by the square footage of the size board used (i.e., 32 sq. ft. for 4 x 8' boards). If using gypsum board nails, figure about 5¼ lbs. per 1,000 sq. ft. of wallboard. If using Type W buglehead screws, figure about 3 lbs. for every 1,000 sq. ft. of wallboard. Also figure you will need about 40' of roll wallboard tape and about a half gallon of ready-mix joint compound for every 100 sq. ft. of wallboard.*

Poured Footings. *To figure the size of footings under concrete block or poured concrete walls, the general formula is to make the footing width twice the width of the wall and as deep as the wall width. This means that a 12" block wall will require a footing 24" wide and 12" deep. Likewise, an 8" wall will require a footing 16" wide and 8" deep. To figure cubic yards of concrete, see the formula under Concrete Mix. Or, if you prefer to figure in cubic inches, you can divide by 1,728 to get cubic feet.*

Concrete Mix. *To figure the cubic yards of concrete needed, multiply the length, width, and depth of the area to be filled (in feet) and divide by 27 cubic feet per yard (3 x 3 x 3). For example, a driveway 30' long x 12' wide x 5" thick would first be figured as 30 x 12 x 5/12 = 1,800 divided by 12 = 150 cubic feet. Then, 150 cubic feet divided by 27 cubic feet per cubic yard = 5.56, or 6 cubic yards. Always figure some extra for waste.*

Insulation. To roughly figure the square (not running) feet needed when using roll insulation, first multiply the total square footage of the attic or exterior wall area by .90 (if joists or studs are 16" apart) or by .94 (if the joists or studs are 24" apart). This gives the number of square feet of insulation needed. If, for example, the area is 640 sq. ft and joists are 16" apart, then 640 x .90 = 576 sq. ft. If you are using loose-fill insulation, divide that number by the maximum net coverage per bag listed on the label (for the R-value you want) to get the number of bags needed. For example, if the square footage is 640, the joists are 16" apart, and each bag covers 33 sq. ft. for R-30, then 640 x .90 = 576 divided by 33 = 18 bags.

Caulking. For rough estimates, figure that one 11-ounce tube of caulking will produce approximately 13' of seam, if applied in a three-cornered seam extending ½" from each side of the joint. For caulking windows, for example, first figure the total linear feet to be covered, then divide by 13 to get the number of tubes to buy.

Exterior Paint. To roughly estimate the gallons of paint needed for home exteriors, add up the total square footage, including sides, gables, dormers, and soffits. Then subtract the square footage of areas that won't be painted, such as brickwork, doors, and windows. Then divide this figure by 400, which is roughly what one gallon will cover in one coat. Adjust for specific surfaces and conditions. Add 20% if the surface is rough or porous; add 10% for narrow 4" or 5" siding; add 33% for any metal or fiberglass corrugated surfaces. Double the figure for first coats on concrete block.

Concrete Block. To get a rough estimate of how many concrete blocks that will be needed, divide the square feet of the wall by 8 and multiply the result by 9. It takes 9 standard 8" x 8" x 16" blocks (nominal) to make 8 square foot of wall. Blocks are sold in nominal sizes, ⅜" less than the stated size, to allow for the mortar joint. To estimate the number of blocks accurately, it is best to work in inches with your block supplier.

WONDER WORKERS

*Discovering New Ways For Solving Home
Challenges Can Be Half The Fun*

Got a problem around the home? Reach for the WD-40. Thousands of do-it-yourselfers are doing just that, judging by the stacks of testimonial letters piling up at the manufacturer's San Diego headquarters. Many of the letters uncover a newly discovered use for the contents inside the familiar blue and yellow cans found in about 8 of every 10 U.S. homes and garages.

Taking its place alongside duct tape, super glue, and the trusty hammer, WD-40 seems to have become one of the truly indispensable homeowner survival items.

One look on the back of the can gives you an idea why do-it-yourselfers consider it a liquid jack-of-all-trades that often saves the day by displacing moisture, penetrating, protecting, cleaning, and lubricating.

Originally developed to protect Atlas missiles, the product takes its name from the 40th experimental formulation of a water-displacement compound. It was first marketed in 1953 by the company,

WD-40 ranks as high as duct tape as a problem-solver; over a million cans are sold weekly in the U.S. alone, and it's found in four of every five households.

then known as the Rocket Chemical Company.

Since then, do-it-yourselfers have found it is just the ticket for lubricating door locks, hinges, cables, latches, chains, wheels, or gears;

WD-40 was developed in 1953 by Rocket Chemical Co. to protect missile skins from rust and corrosion. Today it has a near cult-like following with users who dream up new applications every year.

loosening lug nuts, stuck bolts, frozen mechanisms; cleaning and protecting metal, chrome, and painted surfaces; removing oil, grime, sap and gummy residue, and preventing rust and corrosion.

And they have discovered that it works wonders in removing tar, grease, decals, stickers, even crayon marks from many types of surfaces. Just soak with WD-40, wait and peel or rub off.

WD-40, say its makers, has a high surface attraction to metal so it completely covers surfaces, even in the presence of moisture. In fact, it goes under surface moisture and establishes a protective barrier between the moisture and metal. And it is especially useful in eliminating short circuits caused by moisture because it is a non-conductor of electricity.

Many do-it-yourselfers consider WD-40 to be 1,001 slick tricks in a can. In response to its almost cult-like following, the WD-40 people now sponsor an annual contest for new ways to use the product. Last year's winner was a California woman whose parakeet was trapped on sticky mousetrap paper until its feet were sprayed with WD-40. Runner-up was a musician who sprayed his guitar strings in order to play faster.

Also among the contest entries was a doctor who used WD-40 to release a child's arm from an elevator door, as well as a little league coach who reported that WD-40 works wonders softening baseball gloves, and someone who found that spraying it on the shower rod kept the shower curtain liners from ripping.

(Continued on page 128)

DO-IT-YOURSELF WD-40 DISCOVERIES

What exactly is WD-40? Company spokesmen call it their "secret sauce." However, technical data in their literature implies that it has something to do with high-grade aliphatic petroleum spirits with a flash point of 110° F. The literature also states that the duration of protection will vary with the type of material and conditions of exposure. On mild steel, for example, the protection to expect would be approximately as follows:

1. Covered or indoor storage: 1 year or longer.
2. Protected exterior storage: 6 months to 1 year.
3. Normal exterior exposure: 30 to 60 days.
4. Severe exterior exposure: 15 to 30 days.

Severe exposure includes being on or very near an ocean beach, subject to high humidity, salt spray or salt fog. If longer protection is desired, WD-40 should be lightly reapplied periodically. The company says that when you want to apply permanent coatings over WD-40, the best results are obtained when the surface is cleaned with mineral spirits, lacquer thinner, or a vapor degreasing or alkaline cleaner.

The following are uses for WD-40 which the company has received over the years. **Note:** While many are discoveries that others can use, the company does not condone or recommend all the uses listed—they are simply ways people say they have used the product.

WORKSHOP & GARAGE

❒ Removes grease and thick roofing cement from hands. Dries tools that get wet. Removes rust, grease, and grime and prevents both rust and squeaks on hedge trimmers, scissors, pliers, jack knives, snow chains, and other metal garden tools.

❒ Frees triggers on electric drills. Loosens bolts and screws on snow blowers. Keeps snow from sticking on snow blower chutes and snow shovels.

❒ Removes dust and debris in drill holes when sprayed on drill bits. Lubricates chainsaw chains. Cleans varnish brushes. Cleans nozzles on spray paint cans. Protects saw blades from rust and makes cutting easier. Lubricates screws to make them easier to drive. Removes oil spots from driveway. Works as an engine starter on cars, lawn mowers, and tractors.

❒ Cleans and protects electric saws. Prevents rain seepage when sprayed on garage door seals. Prevents rust on garden tools and outdoor furniture before putting away for winter. Lubricates sticky hand-held tools. Removes deposit build-up on sanding belts. Helps thread electrical wires through flexible conduit when sprayed on wires.

❒ Penetrates and frees frozen shafts and other parts. Displaces moisture from electrical parts, eliminating shorting and current leakage. Deposits protective film to inhibit corrosion caused by moisture, salt water, acids, caustic cleaners, and other chemicals. Quiets

HOW IT WORKS

While most users just know that it works, the WD-40 Company files are filled with data on their product. Their findings, for example, show that spraying it on rubber has no visible effects.

They have also found that exposing WD-40 to nylon, orlon, wood, dacron, and cotton has no effect except a slight stain readily removed with dry cleaning solvent.

Paints and plastics for the most part are also not affected. Some wax polishes and certain wax coatings may be softened. Besides spraying, WD-40 can be applied by brush or dip methods.

DISPLACES. WD-40 is a non-conductor of electricity so is able to eliminate moisture-caused electrical short circuits.

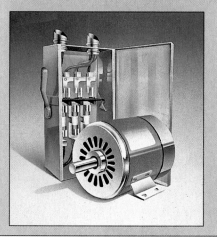

PENETRATES. Its surface attraction for metal helps it to loosen rust-to-metal bonds and free stuck or frozen parts.

and lubricates garage door openers. Lubricates glass cutting tools.

❐ Lubricates and cleans blades of rotary-type lawn mowers. Prevents grass clippings from sticking on underside of lawn mowers. Lubricates lawn mower throttle cables. Protects metal garden tools from fertilizer and garden chemicals. Cleans contacts on electric weed trimmers. Lubricates sprinklers.

AUTOMOTIVE

❐ Releases gummed-up cruise controls. Removes grease and dirt on cars and motorcycles. Displaces moisture in engines or electrical parts. Removes plastic tint film and glue from windows. Lubricates exterior linkages of auto carburetors. Lubricates ignition switches. Removes tar on cars.

❐ Helps keep paint from fading on fiberglass truck cabs. Protects cylinder heads from rust and corrosion. Cleans spark plugs. Quiets squeaky car door hinges. Lubricates and cleans battery terminals and poles from oxidation. Lubricates and helps remove wheel lugs on trucks. Loosens hinges of convert-

ible tops. Helps remove oxidation from paint.

❐ Lubricates car cassette mechanisms. Cleans chains, brake cables, and jammed throttles. Softens and preserves leather seats. Lubricates rubber parts. Stops squeaking of windshield wipers. Cleans whitewall tires. Helps prevent rust on auto side trim. Cleans chrome and restores luster. Cleans black grease from vinyl or velour seats.

❐ Frees stuck accelerators when sprayed on carburetors. Frees electric windows in cars. Frees stuck antennae. Prevents rust on door panels and undercarriages. Loosens springs on hoods when they won't close. Cleans sticky debris from steering wheels and columns. Removes pine sap and bugs from cars. Prevents buildup of mud and clay. Protects tow chains from rust.

HOUSEHOLD

❐ Softens leather on shoes and boots and helps shed moisture. Removes tile adhesive from new no-wax floor. Removes baked-on food from cookie pans. Removes stickers and adhesives from glass. Removes

hard water deposits. Loosens stuck light bulbs.

❐ Removes scuff marks, rust, gum, and stubborn stains from carpets, linoleum, and tile floors. Removes tough grease and oil stains from clothes. Loosens stubborn zippers. Removes dirt and grime from sliding glass door tracks, sewing machines, barbecue grills, bathroom and kitchen fixtures.

❐ Lubricates clock gears. Loosens and lubricates storm windows. Removes pine pitch from hands. Aids in restoring vinyl floors. Removes gum from clothing. Removes built-up mineral deposits from freezer grids. Keeps dogs, flies, and maggots out of trash cans.

❐ Removes make-up stains from clothing. Makes window shades roll easier. Removes crayon and other marks off walls and floors. Lubricates push-button light switches. Fixes over-wound watches. Protects and cleans electric shavers. Removes water spots from metal surfaces.

❐ Releases jammed plastic containers. Protects and cleans antiques from rust. Lubricates tuner on stereo when it is hard to turn and

PROTECTS. It gets under surface moisture and establishes a protective barrier between the moisture and the metal.

CLEANS. Its surface attraction helps it get under dirt, grime, caked grease, and oil to clean surfaces and provide protection.

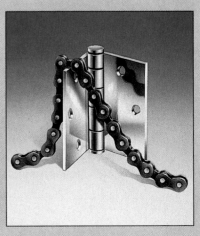

LUBRICATES. WD-40's ingredients disburse and cling to moving parts without attracting dust or leaving residue.

causes static. Lubricates track of fire screens in fireplace. Takes squeaks out of recliners. Stops squeaks and prevents rust on casters. Lubricates crank on barbecue grills.

❑ Fixes push button controls on electric stoves that become frozen. Quiets noisy garbage disposals. Cleans skillets. Takes squeaks out of beds. Frees tank ball in toilet tanks. Unsticks roll-down awnings. Removes oil and grease from shoe bottoms. Unsticks locks and hinges on briefcases.

❑ Removes tape glue residue and marking pen from glass and other finished products. Removes dirt and grease from window screens. Repairs thermostats that are hard to turn on and off. Frees bathroom taps that have seized. Removes corrosion from pressure switch of water pumps.

❑ Takes squeaks out of shoes. Keeps mud from sticking to leather and plastic boots. Unsticks lock on front door. Prevents clothesline poles from rusting. Removes stains like grease, coffee, and chocolate on linen. Lubricates microwave oven doors. Frees swollen storm windows after storms. Shields glass when painting nearby.

❑ Cleans and prevents calcium deposits on water faucets. Removes rubber caulking and paneling glue from hands. Cleans oil burner parts. Helps remove tight rings from fingers. Removes oil-base paint from glasses. Cleans blackboard smeared with color crayons. Renews typewriter, adding machine, and mechanical calculator ribbons and ink pads.

SPORTS & LEISURE

❑ Unsticks keys and hammers on pianos. Unsticks keyboard keys. Removes paint from paint palettes. Silences drum pedals, woodwind sticky valves, and brass slides on musical instruments.

❑ Softens new baseball gloves. Lubricates, removes corrosion, and prevents sticking of fishing reels. Improves fishing results when sprayed on bait. Cleans and protects golf clubs, spiked shoes, hand carts and golf bags. Frees sticky bolts and removes grease and dirt on guns. Protects boat hardware. Cleans and protects metal and brass boat items.

❑ Unfreezes aluminum tent poles. Prevents sticking sleeping bag zippers. Unfreezes pump handles on camp stoves. Cleans out clogged propane holes. Prevents buildup of grease and dirt on camp stoves and lanterns. Cleans flashlight battery contact points. Keeps feathers on archery arrows water resistant. Increases archery arrow velocity and penetration.

❑ Keeps ski boots from squeaking. Protects ski bindings from rust. Removes ski wax from clothing. Lubricates spokes and bike mechanisms such as bearings, chains, sprockets, and brake cables. Starts camp fires. Removes tangles and matted hair on horse tails. Prevents wasps from building nests. Kills thistle plants.

"Ideas for ways to use it just keep rolling in": WD-40 Co.

(Continued from page 125)

In response to the contest, a New York man wrote in to report how well WD-40 works to clean chewing gum from his work boots and driveway. Someone in California used it on an old German cuckoo clock which had stopped working. A Virginia man wrote that spraying WD-40 on old printer and typewriter ribbons makes them work like new.

A woman from California used it to avoid broken light bulbs when changing them. Some people have even claimed that spraying it on their golf clubs, golf balls, and bowling balls has greatly improved their game.

Among the more bizarre uses was the time Denver police extracted a nude burglary suspect who had wedged himself into a vent at a cafe. A Washington rancher freed his stuck finger from a toilet fitting hole with WD-40 during a repair project. And someone else in Colorado used it to remove a dog's tongue from a frozen tractor blade.

These unique applications join other WD-40 use ideas that have been around for awhile—like spraying the distributor cap and spark plug wires if your vehicle won't start after a heavy rain. Or, using it to improve fishing results by spraying it on bait and lures, spraying snowblowers to prevent sticking snow, removing soap and hard-water scum from bathroom fixtures, or spraying it on boat dock posts to quiet them during windy nights.

WD-40 has come a long way since it was first packaged into aerosol cans for the consumer market in 1958. In 1993 the company celebrated its 40th anniversary with almost $109 million worth of sales.

If you aren't already a WD-40 convert, we hope this section will give you some ideas. If you are already a fan and have your own story to tell, you can write to WD-40 Company, c/o Phillips-Ramsey, 6863 Friars Rd., San Diego, CA 92108.

OTHER OFF-THE-SHELF WONDERS

Long before the advent of WD-40, commonly available household products have been pulled off the shelf by do-it-yourselfers and tested as problem-solvers.

One common household product that was tested often for offbeat uses is Mrs. Stewart's Bluing, first marketed in 1883 as a slick way to remove dingy gray from white clothes. Over the years, people have discovered that the non-toxic, non-polluting product also can be used in the rinse water to make white hair sparkle, to spray on greenhouses to cut down solar rays, to trace the location of drain pipes, even to sooth insect bites, plus a host of other uses claimed by at-home experimenters.

Two other common products that also have gained reputations as wonder workers are bicarbonate of soda (baking soda) and vinegar. Today just about everyone knows that a box of baking soda kept in the refrigerator will reduce odors, but this is just one of many uses.

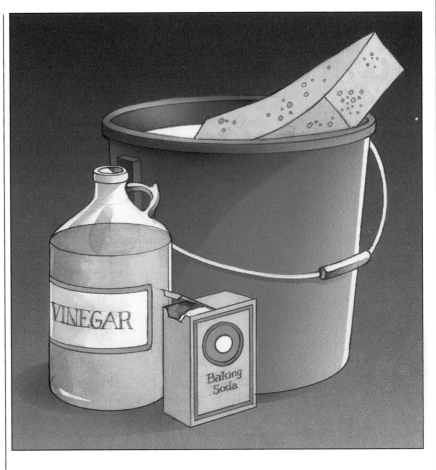

USING BAKING SODA

Packaging baking soda began about 130 years ago in New England when John Dwight and Austin Church hand-filled paper bags in Church's kitchen to sell throughout the United States. By 1896, their enterprise became known as Church & Dwight Co., Inc., the company with the Arm & Hammer Brand trademark.

Baking soda, like vinegar, can be called one of the most useful 100% natural products. It can be chemically produced by passing carbon dioxide and ammonia into a concentrated solution of table salt. Crude sodium bicarbonate precipitates out. It is also mined from an ore called trona, a peculiar mixed salt which can be converted to baking soda. The state of Wyoming contains enough trona to continue supplying baking so-

da for hundreds of years to come.

Besides its uses in baking, this simple, low-cost product lends itself in either wet or dry form to multiple jobs around the home. You can use baking soda in a dry state, sprinkled right from the box. You also can use it as a paste mixed as 3 parts baking soda to 1 part water, or in a solution by dissolving 4 tablespoons of baking soda in a quart of water. Here are just some of the ways you can use it:

To clean corrosion from battery terminals without a wire brush, apply a paste solution. The slightly alkaline paste neutralizes the corrosion. After cleaning, wipe with petroleum jelly.

To remove grime and salt deposits on chrome, use as a solution.

For extra tough spots, use dry sprinkled on a damp sponge. Rinse with water and polish with a soft cloth.

To clean vinyl seats, use a baking soda solution. Rinse and dry. For stubborn spots, use right from the box on a damp sponge.

To clean car floor mats, use as a solution. For tough spots, use sprinkled on a soft-bristled brush. Scrub, rinse, and dry.

To remove stubborn road dirt, tar, and grease from auto glass without scratching, wipe with a damp cloth or sponge sprinkled with dry baking soda. Rinse with water and dry.

To clean, deodorize and remove mildew from fiberglass without scratching, sprinkle on a damp sponge and gently scour. Sponge clean and wipe dry.

To clean and remove onion, garlic, and other odors from wood chopping boards and other porous surfaces, sprinkle dry on a damp sponge and rub. Rinse with water.

To freshen RV water tanks, flush periodically with one cup of baking soda dissolved in one gallon of warm water. Drain and flush with clean water before refilling.

To help septic systems, pour one cup baking soda down the toilet every week. This creates a favorable pH for better sewage digestion of household solid wastes. It also helps avoid clogging, backups, corrosion, and septic odors.

To remove buildup of coffee oils and sweeten coffee pots, wash with a solution. To remove stubborn stains, shake on a damp sponge and rub until clean. Rinse and dry. This procedure works for vacuum bottles, too.

To remove tarnish from silver, apply a paste with damp sponge or soft cloth. Rub until clean, then rinse and buff.

To extinguish small grease or electrical fires, toss handfuls at the base of the flames. Baking soda releases carbon dioxide which helps smother the flames. **Caution:** Don't use baking soda for fires in deep fat fryers.

Other uses for baking soda include relieving acid indigestion; as a mouthwash; treating insect bites, poison ivy, windburn, sunburn, minor burns; as a bath soak and dentifrice; and as a body, carpet, refrigerator, or cat litter box deodorant. For more information, you can write Church & Dwight Co., Inc., P.O. Box 7648, Princeton, NJ 08540.

USING VINEGAR

Like baking soda, vinegar also can be used as a home troubleshooter, beyond its traditional use as a cooking ingredient or for pickling. Here is a sampling of other ways you can put vinegar to good use around the home:

To clean plastic tile, use a few drops in a water solution.

To help loosen rusty bolts, put them in vinegar in a plastic bag or other container.

To get more light from propane lanterns, put the new mantles in vinegar for a couple of hours and dry before installing them.

To clean brick or stone, clean with a brush and a solution of half vinegar, half water.

To unplug shower heads, take off the head and soak it in a container of vinegar. If you can't, or don't want to take it off, fill a plastic bag with vinegar, tie over the shower head, and leave it on overnight.

To remove onion odors or fruit stains from your hands, use full strength.

To make chrome or stainless steel shine, try rubbing with a cloth dampened with vinegar.

To get rid of water rings on furniture, try rubbing them with the grain with a solution of half vinegar and half olive oil.

To make your own window cleaner, mix a half cup of white vinegar with one gallon of water.

To keep ants out, wash the area down with a solution of water and vinegar, half and half.

To get stains out of copper-bottom pans, mix up a paste of salt and vinegar and use with fine steel wool.

To clean leather, rub it with linseed oil and vinegar (half and half) then polish with a soft cloth.

To get mildew off shower curtains, rub with full strength vinegar.

To brighten carpets, mix a cup of vinegar in a gallon of water and brush.

To get film out of bottles, shake vinegar inside them.

To get rid of grass where you don't want it, pour vinegar on full strength.

Vinegar, in combination with baking soda, can help you avoid using commercial household products that contain toxic chemicals. For example, in place of deodorizers or air fresheners, put baking soda or white vinegar in small dishes. You can also sprinkle baking soda in trash cans and kitty litter pans.

Instead of drain cleaners that contain lye, you can clear clogs with ¼ cup baking soda, followed by ½ cup vinegar. Keep the drain and sink overflow vent covered until the mixture stops fizzing, then flush with boiling water. To keep drains clear, pour ½ cup baking soda, ½ cup salt, and ⅛ cup cream of tartar down the drain and follow with hot water. (Note: Use this mixture immediately since it won't remain effective if stored.)

To avoid using mold and mildew cleaners, treat problem areas with a solution of vinegar and water. Or, use baking soda sprinkled on a damp sponge to remove mold. Instead of toilet cleaners that contain hydrochloric acid, you can clean the toilet with liquid soap or Borax. White vinegar or a pumice stone can be used on stubborn rings and lime buildup. Use ½ cup baking soda to freshen the toilet and absorb odors.

Vinegar also can be useful in softening old hide-based glue in antique furniture. For other slick solutions using common household products, check "Furniture Troubleshooting," page 169.

ON-THE-BLINK

Tips On How To Be Your Own Troubleshooter
When Home Appliances Quit Working

Enjoying the benefits of increasingly sophisticated technology in our homes comes with a price. Because most home systems are mechanical or electrical in nature, they are susceptible to the dark side of technology: breakdowns, malfunctions, and/or complete outright failures. The price of reaping high-tech benefits is taking the time, and making the effort, to learn how to live in harmony with these systems.

Home system breakdowns, however, don't always have to spell disaster. What one homeowner might consider a major disruption, another might dismiss as a simple technological glitch. Your reaction will depend on whether you know how to correct, or at least minimize, the kind of malfunction that occurs in homes across America every day of the year. Depending upon your experience level and the tools you have or wish to buy, many home breakdowns can be fixed by the do-it-yourselfer.

You don't have to be a technical expert to learn how to handle the more common household problems. By tackling selected repairs and corrections yourself, your payback will be much more than the money you would have spent to have someone else do the work. By taking care of more things yourself, you will likely enjoy the benefits of living in a home where everything is in working order. You will likely learn to appreciate the value of reg-

Paying attention to appliances can reduce emergencies. The pilot and burner here are accessed through the door below the drain valve.

ular maintenance and care that heads off major breakdowns. And, as simple maintenance is done on a more regular schedule, you will end up with fewer mental notes to clutter your mind. Even more important, by becoming a manager of your home's mechanical systems, in some cases you will be able to prevent situations which could, left unchecked, potentially cost you thousands of dollars.

The listings presented here come from a handy book called *The*

Home Repair Emergency Handbook, published by Taylor Publishing. When things break down, the book advises that major disasters can be averted by simply knowing how to turn things off in your home. If residents of your home, for example, know how to turn off the main electrical switch, the main water valve, and the main gas valve, what ordinarily might have become a costly situation can be easily reduced to a smaller, simply-get-it-fixed problem.

A special form is provided at the end of the listings for you to identify and write in where these critical shutoffs are located in your home. Write them directly in the book, or on a photocopy of the page. After filling it out, it's a good idea to go over the Critical Shutoffs list with others in your family, and to make sure everyone knows where the sheet will be posted in your home. Tip: Also take time to assemble the phone numbers to call for emergency services for the electrical, plumbing, and heating and cooling systems in your home—preferably companies that offer service on a 24-hour basis. That way, when you are on vacation in Hawaii and a pipe decides to burst, those at home will know exactly what to turn off and who to call.

STOVE ELEMENTS

Problem: Plug-in surface element doesn't work or doesn't work at normal capacity.

Background: Heating elements which are plug-in units can be removed for cleaning and for replacement. (Some newer tilt-lock surface units are not designed to be removed from the top; however, they can be lifted upward about 6″ and they will lock in an up position.) Replacement of three-wire elements on older ranges is more complicated; consult your owner's manual, appliance repair books, or appliance part retailer for advice. Before replacing an element, make sure it is plugged in solidly, controls are properly set, and that trim rings and drip pans are set securely in the range top.

What To Do: Be sure all controls are turned to OFF and surface units are cool before attempting to lift or remove them. Lift the plug-in unit about 1″ above the trim ring, enough to grasp it and pull it out. Don't lift the plug-in unit more than 1″. If you do, it may not lie flat on the trim ring when you plug it back in. (Repeated lifting of the plug-in unit more than 1″ above the trim ring can permanently damage the receptacle.) To make sure the element is defective before you buy a new one, try another element of the same size which is working. If it works when plugged into the receptacle where the non-working element was, you will know the element in question is defective.

Special Advice: To replace a plug-in element unit, first place the drip pan, then the trim ring into the surface unit cavity so the unit receptacle can be seen through the opening in the pan. Insert the terminals of the plug-in unit through the opening in the drip pan and into the receptacle. Guide the element into place so it fits evenly into the trim ring, making sure the drip pan is under the trim ring.

Helpful Hint: Don't attempt to clean plug-in surface units in a dishwasher or immerse them in liquids of any kind. Also don't bend the plug-in unit plug terminals or attempt to clean, adjust, or in any way repair the plug-in receptacle.

OVEN THERMOSTAT

Problem: Oven thermostat setting is off and needs adjustment.

Background: If, when using the recommended cooking time given in recipes, foods consistently brown too little or too much, the oven thermostat may be out of adjustment. Oven thermostats over time may "drift" from the factory setting; differences in timing between an old and a new oven of 5 to 10 minutes are not uncommon. To correct the situation, on many ovens you can make a simple adjustment in the thermostat (Oven Temp) knob. Small adjustments can be made at a time, or a precise temperature tester available at an appliance parts store can determine the actual temperature inside the oven when in use.

What To Do: Pull the Oven Temp knob off of its shaft and look at the back of the knob and note the current setting of the pointer before making any adjustment. To increase the temperature, move the pointer toward HI or RAISE; to decrease, turn toward LO or LOWER. Each notch should change the temperature 10°. On some knobs you need to hold the "skirt" of the knob firmly in one hand and turn the knob with the other hand to move the pointer. The pointer is designed to move hard. If it is seated so that it is quite difficult to move, you can loosen it slightly by lifting up the end of the pointer slightly with a thin screwdriver, knife, blade or similar instrument. On other knobs you may have to loosen two screws on the back to move the pointer one notch in the desired direction. Replace the knob to the shaft, and recheck the oven's performance before making any additional adjustments.

Special Advice: If you are using a temperature tester to calibrate the oven, allow the oven element to cycle on at least twice. Then, with the oven set at a specific temperature, take four readings to get an average temperature. Take two readings when the element cycles on, and two readings when it cycles off. Add up the readings and divide by four to get the average temperature. The average should be within 25° of the knob setting. If it isn't, recalibrate the setting.

Helpful Hint: When testing the oven temperature, do not rely on the inexpensive thermometers you can buy at discount stores. Their readings will not provide the accuracy needed.

OVEN LIGHT

Problem: Oven light does not work when switched on.

Background: If the oven light will not work, first make sure the stove is getting power. Check that the plug from the range is completely inserted in the electrical outlet. Also, the circuit breaker in your house may have been tripped, a fuse may have blown, or the light bulb may also be loose in its socket.

What To Do: Before replacing the oven lamp bulb, disconnect the electric power for your range at the main fuse or circuit breaker panel. Let the lamp cover and bulb cool completely before attempting to remove or replace them.

On many stove models, the oven lamp bulb is covered with a removable glass cover which is held in place with a bail-shaped wire. (On other models, you may have to remove screws to take off the glass cover.)

With the bail-type, hold your hand under the glass cover so it doesn't fall when released. With fingers of the same hand, firmly push back the wire bail until it clears the cover. Lift off the cover and try tightening the bulb, in case it was loose. If it doesn't work, replace it with a home appliance bulb of the same wattage.

Special Advice: To replace the glass cover, place it into the groove of the lamp receptacle. Pull the wire bail forward to the center of the cover until it snaps into place.

When in place, the wire should hold the cover firmly. Be sure the wire bail is in the depression in the center of the cover. After the cover is in place, restore electric power to the range.

Helpful Hint: If a new bulb doesn't work, the problem may be that the switch operating the oven light is defective. Call for a technician or consult an appliance parts retailer.

DISHWASHER

Problem: Dishwasher won't work, or doesn't operate properly.

Background: Dishwashers, to do a good job, need water that is hot enough, water that is supplied with enough pressure, and water that is not too hard. Manufacturers recommend that water temperature be at least 140°, though some energy specialists say 130° is high enough. Because a dishwasher fills with

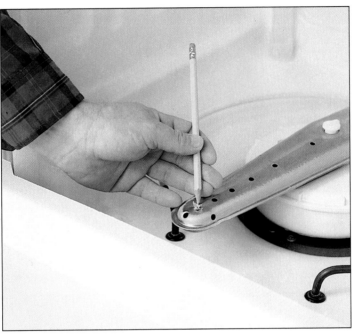

If your dishwasher isn't working properly, check the spray arms for clogs; this one is removed by loosening the white knob at its center.

wash or rinse water for only a limited length of time, it will not get enough water if the water pressure is too low. Pressure should be between 20 and 120 psi. A simple test for pressure is to close all other faucets and put a half-gallon container under a fully opened hot water faucet nearest the dishwasher. It should be full in less than 14 seconds. Review the suggestions below before calling a technician.

What To Do: If the dishwasher will not run, make sure it is receiving electrical power and that the controls are set to ON. If the unit doesn't fill, first check to see that the water is not shut off; the valve on the incoming water line should be in an open position.

Also check to see that the unit's float is not stuck. (To prevent the float inside the unit from sticking in the up position, where it stops a water fill, periodically lift it out and clean around the tube it fits into. Make sure the float moves freely up and down after it is replaced in the tube.)

Special Advice: A small amount of clean water in the bottom of the unit after each cycle is normal and serves to lubricate the water seal. However, an excessive amount left in the bottom may be caused by an improperly installed drain hose.

If water won't drain from the machine, check to see if either the house drain is plugged or if the drain air gap (if used) is stopped up and needs cleaning.

If the dishwasher leaks, it may be because the dishwasher is not level, or an inappropriate detergent was used and caused excessive sudsing.

Helpful Hint: Plugged spray arms, or spray arms that do not turn freely, can keep dishes from getting clean. If necessary, clean openings in spray arms of any collected food fragments.

Also make sure the spray arm unit rotates freely prior to starting the wash cycle; large dishes or utensils can interfere with its rotation.

MICROWAVE

Problem: Microwave won't operate, or takes longer to cook food than times suggested in cookbook.

Background: Microwaves are like radio or radar waves. They will pass through glass, plastic, paper, and most other containers that are not of metal. Metal containers are never used in microwave ovens.

As the food absorbs microwaves, heat is created because water molecules in the food bounce around, colliding with each other. Heat is created by these collisions, much like when warming your hands by rubbing them together. For minor problems which you can solve yourself, see the suggestions below. For other problems, check your owner's manual or call a service technician.

What To Do: If the microwave will not operate, first make sure the unit is plugged in. If it's plugged in and still doesn't work, the cause may be faulty wiring, a blown fuse, or a tripped circuit breaker. Check that the oven door is securely closed and that the controls are correctly set. Also check to see that the air vents are not blocked. The oven may overheat and turn off if the air vents are blocked. Let the oven cool for an hour, then restart it. If it still won't operate, call a service technician.

If it takes the microwave longer than it should to cook food, check with your local utility to see if the voltage in your area is fluctuating below the normal operating range. Next, check to see if the microwave is operating on the same electrical circuit as another appliance. If so, the cooking times will increase when both of the units are on at the same time. (Note: It's best if the microwave has its own circuit which is not shared with any other appliance.) If the unit has a glass shelf, check to see that it is in place. If it isn't, cooking time may be affected. Cooking time will also increase if more or larger amounts of food are placed in the oven than the recipe called for, if the food is frozen or was refrigerated immediately before being put in the oven. (Some recipes reflect the time needed to cook based on food which is at room temperature.)

Special Advice: Microwaves should not be adjusted or repaired by anyone except properly qualified service technicians. After a repair is made, the technician should check for microwave leakage. To avoid potential harmful exposure to microwave energy, don't attempt to operate with the door open. Don't tamper with safety interlocks. Don't put any object between the oven front face and the door, or allow soil or cleaner residue to accumulate on sealing surfaces. Also, don't operate microwaves if the door doesn't close properly, if the door is bent, if the hinges or latches are broken or loose, or if the door seals or sealing surfaces are damaged.

Helpful Hint: Metal ties from plastic bags must be removed before placing the bag in the oven; also check carry-out food for metal before reheating. For cooking times longer than four minutes, avoid using paper containers which may char, and be careful of plastics since some may melt. Don't attempt to cook eggs in the shell since steam build-up inside the shell may cause them to burst.

REFRIGERATOR

Problem: Refrigerator doesn't work, or doesn't work properly.

Background: Newer refrigerators are largely self-sufficient, and many models have electronic monitor and diagnostic systems. Added features, such as ice makers, complicate the mechanical system and require more attention. Keep your owner's manual handy; if you don't have one, order a copy to have on hand. For efficient operation, try to avoid locating the unit next to a range, a heating vent, or where the sun shines directly on it. The tips below include some suggestions on handling minor problems you can correct yourself. For other tips, see your owner's manual, or contact a qualified technician.

What To Do: If there is no touch panel response, or if the unit does not operate, check to see if the interior light is on. If not, the unit may not be plugged in at the wall outlet. If the plug is secure and the refrigerator still doesn't operate, plug a lamp or small appliance into the same outlet to see if there is a tripped circuit breaker or burned-out fuse. Also check that the temp control is not in the OFF position. (Note that the unit may be in a defrost cycle when the motor doesn't operate for about a half hour.)

If the unit is getting power, and an interior light doesn't come on, a light bulb may be burned out or the door switch may be defective. If the motor runs for long periods, it may be caused by large amounts of food placed into the unit to be cooled or frozen, by hot weather, frequent door openings, door left open, or temp controls set too cold. The grille and condensor may also need cleaning. Remove dust from the fin-and-tube assembly either on the back or underneath the unit at least once a year; more often if you have pets that shed hair. A special brush designed for the job is available at appliance parts stores.

If the door doesn't close properly, check to see that the door gasket on the hinge side isn't sticking or folding over. To fix, put a small amount of petroleum jelly on the face of the gasket. If water leaks onto the floor under the unit, the drain from the freezer may be clogged. On newer models, remove ice from the freezer bottom and clean the drain by flushing a solution of one teaspoon of baking soda and two cups of hot water through the drain line using a meat baster.

If an automatic ice-maker doesn't work, make sure its feeler arm is not in the OFF or up position; that the water supply is connected, turned on, and not clogged; or that ice cubes haven't piled up in the bin, causing it to shut off. If the cubes don't dispense, irregular ice clumps in the bin may be the cause.

Interior Temperature Check: Generally temperatures inside the refrigerator compartment are kept at from 35 to 40°; those inside the freezer at near 0°. You can test the refrigerator compartment by keeping a thermometer set in a half glass of water on a shelf for eight hours, or you can use the "milk test." Put a milk carton on the top shelf and check it a day later; if it's too warm or cold, adjust the controls. You can test the freezer compartment by putting a thermometer between two packages of frozen food overnight, or by using the "ice cream" test. Put the ice cream in the center of the freezer compartment and check it after a

day. If it's too hard or soft, adjust the controls. Premium ice creams with their high cream content normally require slightly lower temperatures than the more "airy" brands.

(Note that if the temperature in your home drops below 60° at night, it may cause the compressor to operate less often, allowing the freezer compartment to warm somewhat. You may want to adjust the freezer control one setting colder to protect frozen food, especially

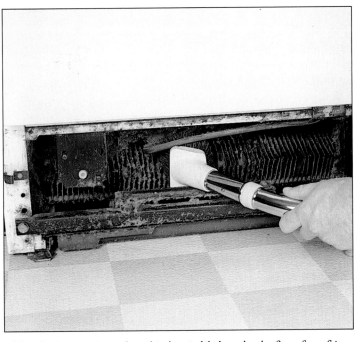

The dirtiest spot in a clean kitchen is likely to be the fins of a refrigerator. Keeping them clean will improve its operating efficiency.

when the thermostat is turned down for an extended period. If freezing occurs in the fresh food compartment, adjust the control for that side one step warmer.)

Helpful Hint: Unplug the refrigerator before making any repairs, even to replace a burned-out light bulb. A light bulb can break when being replaced; unplugging allows you to avoid any contact with a live wire filament. Note that turning controls to OFF position does not cut off power to the light circuit.

ROOM AIR CONDITIONERS

Problem: Air conditioner does not operate, or turns off and on.

Background: Regular care and light maintenance of compact room air conditioners helps assure longer service life and lower operating costs. Most important for maximum cooling is the regular cleaning of the permanent, washable filter which removes dust, lint, and other airborne particles. It should be checked at least every 30 days of operation. The unit should also be given an annual inspection by yourself or a technician.

What To Do: If the air conditioner is not operating, first check to see if its cord is properly plugged into the outlet. Check the main electrical panel to see if a fuse has blown, or if a breaker has tripped. If not, try turning on a light to find out if the local power supply has failed. If not, check to see if the air conditioner was accidentally turned off.

If the air conditioner operates intermittently (turns off and on), or does not cool the room, first remove anything blocking the front of the unit. Close the doors to adjoining rooms and, if the thermostat is set at less than the coldest position, turn it to that position. Check the filter and coils for dirt accumulation. And, if the air conditioner is being fed power through a long extension cord, it may not be getting enough power to operate properly.

Special Advice: You should be able to remove the permanent, washable-type filter, and clean it by using a vacuum cleaner. If the filter is extremely dirty or clogged, clean in warm water with a small amount of detergent and dry before replacing. Plastic parts of the unit may also be cleaned in a soapy water solution, using a soft cloth.

Helpful Hint: The coils and condensate water passages should be inspected and cleaned every year, if necessary. Although the compressor is the hermetically sealed type and the fan motor likely is permanently oiled, these parts should also be checked annually to see that they are in good operating condition.

WATER HEATER

Problem: Heater appears to be leaking into burner area.

Background: The water heater tank may be leaking onto the burner, or water caused by condensation may be dropping into the burner area. Whenever the heater is filled with cold water, a certain amount of condensation will form while the burner is on. This usually happens 1) when a new heater is filled with cold water for the first time, 2) when gas burns and water vapor is produced in heaters, particularly high-efficiency models where flue temperatures are lower, and 3) when large amounts of hot water are used in a short time and the refill water is very cold.

What To Do: Heaters with tank leaks should be replaced. However, don't assume a water heater is leaking until there has been enough time for the water in the tank to warm up. A water heater may appear to be leaking when, in fact, the water is condensation. Excessive condensation can cause water to run down the flue tube onto the main burner of a gas-fired heater and put out the pilot. This condition may be noticed during the winter and early spring months when incoming water temperatures are lowest. After the water in the tank has warmed up (about one to two hours), however, the problem should disappear.

Special Advice: If condensation is heavy, also check the venting system of a gas-fired heater. Good venting is essential for the heater to operate properly, as well as to carry away products of combustion and water vapor. Inspect the venting system once a year, looking for obstructions blocking combustion and ventilation air flow, or damage or deterioration which could cause improper venting or leakage of combustion products. If discovered, have the flue and venting cleaned or replaced before resuming operation of the heater.

Helpful Hint: An undersized water heater will cause more condensation. The heater must be sized properly to meet home demands, including dishwashers, washing machines, and showers.

PORTABLE HUMIDIFIER

Problem: Portable, belt-type humidifier doesn't run, or continues to run for extended periods.

Background: Portable humidifiers which use wide belts of porous material partially submerged in a tank reservoir to evaporate moisture into the room usually will have a variable speed control (controlling how fast the belt turns), as well as an automatic humidity control. Some units use colored pilot lights, one which signals when the cord is plugged in and the variable speed control is in the operational range, and another which signals when the unit has shut down automatically because the water level in the reservoir has gotten too low.

What To Do: If the unit does not run, make sure it is plugged into a live outlet. If it does not turn on, it may be because the humidistat is set below the relative humidity of the room, or the humidistat has not had time enough to adjust to the conditions in the home (this may take several hours). If the home and furnishings are exceptionally dry, the humidifier may operate for an extended period of time. After proper humidity is reached, the operation time of the unit will be shorter. If the humidifier continues to run excessively, check for open doors or windows, as well as for an open fireplace damper. The air escaping up the chimney can cause two or more complete air changes in the home per hour; the more air changes, the greater the humidity requirements.

Special Advice: For the most effective humidification, keep doors open to all rooms to be humidified. Do not place the unit with its back grill too near drapes or curtains. Air movement could pull the drapes against the grill and cut off air flow, resulting in possible damage to the humidifier or the drapes. For maximum efficiency, the evaporator belt should be replaced at least once a season, or more often under severe conditions. The unit should be cleaned periodically, and emptied and cleaned at the end of the season. Also, once a season, put two to four drops of oil in any oiling tubes provided on the fan motor.

Helpful Hint: All humidifiers containing water for extended periods will eventually develop odors. Periodic cleaning, and the use of water treatment tablets, can help prevent odors. For very persistent odors, use two tablespoons of chlorine bleach diluted in a gallon of water to clean the tank and the evaporator belt. Use proper safety precautions.

CENTRAL HUMIDIFIER

Problem: The humidifier installed in a forced-air furnace is leaking or overflowing.

Background: A furnace-installed humidifier can overflow for a number of reasons, including a defective float valve, a defective float valve seat, or a unit that is not mounted level or in the right position in the furnace. Sometimes a humidifier may create minor overflow when the media pad needs replacement or is rubbing against the side of the unit.

What To Do: First check to see that the humidifier unit is level both horizontally and vertically using a carpenter's level. If the unit is not level, adjust the mounting. Check the float valve and its adjustment to see that it is not set for too deep of a water level. (Also check to see that the float itself is not defective; if it is leaking water, it must be replaced.) Inside the float valve mechanism there may be a small black rubber button which seals the valve water outlet. If the button shows wear from water erosion, reverse the button or replace it. Then make sure the button seats properly and evenly on the float valve water outlet.

Special Advice: In some cases a central humidifier may be installed incorrectly so that its opening is located inside the "A" frame of the air conditioner coil in the plenum of the furnace. In this case, overflowing may be the result of the high static air pressure in this location and the unit should be relocated above the "A" coil.

Helpful Hint: When replacing the media pad on the media wheel of the humidifier, make sure that it

Don't use fabric softener in the pre-wash cycle, which requires another rinse. To remove the dispenser shown, pull up on the blue ring.

does not extend past the wheel edges. Do not turn the wheel while attached to the motor; damage to the gears may result. To dissolve lime build-up in the humidifier you can use a solution of household vinegar (1 part) and water (3 parts), or a commercial mineral dissolving cleaner.

CLOTHES WASHER

Problem: Clothes washer is not working, or does not work properly.

Background: Clothes washers use three basic systems, all controlled by electricity: the water fill, water drain, and the drive. Before calling for service, check the possibilities below. If the washer still doesn't work right, check detailed appliance repair handbooks available, or call for a technician. If the machine won't fill, for example, the problem might be dirty water-sediment screens, or a defective water temperature switch or water-mixing valve solenoids. If the water won't shut off, the problem could be dirt inside the mixing valve, a bad water level control switch, a defective timer, or a short circuit. For no agitation or spin, a faulty water level control switch or agitator solenoid may be the problem. If the machine won't spin, the problem may be a faulty drive unit or timer. If the machine does not drain, the problem could be "suds lock," a damaged water pump impeller, or the water pump belt.

What To Do: If the clothes washer won't fill or agitate, won't spin or drain, or stops, make sure that the power cord is plugged into an electrical outlet, that a fuse hasn't blown or a circuit breaker tripped, and that the control knob is not on OFF. If the washer fills slowly, make sure that the inlet hoses are not plugged or kinked, that the water faucets are on fully, and that water pressure is sufficient.

Special Advice: If the unit won't fill or agitate, also doublecheck that the inlet hoses are not plugged or kinked, and that the water faucets are turned on.

If the washer won't spin or drain, also check to see that the lid is not open and the water faucets are on.

If the unit drains when not running, make sure the drain hose is not lower than washer or not fitted too tightly in any standpipe used.

Helpful Hint: A clothes washer should drain into a 20-gallon tub or a 2″-diameter standpipe. If run to a floor drain, a siphon break must be installed.

The drain should be able to carry away 17 gallons per minute. The end of the drain hose should be more than 34″, but less than 72″ above the base of the washer.

If you use less than a 2″-diameter standpipe, there must be an air gap around the hose inside the standpipe to avoid siphoning action.

*Note: To find out how to handle other home problems, consider ordering the valuable 200-page **Home Repair Emergency Handbook**. An especially helpful guide to tracking down and solving problems relating to all aspects of a home, it's available in soft cover format at bookstores for $14.95 or, it can be ordered by writing Taylor Publishing Co., 1550 W. Mockingbird Ln., Dallas, TX 75235, or calling (800) 677-2800.*

CRITICAL EMERGENCY SHUTOFFS

EMERGENCY SWITCH LOCATIONS

ELECTRICAL MAIN SWITCH _____

LOAD CENTER SWITCHES _____

FURNACE POWER _____
AIR-CONDITIONER POWER _____
WATER HEATER POWER _____
RANGE/OVEN POWER _____
CLOTHES DRYER POWER _____
OTHER POWER SWITCHES _____

EMERGENCY VALVE LOCATIONS

GAS MAIN VALVE _____

SECONDARY GAS SHUTOFFS _____

FURNACE GAS _____
WATER HEATER GAS _____
RANGE/OVEN GAS _____
CLOTHES DRYER GAS _____
OTHER GAS SHUTOFFS _____

WATER MAIN VALVE _____

SECONDARY WATER SHUTOFFS _____

OIL LINE SHUTOFFS _____

ELECTRIC MOTORS

*Tips On Selecting And Harnessing
The Workhorses Of The Modern Home*

When was the last time you saw someone using a bit and brace to bore holes in wood? Be honest, this is the age of power tools. If you walk around places where things are being built, you will notice that even the ubiquitous hammer is in danger of becoming an orphan, left in the toolbox or on the tool belt in deference to faster power fastening systems.

The work of the home do-it-yourselfer and workshop craftsman is increasingly motorized. Electric motors work so well we don't often need to think about them until we need to replace one or when we need to power some special tool or device. In these cases, some basic facts about electric motors, plus how to harness them for specific applications, can be helpful.

Motors are classified by their operating characteristics and/or the type of power required. For example, universal motors are the high-revving motors (usually 5,000 rpm or more) used in smaller electric power tools and appliances such as vacuum cleaners and electric blenders. They get their name from the fact that they can operate on AC or DC power. The speed of these brush-type motors drops rapidly as load increases. But universal motors are useful for drills, saws, and other applications where high output and small size are needed, and where the high rpms and limited life (due to the use of brushes) is acceptable.

You may have up to a half-dozen types of electric motors powering the appliances and power tools in your home and workshop.

Other than the smaller universal motors, most other motors found powering tools in the workshop are induction motors which operate on AC power. They are available in three-phase versions which operate only on three-phase power, primarily in industrial uses. They are usually of simple, rugged design and offer long life. However, most induction motors used in the home workshop are single-phase motors, since single-phase power is what is found in most homes.

Single-phase motors of correct voltage can operate from a three-phase system when properly connected to any one of the three phases. However, three-phase motors cannot be connected to single-phase power.

While a three-phase motor is less expensive and more durable than a single-phase, the extra cost of installing three-phase lines is usually prohibitive. Converters are available to alter single-phase power to three-phase, but their cost also can be impractical.

Single-phase motors are available in the following types:

Shaded pole. This type offers low starting torque and low cost. They are typically used in direct-drive fans and blowers, and in small gear motors.

Permanent split capacitor. These provide performance similar to shaded pole motors but are more efficient, require lower line current, and offer higher horsepower capabilities.

Split-phase start, induction-run (or simply split phase). These offer moderate starting torque and are often used on easy-starting equipment such as belt-driven fans and blowers, gear motors, centrifugal pumps, and grinders.

Split-phase start, capacitor-run. These offer the same performance as split-phase, induction-run motors, except they provide higher efficiency. Split-phase motors can also be used where the load is not applied until operating speed is reached, such as with table saws and drill presses.

Capacitor-start, induction-run (or simply capacitor start). This type offers high starting torque and is used on hard-starting applications, such as compressors and positive displacement pumps.

Capacitor start, capacitor-run. These are similar to capacitor-start, induction-run motors except that they offer higher efficiency. They are generally used in higher horsepower applications.

When replacing motors, be aware that, in some applications, more than one motor design can work. In other cases, you may not be able to find an exact replacement but a similar motor with slightly different mechanical and electrical characteristics may work. To choose an appropriate motor for an application, much of the information you need can be found on the existing motor's nameplate, including horsepower, which for very small motors may be rated in watts. Choose one with equal or higher horsepower.

Speed is given in rpm; try to match it within 5%. Try to exactly match voltage, physical size/frame, frequency (HZ), phase (single- or three-phase), and bearing type (sleeve or ball). If the motor is rated for intermittent duty, you can upgrade to continuous duty. Choose a motor of equal or great number Service Factor.

Motors that start automatically, such as those that are thermostat controlled and are located out of sight, must be protected against

"Use a straightedge to check for proper pulley alignment."

dangerous overheating due to failure to start or overloading. This protection can be a separate overcurrent device, such as a motor starter complying with National Electrical Code regulations, a thermally protected motor with integral motor protection, or an impedance protected motor.

Motors with automatic reset thermal protection must not be used where automatic or otherwise unexpected starting of the motor could be hazardous. Applications where automatic restarting could be hazardous include power tools, compressors, and conveyors. Always use a manual-reset thermally protected motor for such equipment.

When buying an electric motor as a replacement, follow the owner's manual for connecting it to your power supply. The new motor, when energized, should operate with only a small amount of electrical "hum" and very low bearing noise. If the motor's shaft rotation is not correct, the manual should provide instructions for changing the position of the black and red motor leads to reverse the direction. The motor should be installed in a location as cool and dry as possible, and should be protected against excessive dust, dirt, and moisture.

When tightening the motor mounting bolts, make sure all four mount points of the base are in contact with the surface the motor will rest on. If the base doesn't contact the surface properly, the base (or support) may be warped or cracked when the mounting bolts

are tightened. Make sure all pulleys are secure on their shafts and correctly aligned. To check for proper pulley alignment, hold a straightedge across the flat sides of the pulleys and adjust to it.

Also adjust the belt tension so the top of the belt between the pulleys deflects a quarter inch when pressed down. Excessive belt tension can increase the load on the motor and decrease bearing life, while loose belts can reduce operating efficiency and shorten belt life. Also make sure the motor frame or base is grounded to prevent accumulation of static electric charges from belt friction.

Check the data supplied with the motor and/or the nameplate for lubrication instructions. Motors used on woodworking tools are particularly susceptible to the accumulation of sawdust and wood chips and should be blown out or vacuumed regularly. Many motor problems can be traced to loose or incorrect connections, to overloading, or to reduced input voltage which results when wires too small are used in the supply circuit. Always check the connections, load, and the supply circuit when the motor doesn't perform satisfactorily.

Low voltage can result if home or shop circuits are overloaded with lights, appliances, or other motors, if undersized wires are used in circuits or extension cords, or if the power company's facilities are overloaded. Suspect low voltage if: the motor fails to develop full power, it starts slowly or fails to come up to full speed, it overheats, or it burns out when operated for long periods.

If fuses burn out or if circuit breakers trip often, the problem could be low voltage, or the result of overload, or because the motor circuit is fused incorrectly.

TECH NOTES: TOOL SPEEDS & PULLEY SIZES

Most home workshop power tools are powered by fractional horsepower motors, the most common being the 1,750-rpm electric motor. Higher rpm motors, such as those running at 3,500-rpm, can be stepped down in speed for use on tools by using belts and pulleys. The tool speed can be varied, while motor speed remains constant.

Formula 1: Speed of Tool. This formula is used to determine the speed of the tool when the diameters of the motor pulley, tool pulley, and the speed of the motor is known. The rpm of the machine will equal the (diameter of the motor pulley x the rpm of the motor) divided by the diameter of the machine pulley.

Formula 2: Size of Tool Pulley. This is used to determine the size of the tool pulley needed for a specific speed when the motor rpm, size of the motor pulley, and the required speed are known. The diameter of the machine pulley will equal the (diameter of motor pulley x the rpm of the motor) divided by the rpm of the machine.

Formula 3: Speed of Motor. This is used to determine the rpm of the motor required to drive the tool at a specified speed when the size of the motor and tool pulleys are known. The rpm of the motor will equal the (diameter of machine pulley x the rpm of the machine) divided by the diameter of the motor pulley.

Formula 4: Size of Motor Pulley. This is used to determine the size of the motor pulley required to drive a tool at a specified speed when the speed of the motor and size of the tool pulley are known. The diameter of the motor pulley will equal the (diameter of the machine pulley x the rpm of machine) divided by the rpm of the motor.

Below are other formulas to use when an intermediate shaft with pulleys (jackshaft) is introduced in the power train. A jackshaft can allow a tool to operate at extremely low or high speeds, as well as most intermediate speeds.

Formula 5: Speed of Tool. This will give you the speed of the tool when all other factors are known. The rpm of the machine will equal the (diameter of the motor pulley x the rpm of the motor x the diameter of the jackshaft driver pulley) divided by the (diameter of the jackshaft driven pulley x the diameter of the machine pulley).

Formula 6: Size of Motor Pulley. This is used to determine the motor pulley size when all other factors are known. The diameter of the motor pulley will equal the (diameter of the jackshaft driven pulley x the diameter of the machine pulley x the rpm of the machine) divided by the (rpm of the motor x the diameter of the jackshaft driven pulley).

Formula 7: Jackshaft Driven Pulley. This is used to determine the jackshaft driven pulley size. The diameter of the jackshaft driven pulley will equal the (diameter of the motor pulley x the rpm of the motor x the diameter of the jackshaft driver pulley) divided by the (diameter of the machine pulley x the rpm of the machine).

Formula 8: Jackshaft Driver Pulley. This is used to determine the jackshaft driver pulley size. The diameter of the jackshaft driver pulley will equal the (diameter of the jackshaft driven pulley x the diameter of the machine pulley x the rpm of the machine) divided by the (diameter of the motor pulley x the rpm of the motor).

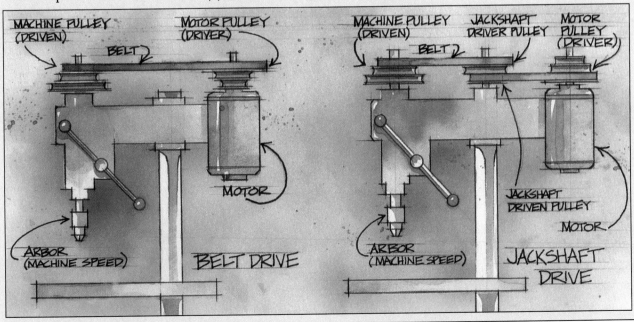

MACHINE PULLEY (DRIVEN) — MOTOR PULLEY (DRIVER) — BELT — MOTOR — ARBOR (MACHINE SPEED) — **BELT DRIVE**

MACHINE PULLEY (DRIVEN) — JACKSHAFT DRIVER PULLEY — MOTOR PULLEY (DRIVER) — BELT — JACKSHAFT DRIVEN PULLEY — MOTOR — ARBOR (MACHINE SPEED) — **JACKSHAFT DRIVE**

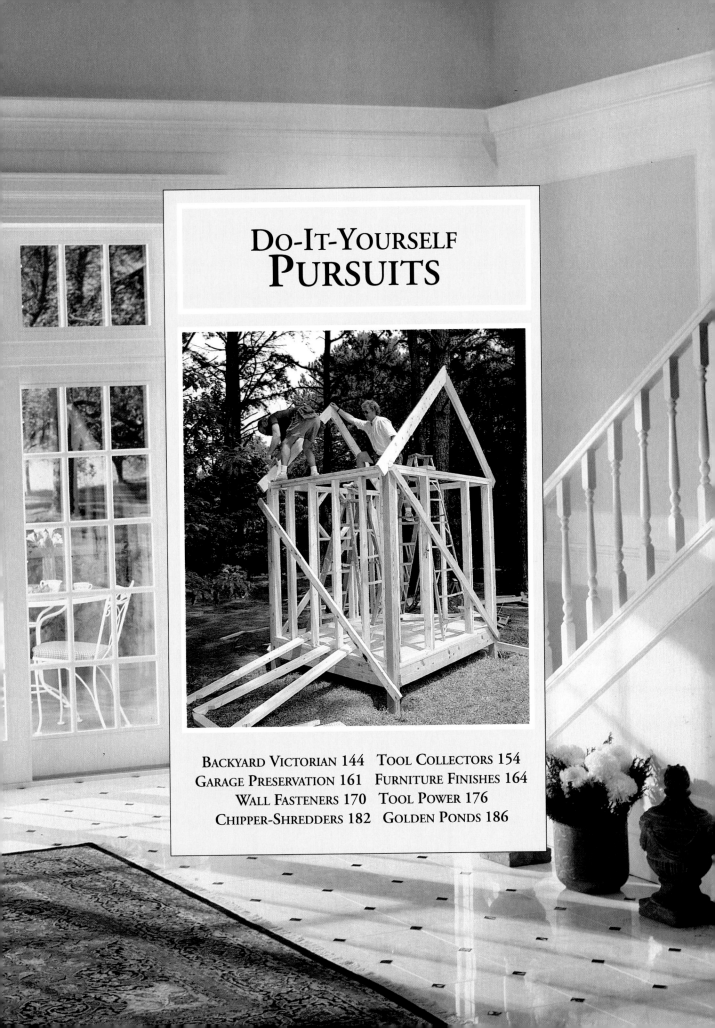

DO-IT-YOURSELF
PURSUITS

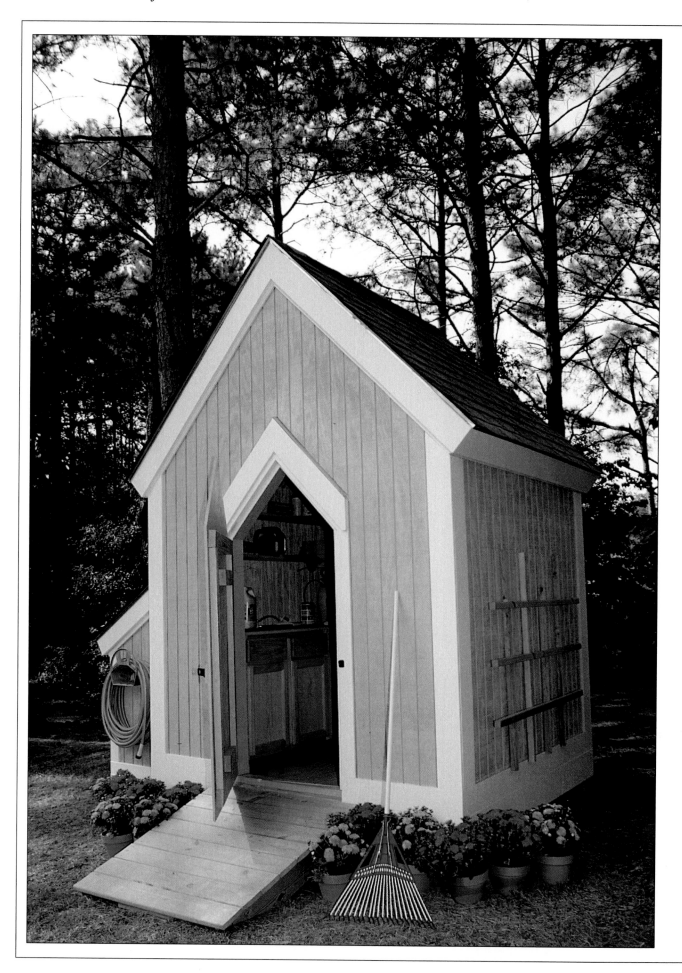

BACKYARD VICTORIAN

*A Unique Storage/Work Structure
You Can Build Just About Anywhere*

Are your garden tools, lawn chairs, and snow-blower taking over the garage? Perhaps you're searching for a quiet place to pot petunias? Whatever the need for more sheltered space in your backyard, you will find this structure unique in both the way it is built and the way it can be customized to fit your needs.

Reminiscent of early Victorian, the design and plans for this spacious backyard shed originated with Georgia-Pacific Building Products division. Its nearly 40 square feet of floor space allows ample room for storing bicycles, lawn mower, garden tools, or play equipment.

The interior is large enough to accommodate a 6′ workbench, and an attractive rear window lets in natural light. The shed design also includes an exterior hutch on one side that can hold several refuse or recycling bins, or be used for additional storage.

Adding insulation, electricity, or running water can give the shed all the comforts of home. And, when built with the premium-quality

This stylish backyard building, built with plywood siding, can help organize outdoor gear. It uses platform construction on 4x4 posts.

materials recommended, the structure will serve as an attractive addition to your backyard for years to come.

The structure is designed to be built by the moderately experi-

The structure is designed to be built by the moderately experienced do-it-yourselfer. Its interior can be made as plain or fancy as you prefer, even equipped with lights and running water.

enced carpenter. If you are a beginner, you may want to enlist the aid of someone who understands how to frame up a building and read technical drawings.

What makes this project unique is that it borrows construction procedures from the way pole barns are built. The framing method is sturdy and bypasses the trouble and expense of digging a foundation.

This project features a platform construction on 4x4 posts which

are sunk in concrete-lined holes, much the same way that a deck is added onto a home. It can be set on any firm soil, whether sloped or flat, without any major site preparation. The optional recycling hutch is built using the same construction techniques and sequence as the shed except that a ledger board attaches it to the shed, much as a deck is attached to a house. Beyond that, 8′ 4x4 posts are cut in half to make the two corner posts, and flashing is needed where the roof meets the shed siding.

The trellis is constructed by laying out 2x2 lattice and marking the overlap of all boards with a pencil line. Cut and chisel out half the depth of the wood between the pencil lines to make half-lap joints and reassemble the layout with the boards lapped together.

When you are satisfied with the size and pattern, screw the joints together. Hang the trellis from screw eyes with hooks to make it easy to detach for fall cleanup or to repaint the wall behind it without uprooting your plantings. Vinyl-coated electrical wire is woven diagonally between the boards to support your plants.

The following pages show the steps of construction, accompanied by comments from the builders.

HOW IT'S BUILT

1 LOCATION. Choose a convenient spot, remembering that the site does not have to be on level ground. When finished, the bottoms of the floor joists should be at least 6″ above the ground, high enough so that water puddling on the ground won't reach them. The ramp should be long enough to slope down at a 45° angle, or less.

2 FOOTING AND POSTS. Lay out the holes to make certain they are square. Dig the holes for the footings; the depth should be below your local frost line. Make the holes larger than the posts to allow for adjustment (approximately 12″ wide.)

Set four full-length 4x4 corner posts in the holes, temporarily bracing them in both directions so they stay plumb. *Do not pour the concrete at this time.* The posts for the hutch should be set after the shed is completed.

3 FRAMING. Hang the 2x8 rim joists on the posts with joist hangers so the outside faces are flush with the 4x4 posts. Then hang the 2x8 floor joists from the side rim joists using joist hangers at 16″ on center or less. Deck the floor with 23/32″ plywood.

Frame the 2x4 stud walls horizontally on flat ground using standard construction techniques, including a sole plate, a single top plate, and studs at 16″ on center.

Frame the door and window openings leaving the sole plate under the door. Add a nailing surface if you will be adding interior

Holes for the 4x4 corner posts, above, are dug below the frost line. Then joist hangers are used to attach the rim joists to the posts. Stud walls are framed, below, after the subfloor is installed.

Rafters, above, are installed with a birdsmouth; the tails are trimmed later. The posts, below, are not set in concrete until after the walls are in place and they have been plumbed and leveled.

sheathing. Nail the walls in place between the 4x4 posts using 16d sinkers.

Check the posts to be sure they are plumb and level, and then fill each posthole with 2 bags of concrete, leaving the top surface sloped to drain water away from the posts.

When the concrete has set thoroughly, cut the four posts off flush with the side wall plate. Add a second top plate on top of the side walls, extending over the post tops. Then add additional top plates on over the front and rear walls, extending them over the post tops, on top of the second top plates which were used on the side walls.

4 RIDGE AND RAFTERS. Toenail the ridge beam in place between the front and rear walls. Cut the rafter birdsmouths so the level (seat) cuts are 3½″ long where they sit on the top plate. The plumb cuts are perpendicular to the seat cuts. Let the rafter tails run wild (long) to be trimmed later. Lay out the rafter spacing on the ridge using five rafters evenly spaced on each side.

5 SIDING. (Optional: Wrap the entire structure with tar paper or building wrap.) Nail band to rim joists, and skirt above band to stud walls.

Before cutting the siding, lay out the cutting lines on the plywood following the patterns on page 154 so that the channels do not fall on a cornerboard and so that the center of the facade is centered between two channels.

Slip the flashing for the shed roof and overdoor trim under the siding before nailing it to the studs, and the Z-flashing under the bottom of the siding and over the skirts.

6 ROOF. To calculate the rafter tail length, mock-up the fascias on the front facade following the dotted lines in the eave detail drawing. Cut the rafter tails so that the fascias will neatly wrap around the building corners. The channels in the siding meet with the sub-fascia and allow the roof to vent. Sheath the roof with $15/32''$ plywood. Apply the roof felt and shingles following manufacturer's instructions. Cover the ridge with G-P Hide-A-Vent ridge vent.

7 DOOR AND WINDOW. Cut the door out of siding and apply 2x4s flat for stiffening and add a diagonal brace from the top hinge down to the lower corner on the swinging side. (Optional for door: Add a small window of Plexiglas, window glass or insect screen trimmed with small-dimensioned window stop and use small strips of lattice for decorative muntins.)

Hang the door in the cased opening using decorative strap hinges mounted on pads so they lay flat with the door trim. Leave the sole plate under the door as a door stop. Install the window in the rear wall.

8 TRIM. Apply the sub-fascia and fascia on top of the siding. Apply cove moulding to trim the bottom and top edges. Add a drip edge at the top of the fascias under the roof deck. Next, cut cornerboards to fit between the skirts and fascias. Add the cornerboards to the front and rear facades, then butt the side cornerboards to them so the caulk joint does not show from the main facades. Add the door and window casing and the overdoor and overwindow trim. Add the drip edge to the side and top edges of the overdoor and overwindow trim.

The building's exterior, above, is sided with eleven 4x8 sheets of 4" o.c. pine plywood siding. Rear window, below, is framed to use a prefabricated 24x24" wood octagonal venting window with clear glass. A window in the door is optional.

9 RAMP. Make the ramp from 2x6 pressure treated joists with ⁵/₄x6 decking nailed on top. Make it long enough that it slopes down at less than a 45° angle. (Optional: If your ramp is long or steep, apply footholds at 12″ intervals or at whatever distance is comfortable for your stride and the angle you have chosen; be sure you are able to move your lawnmower or other equipment easily around the footholds. If you are using the shed for bicycles or a wheelbarrow, two sets of footholds with a space in between for the wheel would be convenient.)

10 INTERIOR. You can finish the interior to suit your planned use. Drywall can be used; however, G-P Clutter-Cutter perforated hardboard would make the walls functional for tool storage. Shelves and cabinets would be useful for a potting shed if there is water available nearby. A serious gardener may want a large sink. The addition of a workbench and a power source would make the structure a functional workshop.

Posts for the hutch, above, are not set until the shed is built and a front ramp is added using 2x6 treated joists. The interior, below, will be more comfortable if the walls and ceiling are insulated.

The final construction steps consist of caulking and painting the exterior. Caulk joints carefully except where the siding meets the soffit, then paint or stain the shed to suit your style preference. Architectural drawings and a materials list are on the following pages.

Note: For more information on materials used for this project, contact Georgia-Pacific Corp., P.O. Box 1763, Dept. Garden Shed, Norcross, GA 30091.

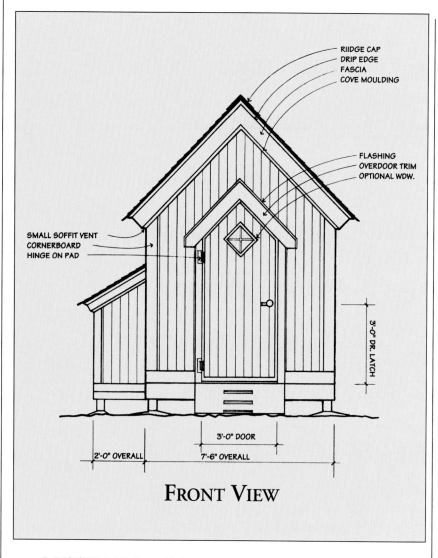

RIIDGE CAP
DRIP EDGE
FASCIA
COVE MOULDING

FLASHING
OVERDOOR TRIM
OPTIONAL WDW.

SMALL SOFFIT VENT
CORNERBOARD
HINGE ON PAD

3'-0" DR. LATCH

2'-0" OVERALL

3'-0" DOOR

7'-6" OVERALL

FRONT VIEW

MATERIALS LIST

PLYWOOD AND LUMBER

Posts:
5–12′ 4x4 pressure treated or cedar posts

Floor and rim joists:
8–8′ 2x8s

Flooring:
3–4x8′x²³⁄₃₂″ thick sheets G-P Southern Gold Premium Sturd-I-Floor

Stud walls, sole plates, double cap plates:
8–14′ 2x4s

Sidewall studs:
18–10′ 2x4s (front and rear wall studs)

13–16′ 2x4s (plates, headers, jacks, etc.)

Door rails and stiles: 3–8′ 2x4s

Rafters: 6–14′ 2x6s

Ridge beam: 1–8′ 2x8

Roof deck:
5–4x8′ sheets ¹⁵⁄₃₂″ Super Blue APA rated plywood sheathing

Interior wall sheathing:
11–4x8′ sheets ¹¹⁄₃₂″ Ply-Bead; 2–4x8′ sheets ³⁄₁₆″ G-P Clutter Cutter perforated hardboard

Ceiling:
4–4x8′ sheets ¹¹⁄₃₂″ Ply-Bead

CONCRETE AND GRAVEL

Concrete: 12–80 lb. bags of concrete mix (2 bags per hole)

Gravel: enough to cover ground under shed (optional)

HARDWARE

Door hinges:
3 pairs–strap style, black

Door latches:
2–with hasp and lock, black

Joist Hangers:
16–to fit 2x8 joists
14–to fit 2x4 joists

Nails:
25 lbs.–16 penny hot dipped galvanized (HDG) sinkers
10 lbs.–1¼″ HDG roofing nails
10 lbs.–8d HDG finish nails for trim
10 lbs.–8d HDG spiral siding nails
5 lbs.–joint hanger nails

TRIM

G-P PrimeTrim engineered wood trim in the following dimensions:
8–16′ 1x6 for overdoor, corner boards, and sub-fascia
7–16′ 1x4 for door and window casing and trim, hutch corner boards, and baseboards.
6–16′ ⁵⁄₄x8 for fascia on shed and band
4–16′ ⁵⁄₄x6 for fascia on recycling hutch and skirts on shed
1–16′ ⁵⁄₄x4 for skirts and band on hutch

SIDING

G-P Southwoods Collection T-1-11 4″ o.c. Pine Plywood siding:
4–4x9′ sheets for front and rear facades
7–4x8′ sheets for side facades and door

MOULDING AND FLASHING

Cove moulding under fascia edge:
96 linear feet of ¾″ or 1″ cove profile

Optional trim (window in door):
1–8′

Drip edge on roof fascia (eave and rake): 5–10′ drip edge

2x2 flashing (overdoor and

window): 10 linear feet
3x3 flashing (hutch roof and shed sidewall): 10 linear feet
Aluminum Z flashing: 36 linear feet
G-P pressure-treated lumber joists: 1–12′ 2x6 pressure-treated (length will vary to accommodate each site)
Decking: 3–12′ ⁵⁄₄x6 pressure-treated
Optional footholds: 1x2s, each 14″ long; number varies with length of ramp, spaced every 12″

WINDOWS
Rear window: G-P prefabricated 24x24″ wood octagonal venting window with clear glass

Optional insect screen

Optional window on door: Plexiglas or glass custom cut to fit

ROOF
Felt: 1 roll G-P 15-lb. residential

Shingles: 4 bundles G-P Summit Series

Ridge cap: 1 bundle G-P hip and ridge shingles to match desired Summit shingle color

Roll Ridge vent: 8 linear feet G-P Hide-A-Vent

OPTIONAL FURNISHINGS
Shelves: 2–16′ 1x10 pine

Cabinets: 2–prefabricated 6′ running feet, 36″ high

Countertop: Approx. 6′–25″ deep x ¾″ G-P Synergite MDF, cut to fit

TRELLIS
Framing: 4–12′ 2x2
Vinyl coated electrical wire
Hooks and screweyes to mount

PAINT AND CAULK
Exterior wall paint: Approximately 2 gallons
Acrylic latex caulk

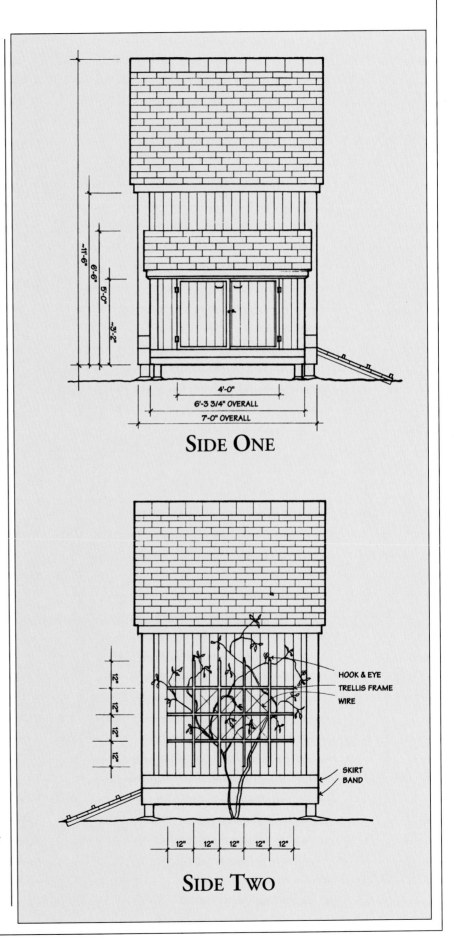

SIDE ONE

SIDE TWO

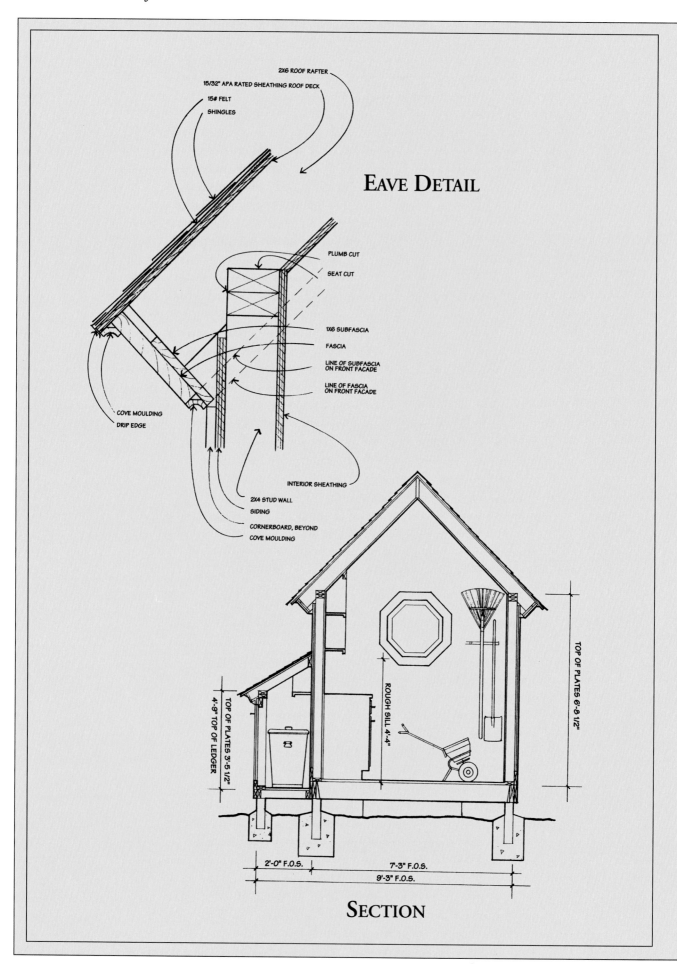

2X6 ROOF RAFTER

15/32" APA RATED SHEATHING ROOF DECK

15# FELT

SHINGLES

EAVE DETAIL

PLUMB CUT

SEAT CUT

1X6 SUBFASCIA

FASCIA

LINE OF SUBFASCIA
ON FRONT FACADE

LINE OF FASCIA
ON FRONT FACADE

COVE MOULDING

DRIP EDGE

INTERIOR SHEATHING

2X4 STUD WALL

SIDING

CORNERBOARD, BEYOND

COVE MOULDING

PLUMB CUT

SEAT CUT

ROUGH SILL 4'-4"

TOP OF PLATES 6'-8 1/2"

TOP OF PLATES 3'-5 1/2"

4'-9" TOP OF LEDGER

2'-0" F.O.S.

7'-3" F.O.S.

9'-3" F.O.S.

SECTION

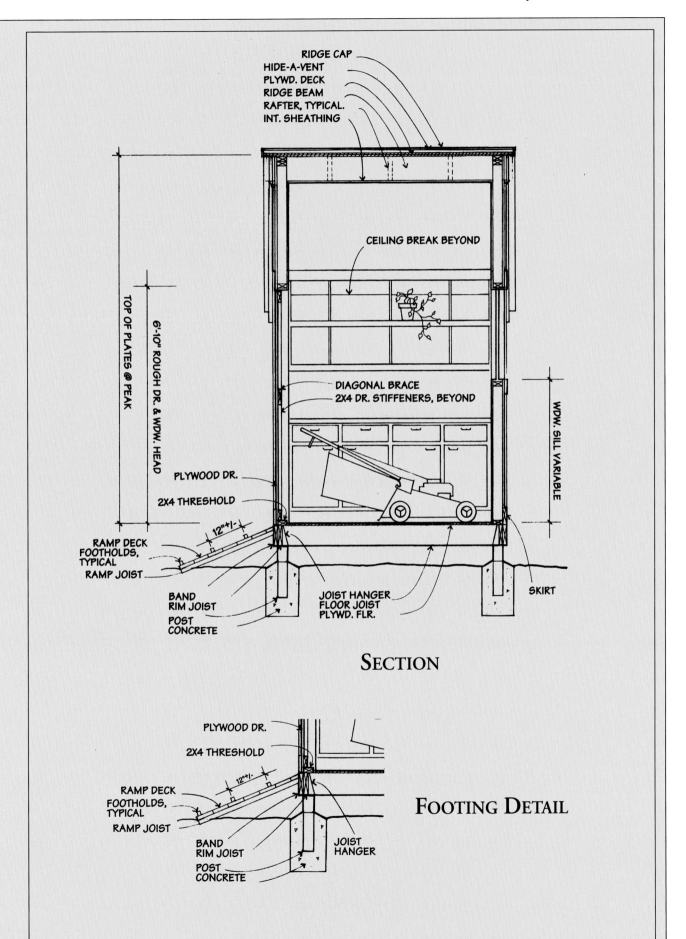

RIDGE CAP
HIDE-A-VENT
PLYWD. DECK
RIDGE BEAM
RAFTER, TYPICAL.
INT. SHEATHING

CEILING BREAK BEYOND

TOP OF PLATES @ PEAK

6'-10" ROUGH DR. & WDW. HEAD

DIAGONAL BRACE
2X4 DR. STIFFENERS, BEYOND

WDW. SILL VARIABLE

PLYWOOD DR.

2X4 THRESHOLD

12"+/-

RAMP DECK
FOOTHOLDS,
TYPICAL
RAMP JOIST

BAND
RIM JOIST

POST
CONCRETE

JOIST HANGER
FLOOR JOIST
PLYWD. FLR.

SKIRT

SECTION

PLYWOOD DR.

2X4 THRESHOLD

12"+/-

RAMP DECK
FOOTHOLDS,
TYPICAL
RAMP JOIST

BAND
RIM JOIST

POST
CONCRETE

JOIST
HANGER

FOOTING DETAIL

SIDE CUTTING PATTERNS

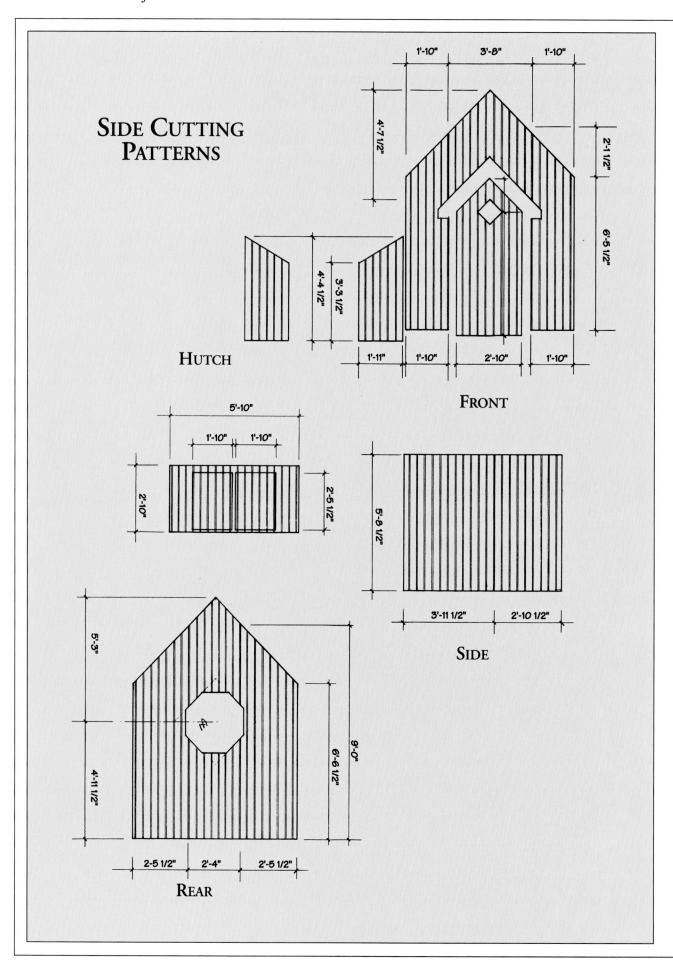

HUTCH

FRONT

SIDE

REAR

TOOL COLLECTORS

*A Beginner's Primer To Collecting And
Restoring Antique Woodworking Tools*

If you haunt flea markets, antique shows, or swap meets, you already know that people will collect, trade, and sell just about anything from Whizzer motorbikes to Elvis posters. Old woodworking tools are no exception—they make up one of the hottest new areas of collecting today.

Long neglected by all but a few sophisticated insiders, old tools are now considered a staple of the antique hunters. Several Stanley-Bailey carpenter planes are already selling in the $500 to $900 range, and early plow planes have been known to sell for over $6,000 at auction. And prices are only going up, says Ron Barlow, who spent three full years accumulating photos, drawings and prices of antique tools from all over the world to produce a 230-page book called *The Antique Tool Collector's Guide To Value* (see the end of this article for ordering information).

Are you a potential tool collector? Ron says you might be if the fragile patina of old iron and brass, coupled with sweat-stained hardwood, make you wax nostalgic. If so, you might soon find yourself tramping through flea markets or sitting for hours at auction barns.

Ron notes that today over 4,000 men and women in the United States belong to half a dozen tool collecting organizations, and he estimates another 6,000 to 8,000 are what you would call active tool collectors. Collector clubs are springing up from coast to coast, and several monthly publications cater exclusively to hobbyists who buy and sell aged tools by mail.

None of this, he explains, should come as a surprise because fine old tools have much in common with traditional antiques: beauty, form, function, identifying marks, and historical significance. Plus, he says, the number of collectors is growing while the supply of old tools is not.

Everything from adzes to band saws to tool chests is fair game for the tool collector. Collectors not only enjoy the "thrill of the hunt," but also gain an appreciation for craftsmen of yesteryear.

His conclusion: Now is the time to carefully begin to accumulate your own collection; tomorrow may be too late.

Planes. Far and away the most popular old tools being collected, he says, are woodworking planes. Prior to 1800, Early Americans mainly used English-made woodworking tools.

Then, between 1810 and 1840, about two dozen plane makers sprang up, mostly around Philadelphia and New York City. The first plane making factories were founded in the 1840s and 1850s, primarily in Connecticut. The average-sized firm employed 15 workers who produced from five to 20 completed tools per day, primarily using beechwood.

Wooden plane production peaked a couple of decades later, and then plummeted when the Stanley Rule and Level Co. began to mass produce Leonard Bailey's iron-bodied planes starting in 1870. A massive advertising program, coupled with aggressive pricing and nationwide distribution, soon eliminated most of the plane-making competition. Stanley went on to manufacture more than 250 different models of woodworking planes. Besides Bailey, some of the names used to identify Stanley planes included the Eagle Trademark, Liberty Bell, Prelateral, Low Knob, Kidney Cap, Sweetheart, and Transition Planes. By the year 1900 Stanley had sold over three million Bailey planes.

Saws. In his research on old tools, Ron unearthed some interesting facts about other tools that commonly adorn the peg-boarded walls of most home workshops. Take saws, for example. According to Greek legend, the first saw was invented by Talus, a nephew of Daedalus who was the 1200 B.C. equivalent of Leonardo Da Vinci. (Daedalus himself is credited with the invention of the hatchet, the wimble brace, and the level.) After creating the saw, Talus went on to develop a woodworking lathe and later invented the first compass.

Archeological excavations show that saws were highly refined tools even in the days of Egyptian tomb builders. Early Roman saws had the "set" teeth of today's crosscut saws. In the late 1600s some types of wooden frame saws began to be replaced with wider-bladed saws whose hammer-hardened steel did not need the support of a stretcher frame. By 1750 the modern backsaw with deep, thin blades reinforced by a heavy brass or steel back bar had been developed.

Both water and wind-powered sawmills employing an up-and-down action began appearing in France during the 12th century. Steam-powered saws were pressed into use about 1800 and within 50 years giant circular blades were invented.

However, Ron's research shows that old traditions do not die quickly among craftsmen. Hardware catalogs of the 1880s offered circular saw blades side-by-side

> "According to Greek legend, the saw was invented by Talus, nephew of Daedalus, the 1200 B.C. equivalent of Leonardo Da Vinci."

with the pitsaw variety of a hundred years earlier.

Foot-powered scrollsaw machines (also called jigsaws) became extremely popular in the era between 1880 and 1900. Some of the heavier machines, such as the Challenge, Empire, and Victor brands, were designed for cabinet makers, printers, jewelers, and other craftsmen who needed saws which were also suitable for delicate work on wood, bone, shell, and soft metal. Some of these pedal-powered machines could slice through 3"-thick wood slabs at 800 strokes per minute.

Rules. Ron also discovered that jointed rules have been around since the days of ancient Pompeii. He found that an Italian architect by the name of Scammozi made a 2′ folding scale for his own use in the late 1500s. However, England became the first commercial center of rule manufacturing. Over 250 firms producing them were listed in 19th century Birmingham directories. Belcher Brothers of New York City became the first American firm to mass produce folding rules in 1822.

Brass and German Silver (a copper alloy) were the most popular binding materials of rules during

the 19th century. Only a scant few presentation pieces were ever bound in actual sterling silver. Ivory was the most expensive material used, but it had definite drawbacks because of a tendency toward shrinkage, staining, and cracking with age.

Boxwood was a favorite wood of rule makers. Most of the early supply came from Turkey and Russia, but by the turn of the century, Stanley Rule and Level Co. was importing a Venezuelan variety.

Automated production of folding rules was begun in the 1860s by Stephens and Company at Riverton, Connecticut. A machine designed by Stephens dressed and marked 8″ boxwood slabs "faster than the human eye could behold," reported Horace Greeley in 1872. Another contraption rolled out the cylindrical brass joints, while yet another cut and spit out 40 binding pins in a single stroke.

The Stanley Rule and Level Co. featured about 80 different boxwood and ivory folding rules in its 1860 catalog, but by 1939 had reduced the number to fewer than two dozen. Inexpensive zig-zag rules introduced in 1903, and push-pull steel tapes appearing in 1922, rapidly cornered the mass market for measuring devices.

*Note: Ron Barlow's book, **The Antique Tool Collector's Guide To Value**, is available for $12.95 plus $1.05 postage (CA residents add tax) from Windmill Publishing, 2147 Windmill View Rd., El Cajon, CA 92020. The author observes that just one tool "find" could pay for the book many times over. Even if you don't plan on collecting tools, the histories of tools and tool makers make it an excellent reference book for any home workshop.*

TIPS ON HANDLING ANTIQUE TOOLS

If you are a potential old tool collector, Ron Barlow has some suggestions on what to do and what not to do with old tools once you begin your own collection.

First, he says, avoid the use of soap and water. Only the sparest and quickest application will prevent the swelling and rising of surface fibers which takes place after exposure to moisture. Soft, light-colored woods such as pine act as blotters and can't really be cleaned with anything short of bleaching compound.

It's best to rub with fine steel wool and apply a thin protective coat of floor wax if you do not plan to completely refinish a pine piece. Harder blonde woods, such as boxwood or fruitwood, can be safely cleaned using a rubbing compound like Dupont's Green Label. Be sure to leave the delicate surface patina intact. Avoid using oil finishes on light-colored woods. Rules, for example, may become several shades darker.

On medium-to-dark hardwoods, you can safely use turpentine or paint thinner with a fine steel wool pad. Popular among collectors on the West Coast is a product called Restor-A-Finish which also cleans and polishes brass parts as you rub it on surrounding wood surfaces. You can write for a sample from Howard Finish Restorers, Inc., 411 West Maple, Monrovia, CA 91016.

Matching patina is an art, Ron observes. It is usually a lot more trouble to make new wood look old than it is to locate a source of antique lumber. To disguise a large repair in boxwood, you can bake the new piece in the kitchen oven for several hours. The coloring of many decades can be duplicated overnight using this method.

To turn other light woods a sunbleached, water-stained grey color, you can bury them in a manure pile for a year or two, or use the quicker "ammonia treatment." Place a warm tray of of ammonia inside a makeshift plastic tent, along with the piece of oak you wish to fume. (Be very cautious about breathing the foul-smelling fumes.) Remove the piece after about 4 hours and set it aside for a few days. Direct application of a lye paste can also produce a primitive light grey tone in some woods.

Purists will look for original replacement parts. Others find there is nothing wrong with artificially aging a brand-new part (such as a

The interest in fine old tools has led to the issue of these limited edition classic tools. The Craftsman Classic Tool Collection includes a zebra wood bow saw, maple/walnut wood clamp, Birdseye Maple 18" level, and Cocobolo-wood try square. These collectible replicas are hand-crafted with solid brass accents, are numbered through 25,000, and sell for about $40 each.

moulding plane wedge) to match the ancient dark patina of the original. Wood stains alone don't seem to be able to simulate the ravages of time to achieve a pleasing color match. Heat, dirt, oil, grime, sunlight, smoke, fumes, and wax are proper ingredients.

Before applying them you must simulate a century or so of natural wear. Round off sharp corners which would normally be subject to contact with hands, work pieces, other tools, or bench tops. Leave some edges crisp because every surface of a part does not receive equal wear. Add a few short random scratches with a dull knife and maybe even a crooked worm hole or two (straight ones are the mark of an amateur). Smooth the whole thing off with the finest sandpaper or buffing well, perhaps even burnishing some areas to a high sheen.

Now you will be ready to apply several different colors of alcohol or lacquer-based wood stain (oil stains dry much too slowly). After an hour or two of drying, you may further enhance your artistry by passing the piece over the sooty flame of a paraffin-based candle. Wipe away any excess lamp black and spray on a light coat of orange shellac or clear matte lacquer. Finally, dust the whole thing lightly with the residue from your vacuum cleaner.

Old Metal. Most any gun shop can supply browning or bluing chemicals for recoloring shiny metal parts. Most bright iron or steel will revert to its natural brownish-grey state if left bare for a few months. An annual coating with WD-40 or 3-in-1 Household Oil is the only other treatment necessary unless tools are handled often.

An important point to remember when cleaning metal parts is to

TOOL CLASSICS

Left: The bit brace is one of the oldest tool designs, updated with locking chucks, revolving handles, and the rachet brace that allowed use in tight areas. Shown are a 1950s Craftsman brace and a 1966 push drill.

Right: Sanding tools used to be specifically either orbital or straight line. Craftsman was one of the first to offer dual sanding motors in one unit. Shown are a 1949 Craftsman sander/polisher and a 1966 dual-action model #2240.

Left: Circular saws were introduced in the early 1920s and were first used to cut framing lumber for houses. Improvements, especially in reduced saw weight, has resulted in the builder's saw becoming a do-it-yourselfer's favorite. This one is a 1953 Craftsman #2553.

Right: The saber saw, also known as a portable jigsaw, bayonet saw, or scroll saw, is one of the most versatile cutting tools available. Variable speed, improved blades, and automatic scrolling made it more popular. Shown is a 1959 Craftsman #27981.

Left: The electric drill was one of the earliest power tools, at first only available with a single speed. Today, a variable-speed drill is one of the first tools purchased. This one is a 1968 Craftsman #1109.

Right: The first portable routers were developed during World War I, and were called electric hand shapers. Over the years, more powerful motors, variable speed, plus a vast array of bits and accessories, have made it a favorite. Shown is a 1974 Craftsman #1736.

avoid dulling the finely defined edges where wood meets inlaid metal in an almost flawless seam. Too much abrasive on either surface will produce an unnatural gap. Shoe polish or crayons may save the day; use with a heated spatula to fill a crack.

Handling Brass. Cleaning brass can often be accomplished with a simple homemade solution consisting of a half a lemon, or a cup of vinegar, and a few tablespoons of salt. Rub it on with a saturated pad of #00 steel wool, then rinse with cold water, followed by boiling hot water to dry. Buff later with #0000 steel wool or a jeweler's rouge-impregnated cloth.

If a lemon juice treatment seems too mild, try immersion in a 50/50 solution of Lysol liquid toilet bowl cleaner and water. Using proper precautions, rub with steel wool and rinse as above. Brass founders use a standard pickling solution of 2 parts nitric acid and 3 parts sulfuric acid with a handful of table salt added to each quart. Castings are dipped and removed at once and water-rinsed. You can get any color, from rose to green to blue and even brown or black, by dipping polished brass into various potash and salt solutions described in the book, *Henley's Twentieth Century Formulas*. You may be able to find it at a used bookstore.

Removing Rust. This is easiest if all parts are disassembled prior to cleaning. They can be soaked in kerosene overnight to loosen stubborn particles before steel wooling or soft wire brushing. The idea is to remove only the surface rust which stands away from the old finish.

If you use a coarse wire wheel or sandpaper you will create pits and scratches which are more objec-

tionable than what you were trying to eliminate.

Purists use a soft knife or dull chisel to remove surface rust. Anything these tools don't get off is best left to preserve the patina. Pits and pores look best when left filled, not cleaned to their shiny bottoms.

Removing Old Screws. This job can be touchy business. A few are bound to break off no matter how careful you try to be. Start by cleaning out the screw slot with an X-acto knife or a jeweler's file. Make sure the bottom corners of the slot are well defined so they will match the head of your screwdriver. Also be very particular about the size screwdriver you use; regrind it to fit if necessary.

Add a drop of Liquid Wrench to the screw and let it soak into the threads below. (Protect fresh wood around the head with a preliminary coating of clean linseed oil, which

---

CAUTION

Make safety your first priority. When using chemicals to recondition old tools, Ron Barlow emphasizes to put safety first. Use proper personal protection, heed all label precautions, provide for proper ventilation, and use common sense, including:

• Keep bleaches far away from bowl cleaners; deadly chlorine gas can result from their mixture.

• Never add water to acid. Always add the strong solution to the weaker one to avoid a violent eruption.

• Do not use any paint thinners or restoration products in the same room as a hot-water heater or other open-flame appliances. A careless refinisher ignoring this precaution can risk being blown into the next world or, at least, suffer premature loss of eyebrows.

---

is also a good precaution before buffing brass inlays.) Now inset the screwdriver and tap it smartly with a hammer blow. Hope for the best. If you are not lucky the head will probably twist off and you will have to drill it out, or epoxy in a replacement head after removing any trace of oil in the recess.

Tumbling. If all of these time-consuming conservation processes leave you cold, you might be interested in a unique rust-removal method developed by a retired chief petty officer. Out behind his barn, he keeps an electric-powered cement mixer full of nice round pea gravel. When enough rusty old tools have accumulated, he tosses them in and flips the switch. Three or four hours later he checks the load and removes any brass or copper parts for buffing. Then the mixer is kept churning for a least a day or two. He uses his tumbling treatment for old wrenches, mule bits, horseshoes, rusty keys, and other farm primitives.

Any tool too good to go in the cement mixer is soaked in a special concoction overnight and rubbed with a pad of #1 steel wool the next day. The basic ingredient is filtered crankcase oil combined with two gallons of paint thinner, a quart of Old English Black Walnut Scratch Remover, a pint of Lemon Oil furniture polish, a tad of lacquer thinner, and the leavings from whatever can of oil stain he can scrounge up. With the exception of a few melted or broken hard rubber knobs, his restored tools look every bit as good as those processed with other methods.

GARAGE PRESERVATION

A Quick Solution To Keeping
Concrete Garage Floors Looking Like New

Protecting the floor of your garage from the abuse it gets every day of the year would seem simple enough. Typically, you would clean it as well as you could, then roll on a couple of gallons of enamel porch and deck paint. That is how it has been done for years, but the results have often been less than perfect.

Ideally, a surface coating for a garage floor should repel road salt and oil leaks and still hold up under foot and tire traffic. The water-based epoxy enamels work reasonably well when applied to concrete floors in basements or workshops. However, vehicles have a tendency to leak fluids, and on hot summer days they also subject the floor of the garage to sizzling-hot tires.

Paint Challenges. One problem is that no conventional paint will stand up to oil, gasoline, brake and transmission fluids, or any of the petroleum-based lubricants used in vehicles. Drips on a painted floor will cause the paint to blister, and then it is difficult to apply a second coat that will adhere any better.

A second problem is that conventional paints are thermoplastic, meaning they soften with heat. A vehicle's hot tires will soften the

paint and cause it to stick to the tires. Whenever you back out of the garage, a patch of floor leaves with your tires. To avoid this problem, you would need a paint that is not thermoplastic, but thermosetting.

Garage floors receive daily abuse. Though epoxy-based paints do the job, a better solution for the homeowner is a latex sealant.

Thermosetting paints cure with heat and won't soften beneath hot tires. These specialty paints are used commercially and work well when properly installed. The catch is that they aren't made for use by homeowners, and suppliers don't like selling them to the uninitiated.

These paints are generally two-part epoxies, which must be mixed on-site and applied very quickly. Once mixed, the pot life is 30 minutes. Also, such paints require extreme caution. To apply them

safely, plenty of ventilation, protective clothing, and a good respirator are required. In other words, you need both professional equipment and expertise.

As with all other paints, surface preparation is also critical with the expoxy-based paints. Sandblasting or acid-washing the concrete floor before application is recommended even on new floors, especially if they've been coated with curing agents. Since two coats are usually applied at specific thicknesses, the cost of the paint plus the sandblasting job could run more than $500 for a typical garage floor.

A safe, easy alternative to thermosetting paints—something that will repel oils and protect the surface from road salts—is a latex sealer. Though it doesn't have any pigment, a clear latex sealant offers both adequate protection and easy cleaning, each of which are high-priority items for maintaining the floor of your garage.

Using Latex Sealants. The latex sealants available, unlike deck and patio sealers, repel oils and antifreeze. Road salts do not penetrate them. Any spills just bead up and can be swept or wiped away. When applied, they are thin and milky, but cure clear in 3 to 4 hours. Best of all, their fumes are not hazardous to breathe, plus all tools can be cleaned up with water.

Latex sealers can be costly. Coverage ranges between 150 to 200 sq. ft. per gallon, depending on surface roughness, and each gallon can cost as much as $65. Because the smallest container available may be five gallons, it can be cost-effective if you can arrange a joint project and split the cost with a neighbor. Or, if the sealant contains a UV stabilizer, you might use the remainder to treat your driveway.

The sealant used in the photos was applied with a low-pressure garden sprayer, though it can rolled or brushed on, too. Once applied, it was allowed to penetrate for about five minutes to a depth of $\frac{1}{16}''$ to $\frac{1}{8}''$. It was then worked in with a broom and brush.

The garage floor shown was less than a year old, but still required a good pre-cleaning. (If the floor had been treated with a curing agent when poured, it would have required stripping with a power washer.) The first step was sweeping the entire floor, then scraping up all paint drips left behind during construction. The entire floor, including the control joints, was vacuumed. Then all soiled areas and oil spots were washed with a commercial concrete cleaner. You could also use a solvent degreaser or even an oil-lifting dish detergent.

It is best to scrub the areas until only a faint trace of any spot remains. For fresh oil spots, you can save time by first working cat litter or portland cement into the spot with a brick. A final step is to hose down the entire area with water and allow it to dry for 24 hours.

1 A putty knife can be used to scrape up paint spatters or construction adhesive from the concrete floor.

2 Vacuum the debris from control joints because any dirt left behind will become permanently sealed in the joint.

3 Use a concrete cleaner or degreaser to scrub oil spots and tire grime from the surface.

4 Sealant contents can separate in storage; stir vigorously with a drill-powered mixer or a stirring stick.

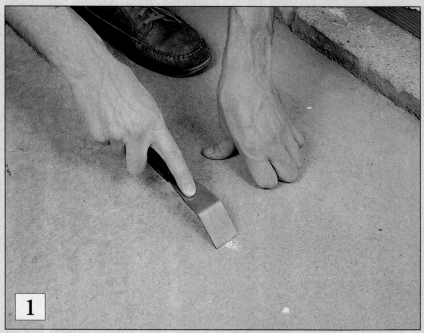

1

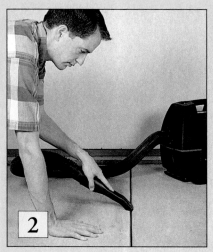

2

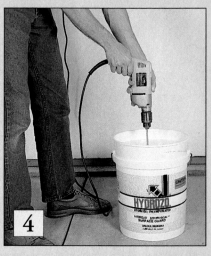

3

4

You can use a drill-powered paint mixer to blend the sealant components, which separate out during storage. To apply the mixed sealant, a good procedure is to pour a quart or so of the sealant into a paint bucket and about two gallons into a garden sprayer.

Working from the bucket, you can use a 3″ brush to cut-in around the walls, about 6″ out from the wall edge. Also carefully cut-in along the expansion joint between the garage floor and drive, and around all permanent floor features, such as the overhead door tracks.

Then, with the perimeter cut in, you can use the tank sprayer to apply a fairly thick layer of sealant to manageable sections of the rest of the floor. Before moving on from each section, allow that area to saturate for five minutes, then work it in with a medium-bristle push broom. Brooming the area can increase penetration and can also help eliminate any voids created by air bubbles.

The sealant does not become slick or slippery *if it is not allowed to puddle* during application. Puddling can be avoided by pulling any excess sealant into the dry areas. Despite your best efforts, some puddling may still occur in control joints where permanent cracks have not yet formed. To pull excess sealant from these joints, you can simply sweep them out using your cut-in brush.

A final note. The above describes a general procedure for using a latex sealant. How you proceed will depend on the latex sealer you buy. Always use all proper safety precautions, including ventilation, and always follow the directions given on the container's label.

5 Pour some sealant into a paint bucket for cutting-in, then pour more into a low-pressure sprayer for the larger areas.

6 Using a soft-bristle brush, carefully cut-in the floor edge where it meets exterior walls.

7 A hand-operated garden sprayer was used to coat the floor in manageable segments, followed by brooming to work the sealant into the surface.

8 Any excess sealant in un-cracked control joints can be swept out with a cut-in brush.

FURNITURE FINISHES

Tips On How To Find, Restore, and Refinish Valuable Old Furniture

A basic rule in working with furniture finishes: Don't ruin it. Experts agree that you are better off leaving a piece of furniture alone than to mess it up or destroy a finish, turning a potentially valuable antique into a piece of junk.

But that does not mean a do-it-yourselfer's hands are tied if the goal is to improve the appearance and value of either antique or newer furniture. The key is to use proven techniques that not only work well, but are safe, effective, and easily accomplished.

If you have been on the verge of dragging Grandma's old table out of the attic for restoration, the man who first created the Formby line of wood care products has some advice: Do your research on products and techniques first. Many do-it-yourselfers still end up using the wrong approach and actually ruin fine furniture with harsh chemicals that are difficult to use, messy, and time-consuming.

Furniture restoration is a rewarding project with immediate visual results. Always dispose of materials such as rags used in the process with utmost care; soak in a water-filled, covered metal can to prevent spontaneous combustion.

Homer Formby grew up in a family of furniture craftsmen and during his childhood spent long hours in a workshop learning how to hand-rub wood until it glowed and felt like satin.

This small dresser was found at a garage sale, covered with antique paint. Below the paint was a treasure of beautifully grained, rich-looking wood.

While amassing a chain of antique shops where craftsmen were kept busy restoring old furniture, Formby developed a refinisher which would easily remove finishes from old furniture without ruining it. Today he has left a legacy of Formby's products which include a full wood care line sold in more than 30,000 home centers and hardware stores, as well as a storehouse of refinishing tips, tricks, and shortcuts.

According to the marketers of these products, a piece of furniture doesn't have to be 100 years old to be worth restoring. Many 50-year-old reproductions can be worth as much or more than some antiques twice as old.

Though restorable pieces can be found just about anywhere, it pays to know what to look for.

Pieces with good lines, mouldings, and turnings are better candidates for restoring. Give priority to furniture with joints that are dovetailed (interlocking), and not held by staples or nails. Also look for furniture that doesn't need much structural repair.

TRY CLEANING FIRST

Once you have the piece at home, first check whether you really need to refinish it. Old furniture is often covered by a build-up of pollution and all that is needed to restore its appearance is a thorough cleaning.

To determine this, rub the dirtiest spot on the piece with furniture cleaner (not furniture polish) on a cotton cloth. Try several times, letting the cleaner dry between applications.

If you can clean the spot well, and the wood grain turns out clear, you can be better off simply cleaning rather than refinishing.

If, after cleaning, the wood still is dull and lifeless, you can avoid refinishing by using a product like Formby's Furniture FaceLift (see below).

If the finish is dark, ugly, badly marred, or "alligatored," refinishing may be the only answer. Old furniture will naturally darken over the years. This process is called ambering and is caused by exposure to light. However, it is the finish, not the wood, that is discolored.

To determine what type of finish is on the piece you can use the cotton-ball test. Moisten a cotton ball with nail polish remover, then touch it to a glossy area in an out-of-the-way place. If the ball sticks, the finish is varnish, lacquer, or shellac, and you can use a refinisher. If it doesn't stick, the finish is probably a synthetic resin or paint, and you need a paint remover.

DIY TIP:
"If a cotton ball dipped in nail polish remover sticks, you can use a refinisher."

Formby's refinisher formula is applied with fine steel wool. Pick an area to work on about the size of a dinner plate. Then just overlap the areas until you are done. An old paint brush trimmed to a stubby length will help work the refinisher in carved and fluted areas.

As the refinisher is applied, swirls and streaks can be eliminated by rubbing fresh refinisher on steel wool from one end of the piece to the other, going with the grain. Wipe the surface with a clean cotton cloth, and let it dry for 30 minutes. The final step is to buff well, but not hard, with dry steel wool.

USING PAINT REMOVERS
An advantage of refinishing without stripping is that it can help preserve the glow brought on by age, or what is called the wood's patina. If the piece needs stripping, try to avoid dip tanks and strippers if possible; they may loosen the joints forcing you to reglue it yourself or to hire a professional.

If you must remove the old finish, also try to avoid paint removers requiring a water rinse. Water can cause wood to warp or mildew, even loosen veneer and wood joints, or open the grain of the wood. Look for a heavy-bodied paint remover. Shake it at the store—it should feel like molasses in the can.

When applying a paint remover, don't use a "painting" stroke. This tends to fan the gases that do the removal work into the air, cutting down on the effectiveness of the remover. Instead, apply it by drag-

DOES IT NEED REFINISHING?

Formby's Furniture Face Lift uses a unique three-step system to restore a permanent shine to tired wood in less than an hour without refinishing. It first cleans the surface, then buffs away minor damage, such as scratches and white rings, and, lastly, floats on a permanent new shine.

1 If a refinisher is necessary, it is put on with fine steel wool, one section at a time.

2 The refinisher is allowed to dry, then the surface is buffed with dry steel wool.

3 If a paint remover is used, a good procedure is to "wash" the wood with a paint remover wash or denatured alcohol.

1

ging a filled paint brush across the wood for about 4". Then stop, refill the paint brush, and make another small stroke. You will get the most out of remover if you brush only in one direction and don't touch it until all the bubbling action stops.

Don't scrape or gouge the wood. Lift the old paint off gently with a wide plastic putty knife or scraper, rather than a metal tool. Formby's Plastic Paint Lifter provides a gentle lifting action that won't scratch the wood. The remover will do a better job if the temperature is between 65° and 85°; the moderate temperatures of spring and fall are ideal. If some spots of paint don't come off, don't panic and try to scrape them off. Instead, apply another layer of paint remover and let it do the work for you.

Some pigment may remain even after most of the old paint is removed, especially in woods like oak and pine that have "valleys" of open

DIY TIP:
"The moderate temperatures of spring and fall are ideal for using paint removers."

grain. To get paint out of these areas, scrub the area with a paint brush (trim the bristles to make them stubby) dipped in paint remover wash or denatured alcohol. Using proper hand protection, have a cotton cloth in your hand to absorb the wash and the paint. It is important that you do this immediately after lifting off the paint remover, while the paint in the crevices is still softened.

Some furniture may have been "pickled" by having paint rubbed into the grain of the wood. To remove this kind of paint, which is

deeply embedded in the wood grain, apply a 50/50 mixture of shellac and denatured alcohol on the wood with a brush. Let it set for a few days, then remove the mixture and the old paint with another coat of paint remover.

If the paint remover you are using fails to bubble and lift the paint when applied, it could be that you are dealing with "milk paint." Milk paint was often used during the 1930s and 1940s on kitchen cabinets or on furniture used in the kitchen. It is a very thick paint, and can be difficult to remove. However, if you encounter milk paint, don't try to remove the first coat of paint remover yet. Instead, spray on a coat of an aerosol paint remover directly over the first coat of paint remover, then let this combination work on the paint.

If the piece has multiple layers of paint, the key word is patience. Don't expect one coat of paint re-

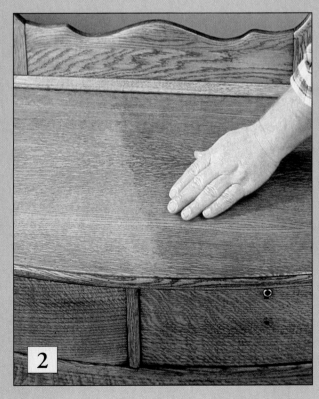

mover to take off three or four (or more) coats of old paint in one shot. You will probably need to apply multiple coats of remover to take off all the paint layers.

Once the paint is off, immediately "wash" the wood with a product like Formby's Paint Remover Wash or denatured alcohol. This removes any remaining paint pigments and prepares the wood for staining and finishing.

APPLYING FINISHES

A tung oil varnish finish is a favorite with many restorers. If you use it, try rubbing the tung oil varnish in by hand. This makes it easier to get into all the nooks and crannies of a small piece and also eliminates brush marks. Clean up can be aided by slathering hand lotion on your hands before the tung oil dries, then simply wiping off the lotion and the tung oil.

Stains are used when you want to change the wood's color. You can also use stain to even up different wood colors. Deciding on which stain to use can be frustrating, but there are a few basic principles you can follow.

• Brush-on pigment stains can work well, but can often be runny and difficult to control. Using a hand-rubbed jelled wiping stain, such as Formby's wiping stains, assures you of good color control.

• Try to stick with a stain that contains a pigment, instead of a dye. Dyes can fade more quickly in sunlight, plus both dye and alcohol stains can leave marks if you apply them in patterns.

• The real trick in staining can be presealing the wood if you are working with soft wood like pine, fir, or poplar. Push your fingernail into the wood. If it dents easily, it is soft wood. If it doesn't, it is prob-

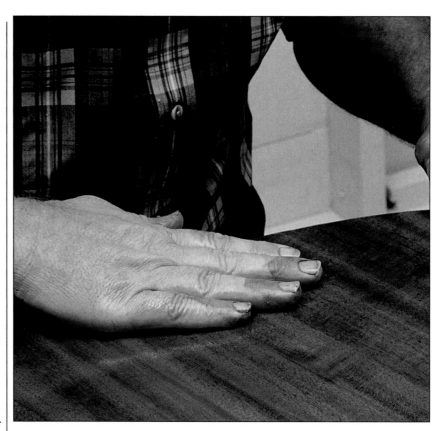

Once the old finish is off of a piece of furniture, it's time for the new finish. Tung oil varnish, above, is a favorite way to go for many restorers. If you want stain, a hand-rubbed, jelled wiping stain, below, is easy to use and leaves few streaks.

ably a hardwood like maple, oak, or walnut.

With soft wood, it is critical to first apply a thin coat of wood seal with a brush or cloth. Stains can penetrate unevenly on unsealed soft wood, leaving streaks, botches, or uneven color. Even if you are working with hardwood, a wood seal can help you do a better job of staining certain problem areas, such as knot holes, unfinished corners, edges, or sides.

• To get the right color, don't go by the name of the stain, but by a stain chart. A maple stain from one company can be much different than the next company's maple stain. Put the stain on darker than you want, using a soft cotton cloth or facial tissue to wipe off, then buff lightly with fine steel wool and brush away any dust. This way you

DIY TIP:

"With soft woods like pine, fir, or poplar, the real trick is in presealing the wood."

can get exactly the right shade.

• A good staining job can be judged by how natural the wood looks. If your project looks like it has been stained instead of looking like natural wood, you have used the wrong stain. The grain should be highlighted by the stain, not hidden by it.

After staining, the wood needs a protective coating. Varnish is a classic finish for sealing and protecting stain; polyurethane is used when you want a hard-wearing surface,

such as for a table top.

Then, once your project is finished, keep it clean. There are two kinds of dirt that can mess up furniture. One kind is water soluble, such as those from most foods and drinks. To clean this type, wipe with a dampened cloth. The other kind is oil-soluble, like greasy spills and body oils. To get rid of these, wipe with a cloth dampened with a furniture treatment (not furniture polish), such as Formby's Lemon Oil Furniture Treatment, Almond Luster, or Furniture Cleaner.

Some good furniture care advice includes three don'ts:

• Don't wax furniture.
• Don't wipe wood with ammonia or other harsh cleaners.
• Don't keep wood in direct sunlight if you can avoid it.

FURNITURE TROUBLESHOOTING

Many home remedies can be used when furniture is accidentally damaged. Some of the best are products you probably already have. Here are some favorites from the folks at Formby's Products:

Color Crayons. For a scratch in a coffee table or other furniture, you can try using a color crayon. Melt a crayon which matches the finish over the gash until it overflows. You can use a soldering iron, or tie a nail to a pencil, heat it over a flame, then put the nail to the crayon. After filling the gash with the melted wax, let the wax cure for a half hour, then gently shave off the residue with a credit card.

Toothpaste. It is a gentle abrasive, ideal for rescuing wood fur-

niture damaged by water spots and rings caused by moisture trapped underneath the wax. To remove them, simply squeeze toothpaste onto a wet cotton cloth and buff the spotted area. For stubborn rings, combine toothpaste with equal parts of another gentle abrasive, such as baking soda. Buff until the spot disappears. Then, with a clean cloth, continue buffing until you can see yourself.

Nail Polish Remover. Char marks from unattended cigarettes don't have to ruin a piece of furniture. Just dip a cotton swab into nail polish remover and rub it lightly across the burn. This will dissolve the black residue. If any remains, scrape it gently with a small knife. If a slight hollow is

left, mix equal parts remover with clear nail polish and apply, one coat at a time, with the nail polish brush. Let each coat dry between applications, and have patience. It may take seven or eight coats to get the job done.

Cedar Chips. Wood acquires a musty odor over time. In fact, it is one way to be certain that a piece of furniture is old and not a reproduction. It can be difficult to get rid of the odor, but you can effectively mask it with cedar chips. Put about a pound of red cedar shavings, not western cedar, in the toe of a nylon stocking, tie the end and cut off the excess. Then tack the sack along the back of a drawer. If there are no drawers, tack it on the back of the piece, or underneath.

WALL FASTENERS

A Guide To Selecting And Using Fasteners
In Home Improvement Projects

Psychologist Abraham Maslow once said that people who are good only with hammers see every solution as a nail.

Although nails have their place, today there is little need to limit yourself when fastening items to the walls of your home. Well-stocked shelves of major hardware stores and home centers abound with dozens of fastener types, and in most cases they come packaged with instructions to show you exactly how they should be used.

How-to experts observe that the average do-it-yourselfer often misses the boat when hanging things from walls either by not selecting the right hardware for the job, or by not installing it correctly.

Selecting wall hardware can be confusing mainly because there are so many variables involved. For example, if you want to hang a shelf above your fireplace, choosing the right hardware will depend on what the wall is made of, how thick it is, what kind of shelf you plan to hang, and how much load it will carry.

Shelving is a homeowner's best friend. With the wide variety of options available, it pays to know how to fasten them to walls properly.

Adding to the confusion is the wide variety of fasteners available, including toggle bolts, Molly bolts, nylon expansion, and masonry fasteners to name just a few. And some fasteners can serve more than

Shelves to hang tools can reduce run-around time. Fasteners for shelves should be selected for type of duty and wall material.

one purpose. Some fasteners typically used for masonry walls can also be used for hollow walls. These include plastic, nylon-expansion, and nylon-drive anchors. They are usually inserted into predrilled holes and expand as either a screw or a threaded nail is driven into them. Generally, however, if walls are hollow and covered with drywall, you will need to use a hollow-wall fastener.

Most hardware for hollow walls actually goes through the outside

surface and anchors against the inside of the hole. The shell expands and grips as the fastener is tightened.

One hollow-wall fastener, the Molly bolt, was invented over 60 years ago. It has a slotted metal sleeve with a bolt going through its center. The bolt threads into a nut or collar on the inside end. To install, you insert the anchor into a hole drilled through the drywall, then tap it lightly to seat the flange or lip against the face of the wall.

When the bolt in the center is tightened, it pulls the far end of the fastener inward, causing it to expand behind the wall and lock the fastener in place. The center bolt is unthreaded and pushed through the brackets or the fixtures to be mounted, then screwed back into the installed anchor for final tightening.

If, on the other hand, your project involves a solid wall, such as plaster or cinder block, one choice is a plastic-lipped anchor. You first drill a hole, then push the anchor into the hole until its flange is flush against the surface. Then, as you insert and drive in a screw, the anchor expands to lock itself firmly in place inside the hole.

SELECTING FASTENERS

Wall fasteners should always be able to support the heaviest load anticipated and do so with a reasonable margin of safety. A good rule of thumb is to use a safety factor of 4-to-1 for general fastening. In other words, if you want to hang something weighing 25 lbs., use a fastener with a holding power of 100 lbs. If there is a possibility that what you hang may be affected by vibration, then go with a 10-to-1 ratio.

If you want to hang objects on a hollow wall, first see if you will be able to place either a nail or a screw into a stud, which can often eliminate the need to buy special fasteners. There are electronic stud finders available to help you locate studs, but there are other ways to find the studs. Try tapping the wall lightly. A solid sound usually indicates you are over a stud.

If that doesn't work, try measuring out from a corner to find studs, which are usually 16″ or 24″ on center. You can also drill small holes in the wall until you find a stud. Or, if the wall has baseboard molding, take it off and punch in nails until you find a stud. One helpful clue is to look where two wall panels meet; they will usually meet over a wall stud.

HOLLOW WALLS

Here is a rundown of some of your options when items must be fastened to hollow walls:

Toggle Bolts. Their main disadvantage is that if you remove a fixture, their wings will drop off and disappear inside the wall. But toggle fixture hangers are great money-savers in remodeling. Their wings spread the load and are useful for attaching electrical junction boxes and light fixtures to ceilings.

Tie-wire toggle bolts are also helpful. These have a spade-end bolt, with a hole to run a wire through, and work well for installing suspended acoustical ceilings.

Molly Bolts. These have a sleeve that stays in the wall after installation enabling you to withdraw and replace the original bolt. Their disadvantage is that Molly bolts must be correctly sized for the wall thickness to work properly. To doublecheck on the thickness of a particular wall, you can insert a bent wire or crochet hook, and pull it back so that the bend or hook catches the inside of the wall.

Nylon Anchors. Sold under Zip-It or Zip-It Jr. brand names, these may be the fastest and easiest hollow-wall anchor for use in wall board. Their unique drill tips use offset blades to drill their own hole into the wall using a Phillips screwdriver. Once in place, a screw can be driven into the anchor.

Picture Hangers. If you need to hang a picture, keep in mind that the hangers which are cemented in place with an adhesive back have limited load capacity. Angled picture hangers have more holding strength, up to 100 lbs. in the bigger sizes. Before driving these into plaster, make an X with two pieces of masking tape where the nail will enter the wall. This will help keep the plaster from chipping out.

MASONRY FASTENING

Fastening to concrete, block, brick, or stone may seem difficult. However, fastener suppliers, such as the Rawlplug Company (see end of article for address) offer you up to two dozen products to help you get the job done. These come in a be-

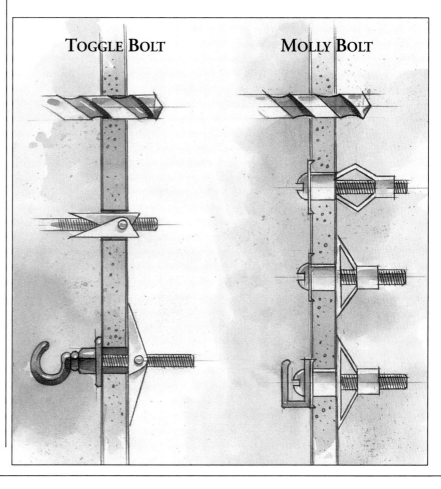

wildering array of configurations, but can be broken down into categories of one-step anchors, bolt anchors, and screw anchors.

Anchor Types. One-step anchors are designed to be installed through a fixture because the anchor size is the same as the size of hole drilled. Bolt anchors are designed to be installed flush with the surface of the base material. They are used in conjunction with a threaded bolt, or in some types, a threaded rod. Screw anchors are also designed to be installed flush with the surface of the base material. They are used in conjunction with sheetmetal, wood, or lag screws, depending on the anchor type.

If your fastening project will be extensive, it will pay you to do some research before deciding which fastener to use. If you have only a few items to fasten to ma-

sonry, one of the simplist types to use is the lag screw anchor, also called the expansion shield. To install these, drill a hole the same size as the outside diameter of the shield. Then insert the lag screw through whatever is being attached and into the anchor. To save drilling time, buy short anchors (1″ to 2″ long), if they will do the job.

Installing Anchors. When selecting the proper anchor, a major factor to take into consideration is the strength of the base material. Anchors installed in stone and dense concrete can withstand far greater loads than the same anchor installed in lightweight concrete, block, or brick. Medium to heavy loads cannot be safely installed in soft material, such as stucco, grout, plaster, or plasterboard. Materials should be fully cured before anchors are installed.

Other factors to consider include what the anchors are made of, the specific loading conditions, and how the anchors work. Most mechanical anchors function by developing a compression force against the wall of the drilled hole, which resists the applied loads. For best performance, expansion anchors should not be spaced closer than 10 anchor diameters apart, and not closer than five anchor diameters to an edge.

Drilling Tips. The holding power of a fastener in a solid masonry or concrete wall depends on making the correct kind of hole. The easiest way to drill a good hole in brick, stone, or concrete is to use a carbide-tip bit designed specifically for the tool you will use, either the common electric drill, the rotary percussion hammer drill which provides an impact of 20,000 to 50,000 blows per minute (BPM), or the rotary hammer drill which provides an impact of up to 6,000 BPM.

When using carbide-tipped bits, make sure the chuck of the drill is in good working order, and, to avoid ragged holes, make sure that the bit is not dull or worn. While drilling, especially in soft or damp materials, don't allow the flutes of the drill to become clogged. Occasionally withdraw the bit to clear out the hole to avoid overheating of the drill tip. Also, don't try to cool the tip of the bit by submersing it in water—this may crack the bit. Since carbide-tipped bits may break or shatter during use, always wear safety glasses and other appropriate protection gear.

If the hole is deep, you can avoid getting dust in your eyes by using an empty plastic squeeze bottle as a pump to blow out the hole occasionally, or you can flush out the

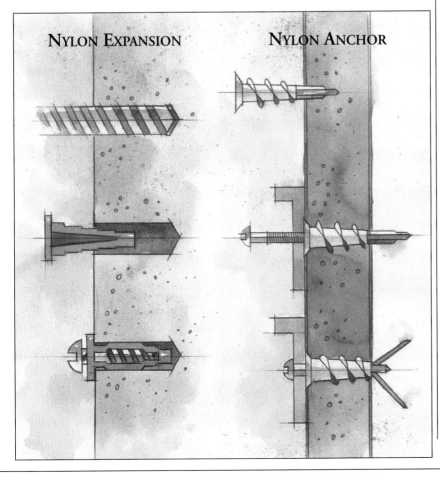

NYLON EXPANSION   NYLON ANCHOR

hole with water. When drilling overhead in any material, you can hold the end of the hose from your shop vacuum next to the hole as you drill, or you can slip a small paper plate over the drill bit to catch the dust as the hole is made.

Star Drills. If you have just a few holes to make in masonry walls, you can use a star drill. The cutting end of the star drill resembles four chisels joined at their edges to form a cross (star). The star drill should be struck only with a heavy drill-hammer or sledge, and should be rotated after each blow. A piece of tape wrapped around the bit will help you know when the hole is the proper depth.

Wooden Dowels. One method of fastening items to masonry is to use sections of wooden dowels, either purchased or made yourself. First make a hole with either a carbide bit or star drill. Then, with a hammer, drive the dowel in flush. Drill a pilot hole in its center, slightly smaller than the holding screw you plan to use. The dowel you use should be slightly oversized; it can be greased, if necessary, to make it go in easier.

USING NAILS

Small nails can be hard to hold while driving into walls. You can hold a small nail by first pushing it through light cardboard or even a small pocket comb.

Another handy way to position a small nail is with a holder made by attaching a pencil clip to a nail set. Put the nail between the clip and the base of the nail set to hold while hammering.

For tacks, one trick is to use a magnetized tack hammer. Or, you can put double-faced tape on the head of a regular hammer and stick the head of the tack to the tape.

If you have many brads to drive, consider buying a brad driver. Some electric staplers can be converted to drive brads. If you are driving them by hand into tough hardwood, you can drill a hole in the wood using a bit made from a brad with the head removed. The nail will go in more easily if dipped in paraffin.

You can keep paraffin handy by drilling a hole in the end of your hammer handle and pouring hot paraffin into the hole. When it cools, you have a ready supply.

Quench-hardened cut nails, used for fastening wood to concrete mortar or masonry, can break, chip, and shatter. Be sure to wear safety goggles and start these nails perfectly straight. Hit the nail squarely with a tapping, one-two stroke with a large ballpeen or hand-drilling hammer. Never use a nail hammer because its face could chip and cause injury.

USING SCREWS

As a general rule, select screws so that at least two-thirds of their length will go into the base material. Try to have the threaded part at least 1/8″ shorter than the thickness of the bottom piece being fastened. For softwoods, such as pine or spruce, drill a hole only half as deep as the threaded part of the screw. For hardwoods, such as oak, maple, or birch, drill the hole as deep as the screw itself.

If a screw is difficult to turn, you can back it out and enlarge the hole slightly. Or you can rub wax or paraffin on the screw. A candle is perfect for this purpose. Never use soap; it may rust the screw, weaken the joint, and cause discoloration of paint or varnish finishes. Don't use oil either; it can penetrate and stain the wood grain for some distance around the screw head.

There isn't a house existing that doesn't have at least one screw hole that has become oversized because the wall material has given way. If you have this problem, try this: Remove the screw and push fine steel wool into the hole, packing it in with a screwdriver. Now redrive the screw. You can also try putting glue on splinters, toothpicks, or burned-out wood matchsticks and drive them into the hole. Let the inserts dry and then redrive the screw.

USING BOLTS

Buy bolts long enough so the nut goes all the way onto the threaded part and leaves some thread showing. When drilling holes for bolts in wood, make them exactly the same diameter as the bolt. Try to use washers under both the head and the nut. Whenever possible, install bolts in metal parts so their heads are up. That way, if the nut is shaken off, the bolt is more likely to stay in place.

You can use lag screws whenever wood screws or nails are too short or too light. To anchor them properly, first drill a hole slightly larger than the diameter of the shank, to a depth that is equal to the length the shank will penetrate. Then drill a second hole at the bottom of the first hole equal to the "inside" diameter of the threaded shank. Make this second hole half as deep as the threaded section.

Note: For more comprehensive information on using fasteners in all types of building materials, a helpful reference is the 147-page **Rawl Drilling & Anchoring Handbook**. *It's available by writing Rawlplug Company, Inc., New Rochelle, NY 10802, or by calling the company at (800) 243-8160. Ask for Catalog Number 0013.*

READY-TO-HANG HOME IMPROVEMENTS

There are great solutions for storage problems, as these photos from Knape & Vogt demonstrate:

1 Decorative brackets for these twin slotted standards can hold from 300 to 450 lbs. Standards are available in lengths from 9″ to 90″.

2 This shelf mounting system makes shelves seem to float on a wall. It accepts ⅝″-thick shelves and, with the right fasteners, can be used on any wall.

3 These decorative clip brackets of heavy-duty steel are covered with high-impact black, red, or white plastic for colorful storage in any room.

4 This tool rack comes in three 2′ sections and can be used singly or as a 6′-long unit. It comes with 18 durable plastic hooks.

1

2

3

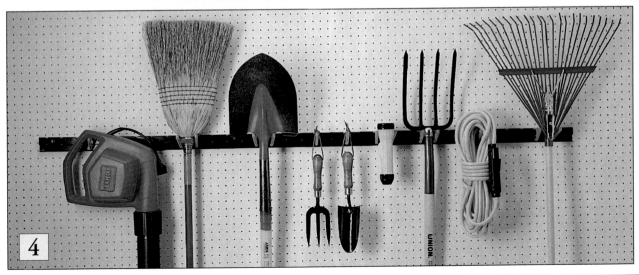

4

TOOL POWER

*Advice On Ways To Make Your Home Workshop
More Productive, Efficient, And Enjoyable*

Setting up a good home workplace is definitely worth the bother, especially since it is the headquarters for most do-it-yourself projects, directly or indirectly.

Some projects, such as building an end table, are completed start to finish in the home shop area. For other projects, such as home repairs and maintenance, the workshop serves as the main base where tools and materials are stored and retrieved.

WORKPLACE IDEAS

How your workshop is set up and equipped will not only reflect on the quality of your home projects, but also on the quantity—how many you will actually end up finishing. You will be more likely to tackle money-saving projects and get more enjoyment out of getting them done if your primary workplace is well organized, adequately equipped, and is a pleasant place in which to work.

Once you begin investigating, ideas for improving your workshop can be found through several sources. The photos here and on the following pages are a sampling selected with the help of workshop experts at Sears and are just a beginning. The trick is to combine your off-the-shelf purchases with an open, common-sense approach to making your workshop work harder for you.

A shop full of capable tools, plus the storage to keep everything in its place, is a worthwhile goal to pursue. The sooner you get started on your dream shop, the sooner it will become a reality.

First, be aware that excellent workshops don't happen overnight; they can be a life-long challenge, and many experienced do-it-yourselfers have rearranged their project headquarters several times over succeeding years. If you work at it, you will continually discover new ways to make better use of the space you have available and to improve your shop's capabilities by selectively adding tools and other equipment that make jobs easier. Also, realize that your workshop doesn't have to look like anyone else's. If it works for you, that is what counts the most.

FINDING SHOP SPACE

Basically, shop space is where you find it, whether it is in the garage, in the basement, or in a separate backyard building. When space is scarce, every square inch counts. Look for unused space in unconventional places. For example, in a basement workshop you might want to consider leaving the ceiling joists uncovered to provide more storage space.

You might also consider the space under the stairway running down alongside a basement workshop for tool and/or material storage. Other places to look for space include between open studs, behind doors, under stationary workbenches, and also in seldom-used rooms and closets nearby.

Outfitted with a full complement of hooks, brackets, and accessories, pegboard is one of the shop organizer's best tools. Consider us-

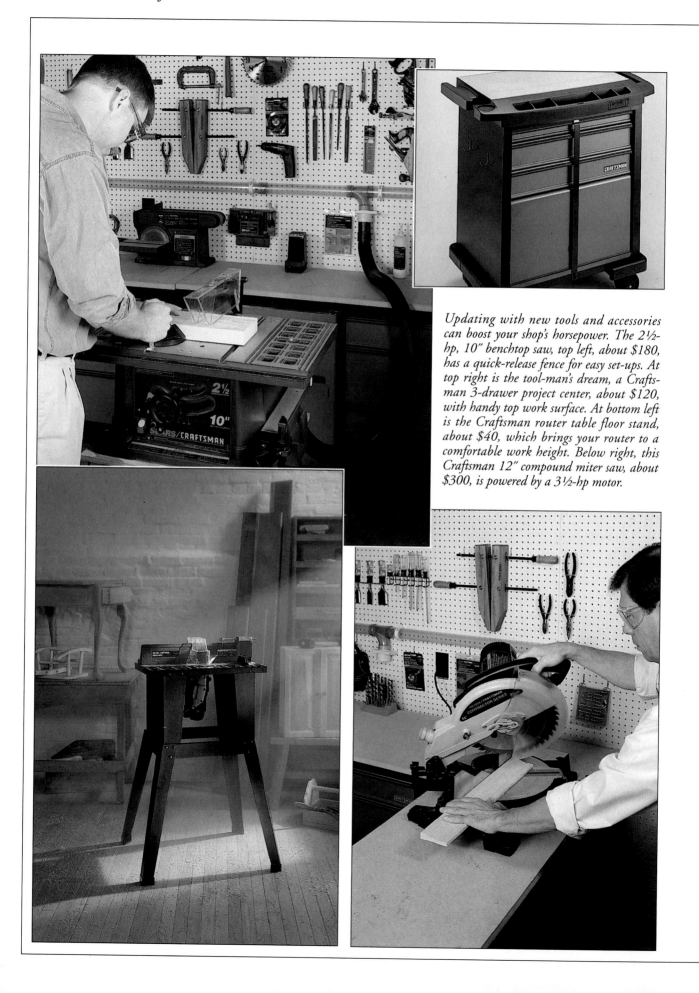

Updating with new tools and accessories can boost your shop's horsepower. The 2½-hp, 10″ benchtop saw, top left, about $180, has a quick-release fence for easy set-ups. At top right is the tool-man's dream, a Craftsman 3-drawer project center, about $120, with handy top work surface. At bottom left is the Craftsman router table floor stand, about $40, which brings your router to a comfortable work height. Below right, this Craftsman 12″ compound miter saw, about $300, is powered by a 3½-hp motor.

ing it wherever you can on the walls of your workplace. You can even make up pegboard sections that hang off the wall like pages in a book. For examples of how to do this, check the swinging panel displays at lumberyards and home centers. You can use the swinging pegboard for either tools or materials, or both.

Tip: Traditional pegboard hooks can have an irritating tendency to fall out when used, so when buying yours consider newer plastic styles which are especially designed to stay in place after they are positioned where you want them. You also can try using short sections of ¼″ dowels pounded into ¼″ pegboard to hang tools.

If you are short on space, consider smaller benchtop shop tools which have been greatly improved over the past decade or so. You can store these scaled-down versions under a workbench and pull them out as needed. Special benches are also available that mount up to three tools on a turret-style revolving center and can free up your regular workbench for other uses. Also consider buying shop tools which combine more than one function, such as combination belt and disc sanders.

SPACE-SAVING OPTIONS
Another option, if you like to experiment, is to consider making your own combination tools. You could, for example, make yourself a sanding table with a disc sander and two belt sanders set up to draw power from a single electric motor. Another combination tool you could build is a grinder-polisher. Then you can attach various grit sandpapers and leather onto wooden discs that fasten to a single shaft.

These Sears measuring tapes, $3 to $9, have easy-to-read, three-color blades.

Accessory manufacturers have been coming to the rescue of the do-it-yourselfer who is short on space. In fact, one power drill outfitted with accessories can give you drill press capability and provide power for bandsaws, sanders, bit sharpeners, small wood lathes, and other basic tool operations. Compact work centers let you clamp portable tools onto one table for light-duty work in small spaces.

The Work Center sold by Sears, for example, can turn your drill into a drill press, your circular saw into a table saw, and your router into a shaper, all on one compact bench complete with woodworking vise, bench dogs, and power switch. Router accessories likewise can help you achieve full shop capabilities in minimal space.

Experienced do-it-yourselfers agree that you can never get enough work surfaces in a shop. Making work surfaces mobile can be handy, especially in a small shop. You can make benches portable by adding casters at one end. Then you can pull them to where they are needed, or push them out of the way when you need more room for a different project.

Consider putting locking casters under some or all of your stationary power tools. They cost money, but pay off big dividends in flexibility. Wheeled tools are easy to arrange, plus they can be dollied over to the workshop door for special operations, such as to rip long lumber, or to take advantage of daylight or good weather.

STRETCHING A BUDGET
In addition to portable workbenches, also consider smaller fold-up benches, such as the one shown on page 180, to help cope with a lack of space. They offer portability plus helpful clamping power.

If you are short on budget, however, keep in mind that you don't have to get fancy. You can pick up sturdy used kitchen tables, for example, and position them as needed around your workshop. Even sawhorses and sheets of plywood can provide portable, temporary workspace. And, recycled appliances can also help you get your

Above, this Craftsman clamping table, about $70, offers handy quick-release jaws. Below, handy benchtop 12½″ planer/molder, about $700, helps save lumber costs.

workshop organized. Because no one wants old appliances like refrigerators, and homeowners are often charged to get rid of them, you can get them for next to nothing. An old refrigerator or portable dishwasher, for example, can be easily converted to provide multiple shelves for storing tools and materials. Or, with the heating element of an old dishwasher plugged in, you will also be able to warm up materials when necessary.

If your checkbook says you can't afford first-class storage right now, you can always find used wooden cabinets at garage sales that will work well to help organize tools and materials. Metal kitchen cabinets, the kind popular in the Fifties, are ideal for storing materials such as glue, paint, nails, and small tools. You can also consider using plastic pans in conjunction with slide-in racks and other kitchen-type organizers. Even items such as plastic milk crates can provide convenient, floor-to-ceiling, cubbyhole storage.

HOOKING UP POWER

Keep in mind that if you are working in small spaces it is essential to figure out ways to minimize the use of extension cords. In addition to the safety hazard of stumbling over cords plugged into hard-to-reach outlets, dealing with tangled cords slows your efficiency and boosts your frustration levels. One idea to consider is to group your power tools in the center of your work area, then install overhead outlets to eliminate having to run cords through walkways.

Outlets directly over workbenches, and selective purchases of cord reels, multiple outlets, and continuous outlet strips are other ways to help you beat cord problems. Also

Above, the Excalibur Elite dado from Sears, about $200, has carbide-tipped scoring teeth to eliminate chipping and produce flat bottoms. The Craftsman Control-Feed blade at right, $10 to $40, also has carbide teeth and eliminates overfeeding in cuts.

pay attention to the light sources in your shop. Don't force yourself to work in the dark.

Make sure you have enough light to make projects enjoyable, and supplement fixed light sources with smaller task lights that can be used when you need more light. If you haven't used them, you will be surprised at how newer halogen task lights will literally shed new light on your projects and elevate your spirits to a professional level.

Don't forget to outfit your workshop with a place to do any figuring that might be necessary. And keep plenty of paper, drawing tools, tape, and other planning aids handy. If your projects require long periods of standing, consider investing in special floor mats to increase your comfort level. Also try to make parts and supplies as visible, accessible, and organized as possible.

Be aggressive about getting your workshop the way you would like to have it. If a modification to your shop increases its efficiency, don't

hesitate to make it. If you need "port holes" in your garage shop to feed lumber to power tools, cut them out and install hinged trap doors. If you don't have room for lumber, consider a bump-out on one side of an inside wall, or use overhead storage boxes attached to the ceiling.

SHOP EXPANSIONS

You may decide you simply have to expand. Garage workshop additions can range from adding a lean-to for a workbench to doubling either its width or length. For example, you can consider doubling the length of your garage and then keep your vehicle in the front with your shop area in the rear. By hanging plastic or canvas between the two areas, you will be able to keep sawdust off the cars while making it easier to heat or cool the smaller shop area when necessary.

Finally, if you live in cramped quarters, don't give up. Even if you live in an apartment or condominium, you can devise a portable work

surface of plywood to use over a kitchen counter or a surface such as a wet bar. Simply cut out a section of plywood to fit the surface, then outfit it as elaborately as you want with tool holders along the back, even a small vise. Another option is to make use of the great outdoors. Canvas-covered workbenches allow some woodworkers to complete dozens of projects outside. Check for opportunities, such as large overhangs, patios, or decks that can be easily covered. Besides gaining excellent light, you will also have a place to perform tasks that are either too dusty, like sanding, or too smelly, like painting, to do inside an enclosed area.

*Note: A valuable resource book to aid you in setting up your shop is **The Home Workshop Planner**, available in bookstores and in the tool departments of many Sears stores. If you can't find a copy in your local area, write to Meredith Books, 1617 Locust, Des Moines, IA 50309.*

CHIPPER-SHREDDERS

New Earth-Friendly Technology Offers
Quick Clean-Up Of The Home Yard and Garden

Our throw-away society has become a recycling society, and that's good news for the environment. Unfortunately, getting rid of yard debris is no longer as convenient as it once was. Most landfills will no longer accept leaves and other yard debris or charge you by the bag. Burning is against the law in many areas, and composting bulky yard waste is often virtually impossible.

Fortunately, manufacturers have come to the rescue with new versions of machines to help homeowners handle yard waste problems and, at the same time, recycle useful organic materials. These new applications of mechanical engineering have now reached the marketplace in three major versions: 1) the leaf shredder, stationary units dedicated to processing leaves only; 2) the chipper/vac, which has the same capability in combination with a powerful vacuum for picking up and mulching leaves, and 3) the chipper/shredder, a roll-about unit that grinds brush and branches into usable mulch.

Shredding organic material breaks it down into nutrient-rich fertilizing matter that can be tucked around plants and flowers.

Leaf Shredders. These units are are usually electrically powered and the lowest in price, costing in a range of about $100 to $250. The chipper/vacs are mostly gas powered. And, while chipper/shredders

Chipper/vacs resemble walk-behind mowers but chip, shred, vacuum, and bag yard debris in a single step. Hose attachments can extend their reach to hard-to-clean areas around the yard.

are available in both electric- and gas-powered versions, the heavier-duty units are all powered with gas engines. For the latter two types of machines, expect price tags ranging from $400 to $1,300 or more.

If leaves are your only concern, there is no need to look further than the low-priced leaf shredders. Most, like the Sears Leafwacker 79685 which has garnered excellent ratings in consumer tests, have wide, open hoppers leading to ny-

lon-filament cutters. This type of device can typically reduce what otherwise would be four or five bags of leaves down to one in short order. A 30-gallon pile of leaves will take less than 40 seconds to shred. However, if you want something that doesn't require bringing leaves to the machine, the logical next step up is to the chipper/vac.

Chipper/vacs. The beauty of these machines is that they have the ability to cut yard work in half. Engineers at Troy-Bilt, a leading manufacturer, point out that with their chipper/vacs you can cut the time it takes to clean up the leaves, branches, and other debris from the average front yard from 30 minutes down to 15. With the portable machines you simply walk around your yard, vacuuming up leaves. If you occasionally run across fallen branches, you drop them into the chipper chute where they feed themselves automatically into the chipper blade.

Chipper/vacs shred and chop yard debris into bits, reducing it down to as much as 10-to-1. This means that instead of disposing of 10 bags, you discard just one and save big if you pay by the bag.

Most chipper/vac models offer an optional hose attachment that allows you to reach leaves hiding deep in tight spots. With a typical 10′ reach, the hose allows easy cleaning of leaves from flower beds, under fences, or behind shrubbery.

Top-of-the-line chipper/vacs further ease the cleanup of exceptionally heavy leaf covers with a special rake-in tray. You sweep the leaves over next to the machine and let its vacuum take over. Just like with newer lawn mowers, chipper/vacs come in push-type or self-propelled versions, and are fitted with an easy on-off collection bag which can hold up to 3½ bushels.

How big of a chipper/vac you may need will depend primarily on the size of your yard. As an example, Troy-Bilt offers 4½-, 5-, and 8-hp gas-powered versions. The smallest is a push-type, vacuums a 20″ swath, and will chip branches up to 2″ thick. The two larger

Chipper/vacs are available in either push-type or self-propelled models.

models are self-propelled, and vacuum a 21″ and 22″ swath respectively. The big 8-hp model will chip branches up to 3½″ thick.

Chipper/shredders. If your yard generates a large amount of brush, a chipper/shredder that is specifically dedicated to reducing brush and branches is worth a second look.

These typically have two hoppers, one for branches and woody material, and another for leaves and other bulky material. Larger 8-hp industrial/commercial models will accept limbs up to 4″ thick. Smaller limbs are drawn down the chute without assistance, eliminating the need to manually feed each one into the machine.

Woody debris is fed into a heavy 22-lb. flywheel spinning at 3,600 rpm which takes up to 60 "bites" per second. On many machines you can control the size of the mulch you create, from fine to coarse, by changing the discharge screen. On some you can use a bar grate to reduce clogging when shredding heavy, wet materials.

When comparing models, check horsepower, chipping speed, shredding reduction ratio, and whether material can be discharged neatly into a receptacle such as a reusable cloth bag. Also ask about noise

produced and check out the safety features; i.e., how easily a hand could inadvertently reach the blade, or tendencies for material to be thrown back into the face of the operator.

With the 5-hp Craftsman 79785, a machine that has received high ratings in independent tests, it is easier to control the last piece fed in than most other models. Its swing-down hopper allows leaves to be easily raked in, and it neatly packages refuse into a reusable bag.

Also consider how easily the unit will be to move, start, stop, or adjust. Some manufacturers, such as Troy-Bilt, offer their largest models (10 hp) set up with wheels and hitch so it can be towed behind a tractor. If you have a higher-horsepower garden tiller, you might also want to consider a Power Take-Off (pto) version to keep costs down.

A final word about safety. All chipper/shredders can cause injury

Roll-about chipper-shredders help reduce unruly piles of brush and debris.

with improper use. Manufacturers have done what they can to design as many safety features as possible into their chipper/shredders. But it's up to you to learn how to avoid the risk of personal injury inherent in using machines of this type. The operator manuals are usually very thorough and are worth studying.

Using Mulch. When figuring whether it will pay to buy a yard waste processor, consider that they are designed to save on the time you must devote to the job, plus money, especially if you pay for hauling by the bag. The processed waste can be used to make your home's landscaping look more professional. Wood chips, for example, can provide a rustic look that blends in with the rest of your landscape while reducing weeds. Larger wood chips can be used where you don't want any natural growth.

Note: For more information on yard debris processors, you can review the options in the yard and garden department at your local Sears store. You can also get a free packet of information outlining the array of choices by writing Troy-Bilt at 102nd St. and 9th Ave., Troy, NY 12180 or by calling 1-800-828-5500 toll-free.

HOW THEY WORK

Chipper/vac. The cutaway at left shows the inner workings of a mid-sized 5-hp model. It uses rapidly spinning fan blades to create a vacuum that draws in debris, shreds it and blows it into a collection bag. Its auto-feeding chipper draws branches in automatically and takes 60 bites per second to whittle branches into wood chips.

Chipper/shredder. The cutaway at right of a top-of-the-line 8-hp industrial-commercial model shows the unit's 22-lb. flywheel, which rotates its free-swinging shredder flails at 3,600 rpm. The large shredder hopper, as well as the chipper chute, both have a rubber retainer flap which helps prevent kickback of materials.

GOLDEN PONDS

*How To Use A Water Garden To
Create A Backyard With Living Color*

Try to imagine one in your backyard: the tranquility of water, the flashes of color from lilies or goldfish, the texture and beauty of water-loving plants in endless varieties. Then imagine calming sounds from a flowing fountain, plus radiant night-time color from under water lighting. The possibilities seem virtually endless.

Specialists at Lilypons Water Gardens, whose photographs are shown here, say once you start a water garden you can find yourself plunged into an absorbing life-long hobby. The key is good planning and designing before you start. You want your new water garden to soothe and relax you, and not cause needless worry.

Virginia Crum of Lilypons suggests you first ask yourself basic questions. It will be a focal point, so you need to decide if you want to locate it at a far point in your garden, have it as a destination for those meandering through your garden, or be close to your picture window, patio, or deck.

Flexible pond liners can be held in place at the edges in a variety of ways using stones, rocks, brick, concrete, flagstone, or treated wood.

Plan for as much direct sunlight as possible. The more sunlight, the more choices you will have when you begin planting your water garden. An exception is the pond of less than 100 gallons which does

Water gardeners find the gracious tranquility of hardy water lilies irresistible. Many lilies available are perennial and frost tolerant.

best with an hour or two of shade during the hot part of the day.

Try to avoid low-lying areas where runoff collects. Any chemicals that you or your neighbors use will ultimately spill into your pond during rains with fatal results to plants and fish alike.

A fairly level site is much better in the long run. Also avoid overhanging trees, if possible. Those leaves dropping into your pond will cause extra maintenance, especially in autumn.

Using flexible pond liners, you can create a pond as your imagination pictures it within certain limitation. Lilypons, for example, carries 32 mil, two-ply liners, tough 45-mil rubber liners, or super durable geotextile-backed 60-mil liners. The cost varies with type in a range from about $50 on up to $500 or more. The liner flaps can be held in place with stones or rocks, or you can edge the new pond with brick, concrete, cut flagstone, even pressure-treated wood.

Once you get the pond made, the fun part is stocking it with such delights as water lilies, iris, reeds, and rushes, as well as underwater plants, snails, tadpoles, and goldfish. Pumps and filters are essential; the water should be recirculated once every two to six hours, depending on your filter selection.

If you prefer to just get a taste of water gardening, companies such as Lilypons offer starter kits which include an 8'x13' liner, small pump, and accessories for about $320. To get a free catalog, you can write to Lilypons Water Gardens at 6800 Lilypons Rd., Lilypons, MD 21717, or call the company at (301) 874-5503.

TECH NOTES: INSTALLING A WATER GARDEN

When installing your water garden, choose a flexible liner from your supplier. If the ground is rocky, excavate first and then measure to determine the liner size. Be sure to check local regulations concerning pools.

1 Outline the desired shape and size of your pool with a rope or hose. Use a string, stakes, and a carpenter's square for pools with sharper angles, such as rectangles and squares. For a circular pond, use a central stake and measure outward evenly.

Excavate soil leaving marginal shelves (optional) in desired areas. These should be about 9″ to 12″ wide and 9″ to 12″ below the top edge of the excavation. The sides should slope slightly inward from top to bottom at about a 75° angle. Pond depth can be checked during excavation by using a board and a yard stick or tape measure.

Most water gardens are 15″ to 24″ deep. The bottom of liner pools should be very slightly sloped toward one end to create an area 1″ deeper than the rest of the pool. This area should be about 18″ across and will facilitate draining and cleaning the pool.

2 If you plan to have sod edging around your pond, trim the excess liner as close as possible to allow maximum rerooting of the sod. For a sod edge/coping, cut the sod in 10″ sections and roll back from the excavation approximately 24″. Wet the sod as you work if it is hot or if it shows signs of drying.

Check the level of the entire rim of the pond by placing a straight 2x4 board on edge across the excavated area. Hold a carpenter's level on top of the board and move it to various points around the rim. Remove soil from high spots until the entire pond edge is level. This step is essential in making the pond edge even.

If your pond is too large to use a 2x4 for leveling, place one to three stakes temporarily in the center of the excavation. All points around the rim should be level with the top of the stake(s). The pond rim must be level, or the liner will be clearly visible on the higher rim.

3 Cut a shallow 12″- to 15″-wide ledge beyond the rim for any intended coping other than simple fieldstones or sod. Complete the final trimming and shaping, and check all depth and leveling measure-

ments one last time. The sides and bottom should be closely inspected for any sharp rocks or protruding tree roots.

Line the bottom of the excavation with about 1″ of damp sand to cushion and protect the liner. An underlayment of geotextile material may also be used to cover the excavation instead of the sand, or you can use simply use sand for leveling your liner bottom. Underlayment is not necessary with some liners.

4 Carefully unfold and drape the liner into the excavation. To avoid damaging it, do not drag the liner across the ground. Most liners take two people to maneuver. The liner will be more flexible and easier to work with if allowed to warm on a paved area in the sun for a few minutes. Do not lay a black liner on your lawn because the warmth from the sun can kill your grass quickly.

Drape the liner loosely into the excavation with an even overlap all around. The liner can be held in place by weighting the edges with bricks or smooth stones. These weights can be eased off as the filling of the pond pulls the liner into place.

5 After the pond is full, cut the surplus overlap. Trim it with a pair of large scissors, leaving a flap 6″ to 12″ wide around the entire pond. Using 10″ spike nails, nail the liner edge (a 6″ to 12″ flap) directly into the ground below to keep it firmly in place as you work on the coping or edging.

6 The pond is now ready for coping. Be sure to extend your coping an inch or two over the pond to protect the liner from ultraviolet rays from the sun. To create the stone coping shown, apply mortar on top of galvanized metal lathe (available from hardware stores) placed on the liner. Lay the stones, watching the evenness of the edges as you go, using as little mortar as possible between the stones. This will give a more natural appearance.

A 2″ to 3″ mortar base (reinforced with additional metal lathe in frost zones) works well in most cases. If the coping will be walked on, use a 12″- to 18″-deep concrete footer. When mortar work is finished, drain, clean, and rinse the pond before stocking to remove any excess mortar.

INDEX

CREDITS

This book was produced by NORTH COAST PRODUCTIONS, with assistance from the following. All text, photos, and illustrations, except as noted, are by NORTH COAST PRODUCTIONS, 650 Mount Curve Boulevard, St. Paul, MN 55116.

DIY PROJECTS (Section I, large photo pages 6 and 7, Marvin Windows and Doors): DO-IT-YOURSELF INDEX (page 8): illustrations, Brian Jensen. ULTIMATE SHOWER (page 10): text sources, U.S. Gypsum Company, Finnleo Sauna & Steam, Amerec Products; photos from U.S. Gypsum Company. WELCOMED WARMTH (page 18): text, photo and illustration source, Village West Publishing; illustration page 20 Don Johnson. HOW-TO CLINICS (page 23): text and photo source, Merle Henkenius. DECK FEVER (page 32): text and photo sources, California Redwood Association and Simpson Strong-Tie Company. California Redwood Association photos: page 32, photo Tom Rider, designer-builder John Hemingway; pages 34 and 35 photo George Lyons, owner-designer James Woodhead; page 36 top, photo Ernest Braun, designers-builders Jain Moon and Scott Foell; page 36 and 37, photo Ernest Braun, landscape architect Scott Smith. DECK CONNECTIONS (pages 38 through 45): text, photos and illustration source, Simpson Strong-Tie Company. USING CONNECTORS TO REJUVENATE A DECK (pages 46 and 47): text and photos, Merle Henkenius. THE HIGH-TECH DECK (pages 48 and 49): text and photos, Sears, Roebuck & Co., Supreme Decking, Vermont American, American Tool, Beckwood Industries.

DIY PROCEDURES (Section II, large photo pages 50 and 51, Marvin Windows and Doors): TRADE SECRETS (page 52): illustrations, Brian Jensen. FENCE BUILDERS (page 60): text, photos and illustration source, California Redwood Association. Page 60, photo Ernest Braun, designer Timothy Jones; page 61, photo Ernest Braun, designer-builder Timothy R. Bitts & Associates; page 62, top photo Rufus Diamont, designer and builder Sierra West Construction; middle photo Karl Rick, architect Robert Engman; bottom photo Barbara Engh, designer Grant Jones; page 63, top photo Ernest Braun, designer Timothy Jones; middle photo Andrew McKinney, bottom photo Tom Rider, designer-builder Mark O'Neil; page 64, top photo Ernest Braun, owner-builder Warren S. Popp; middle photo Jeff Weisman, architect William B. Remick, AIA; bottom photo Tom Rider, designer Eli Sutton; page 65, top photo Clyde Eagleton, builder Timothy Jones; bottom photos (left to right) photo Ernest Braun, designer-builder Richard Schwartz; photo Karl Rick, designer-builder All Decked Out; photo Clyde Eagleton, designer-builder Julian Hodges. MARBLE THRESHOLD (page 70): text and photos, Merle Henkenius. MECHANIZED SANDING (page 73): text and photo sources, Performax Products, Sears, Roebuck & Co., and Hugh Foster. WIRING PROJECTS (page 82): text source pages 83 through 87, David Chapeau; photos page 83 through 87, Sears, Roebuck & Co. and Merle Henkenius; photos, text and illustration source page 88, Merle Henkenius. CLAMP HEAVEN (page 89): text and photo sources pages 89-93, American Tool Companies; pages 94 and 85, Sears, Roebuck & Co.

DIY PROBLEM-SOLVERS (Section III, large photo pages 96 and 97, Marvin Windows and Doors): PROJECT AMMUNITION (page 98): illustrations, Brian Jensen. STRANGE NOISES (page 106): photos, Merle Henkenius. WINDOW SOLUTIONS (page 112): text and photo source, Marvin Windows and Doors. WONDER WORKERS (page 124): text and photo source pages 124 through 128, WD-40 Company; illustration page 129, Brian Jensen. ON-THE-BLINK (page 131): photos, Merle Henkenius. ELECTRIC MOTORS (page 139): text source page 141, Johnny Blackwell; illustration, Brian Jensen.

DIY PURSUITS (Section IV, large photo pages 142 and 143, Marvin Windows and Doors): BACKYARD VICTORIAN (page 144): text, photo and illustration source, Georgia Pacific. TOOL COLLECTORS (page 154): text source, Ron Barlow; photo page 155, Mark Duginske; photos pages 157 through 159, Sears, Roebuck & Co. GARAGE PRESERVATION (page 161): text and photos, Merle Henkenius. FURNITURE FINISHES (page 164): photo page 164, Gardener's Supply Co.; rest of photos, Thompson & Formby Inc. WALL FASTENERS (page 171): text sources, Robert Scharff and Rawlplug Company; photos, Knape & Vogt; illustrations pages 172 and 173, Brian Jensen. TOOL POWER (page 176): text source, Ed Jackson; photos, Sears, Roebuck & Co. CHIPPER-SHREDDERS (page 182): text and photo sources, Sears, Roebuck & Co. and Troy-Bilt. GOLDEN PONDS (page 186): text source, Lilypons Water Gardens; photos pages 186 and 187, Little Giant Pump Co.; photos pages 188 and 189, Lilypons Water Gardens.

ADDRESSES

American Tool Companies, Inc., 8400 LakeView Parkway, Kenosha, WI 53142; Beckwood Industries, Cheeter Div., 889 Horan Dr., Fenton, MO 63026; California Redwood Association, 405 Enfrente Dr., Ste. 200, Novato, CA 94949; Georgia-Pacific Corp., 133 Peachtree St. NE, P.O. Box 1763, Norcross, GA 30391; Knape & Vogt Manufacturing Co., 2700 Oak Industrial Dr. NE, Grand Rapids, MI 49505; Lilypons Water Gardens, 6800 Lilypons Rd., Lilypons, MD 21717; Little Giant Pump Co., P.O. Box 12010, Oklahoma City, OK 73157; Marvin Doors and Windows, 2020 Silverbell Rd., Ste. 15, St. Paul, MN 55122; Performax Products, 12211 Woodlake Dr., Burnsville, MN 55337; Rawlplug Company, Inc., New Rochelle, NY 10802; Sears Merchandise Group (Craftsman Power Tools), D3 181A, 3333 Beverly Rd., Hoffman Estates, IL 60179; Simpson Strong-Tie Company, 4637 Chabot Dr., Suite 200, Pleasanton, CA 94588. Supreme Decking, 10125 Richmond Hwy., Box 1458, Lorton, VA 22079; Thornton Tile and Marble, 612 So. 9th St., Murray, KY 42071; Thompson & Formby, Inc., 825 Crossover Lane, Memphis, TN 38117; Troy-Bilt, 102nd St. and 9th Ave., Troy, NY 12180; Vermont American, Box 340, Lincolnton, NC 28093; Windmill Publishing, 2147 Windmill View Road, El Cajon, CA 92020; WD-40 Company, c/o Phillips-Ramsey, 6863 Friars Rd., San Diego, CA 92108.